REA: THE LEADER IN TEACHER CERTIFICATION PREP

3rd Edition

CSET® ENGLISH
SUBTESTS I-IV

CALIFORNIA SUBJECT EXAMINATIONS FOR TEACHERS®

John Allen

Research & Education Association
www.rea.com

Research & Education Association
61 Ethel Road West
Piscataway, New Jersey 08854
E-mail: info@rea.com

CSET®: English Subtests I–IV with Online Practice Exams

Printed in the United States of America

Library of Congress Control Number 2015954505

ISBN-13: 978-0-7386-1202-7
ISBN-10: 0-7386-1202-2

The content specifications for the CSET® : English Test were created and implemented by the California Commission on Teacher Credentialing in conjunction with Pearson Education, Inc. For further information visit the CSET® website at *www.cset.nesinc.com*. For all references in this book, CSET® and California Subject Examinations for Teachers® are trademarks of the California Commission on Teacher Credentialing and Pearson Education, Inc., or its affiliate(s), which have not reviewed or endorsed this book.

All other trademarks cited in this publication are the property of their respective owners.

Cover image: ©istockphoto.com/monkeybusinessimages

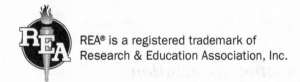

REA® is a registered trademark of
Research & Education Association, Inc.

Preface

As teachers, or aspiring teachers at least, we all know that the best and only way to improve performance on a test is to prepare for it. John Allen and the test prep experts at REA have provided all the resources necessary to prepare for the CSET: English exam. This book is an invaluable resource for anyone looking to take the test, and it provides all the tools you will need to do well.

I have counseled hundreds of students who were preparing to take all kinds of tests, and with every student my advice is always the same. First, get a sense of the content and format of the test—that is, learn what subjects and skills you will be tested on and how you will be tested. Second, take a practice test to determine where you stand on various sections of the test. Then isolate and focus on those sections that need work. This is exactly what REA's test prep allows you to do.

This third edition is completely updated to align with the California Common Core State Standards for English Language Arts, upon which the CSET: English is based. REA's test prep contains a detailed analysis of both the format and content of the CSET: English Subtests I through IV. It also includes subject reviews on all the topics covered by the exam—American literature, literary criticism, the writing process, linguistics, media, dramatic performance, and more.

One of the most beneficial aspects of the REA study system is its adaptability. The book includes two full-length practice tests, presented in the same style as the CSET: English exam itself. Furthermore, these two practice exams are also offered online in a format that allows for instant scoring and diagnostic feedback that lets you target areas of weakness and focus on topics where you need more review. The essay questions for Subtests III and IV include sample answers of varying quality, so that you can get a sense of how your responses will be scored.

Our country and our world can only benefit by having more good educators. I salute you and the noble impulse that brought you to pursue a career in education. It has been an honor for me to be involved with the third edition of this work.

Best of luck to you in your teaching career!

J. Wayne Bass, Ph.D.
Professor of Humanities
San Diego City College
San Diego, California

About REA

Founded in 1959, Research & Education Association (REA) is dedicated to publishing the finest and most effective educational materials—including study guides and test preps—for students in middle school, high school, college, graduate school, and beyond.

Today, REA's wide-ranging catalog is a leading resource for students, teachers, and other professionals. Visit *www.rea.com* to see a complete listing of all our titles.

About Our Author

John Allen has more than 25 years of experience in test preparation. Mr. Allen received his B.A. degree from the University of Oklahoma in 1979. He has written several textbooks in the field of English-language arts and in many other subject areas.

Acknowledgments

We would like to thank REA's Larry B. Kling, Vice President, Editorial, for supervising development; Pam Weston, Publisher, for setting the quality standards for production integrity and managing the publication to completion; John Paul Cording, Vice President, Technology, for coordinating the design and development of the REA Study Center; Kelli A. Wilkins, Senior Editor, for project management; Eve Grinnell, Graphic Artist, for cover design; Ellen Gong for proofreading; and TCS for typesetting the manuscript.

CONTENTS

Introduction

PASSING THE CSET: ENGLISH TEST

Congratulations! By taking the CSET: English test, you're on your way to a rewarding career as an English teacher. Our book, and the online tools that come with it, give you everything you need to succeed on this important exam, bringing you one step closer to being certified to teach English in California.

Recently, the CSET: English subtests were revised to align more closely with the California Common Core State Standards. The subtests also include new material in the areas of writing across the curriculum, reading and analyzing a variety of informational texts, and analyzing the details of dramatic works and performance. Our CSET: English test prep package has been expanded to address these changes. The package includes:

- A complete overview of the four CSET: English subtests

- A comprehensive review of every domain, with updated material

- Two full-length practice tests for each subtest, with online diagnostic tools to help you personalize your study

There are many different ways to prepare for the CSET: English exam. The method that is best for you depends on how much time you have to study and how familiar you are with the subject matter. To achieve the highest score possible, you need a study system customized to fit you: your schedule, your learning style, and your current level of knowledge. This book and its accompanying online practice tests provide the tools that allow you to customize your study and will get you ready to pass the exam!

HOW TO USE THIS BOOK

About the Review

The review chapters in this book are designed to help you hone the basic skills necessary to succeed on the CSET: English test. The exam is composed of four separate subtests, each scored separately and is comprised of multiple-choice or constructed response questions.

This book contains a thorough review of the material featured on each subtest, as well as the specific skills and knowledge associated with each content domain. The skills required for all four subtests fulfill the objectives set by the California Common Core State Standards for English Language Arts and Literacy and the California Commission on Teacher Credentialing.

Remember that your schooling has taught you most of what you need to know to pass the CSET: English exam. The education classes you took provided the background to make important decisions about situations you will face as a teacher. This review is designed to help you fit the information you have acquired into specific domain components. Studying your class notes, textbooks, and other sources together with this review will give you an excellent foundation for passing the CSET: English exam.

To help you navigate through the review, we have used bold type for the first mention of the most important literary periods, literary styles, novels, poems, plays, short stories, and essays. This will help you locate material quickly as you refer back to it while studying. While it is impossible to include everything that might appear on the actual CSET: English exam, we have included a wide range of material to help you with your preparation.

About the REA Study Center

To personalize your study plan, you should first get feedback on what you know and what you don't know. At the online REA Study Center (*www.rea.com/studycenter*), you will find two full-length practice tests for each subtest, along with detailed score reports that will pinpoint your strengths and weaknesses.

Before you begin to study the review chapters in this book, take Practice Test 1 as a diagnostic test. Armed with the information from your score reports, focus your study on the parts of the book where you need the most review.

After studying the review chapters, go back to the REA Study Center and take Practice Test 2 for each subtest. This will ensure that you have mastered the material and are ready for test day.

If you are studying for the CSET: English test and don't have Internet access, you can take the printed tests in this book. The correct answers for the test items can be found at the end of each subtest. These printed tests are the same as the online practice tests offered at the REA Study Center, but without the added benefits of timed testing conditions and diagnostic score reports. When taking a printed test, you are encouraged to simulate the test environment as closely as possible.

AN OVERVIEW OF THE TEST

What's on the CSET: English Test?

The CSET: English test assesses your ability to meet the basic skills requirement and subject matter competence requirement as set out in the California Common Core State Standards for English Language Arts and Literacy. The test combines the expertise of California educators, subject area specialists, and district-level educators, all of whom worked to develop and validate the exam. The CSET: English test is criterion-referenced, which means it is designed to measure your knowledge and skills against an established standard and not in relation to the performance of others taking the test.

CSET: English consists of four separate subtests, each scored separately and composed of either multiple-choice or constructed-response questions. If you choose to take all four subtests in a single session, you are given 6 hours to complete the exam. You may also take any one subtest by itself. A period of fifteen additional minutes is provided to fill out a nondisclosure agreement and tutorial. Time taken for breaks is counted as part of the available examination time. By monitoring your progress on the practice tests in this book, you can find your comfort level and approach the testing session with confidence.

The following chart outlines the subtests, their domains, and the approximate number of questions on the CSET: English test.

Subtest	Domains	Number of Multiple-Choice Questions	Number of Constructed-Response Questions
I*	Reading Literature and Informational Texts Composition and Rhetoric **Subtest Total**	40 10 **50**	none none
II	Language, Linguistics, and Literacy **Subtest Total**	50 **50**	none
III	Composition and Rhetoric and Reading Literature and Informational Texts	none	Subtest III consists of 2 constructed-response questions—1 based on literary text, 1 on nonliterary text. (extended responses)
IV	Communications: Speech, Media, and Creative Performance	none	4 (short [focused] responses)

*Subtest I is a multiple-choice test that covers the two domains of Reading Literature and Informational Texts and Composition and Rhetoric. Subtest III is a constructed-response test that covers the same domains.

FORMAT OF THE CSET: ENGLISH TEST

The CSET: English test is offered only in a computer-based test (CBT) format. The test consists of multiple-choice questions and two types of constructed-response questions: extended-response and short-response.

Multiple-choice questions are designed to assess your knowledge of the domains and related skills reviewed in this book. In general the multiple-choice questions are intended to make you think logically. In most cases you are expected to demonstrate more than an ability to recall factual information. You may be asked to think critically about a passage or excerpt—analyze it, consider it carefully, compare it with other knowledge, or make a judgment about it.

Multiple-choice questions typically will offer a question or an incomplete statement that can be answered or completed correctly by only one of four possible choices. You will choose from among four answers labeled A, B, C, and D.

You should have plenty of time to complete the test, so speed should not be a concern. However, be aware of how much time you spend on each question; maintaining a steady pace will ensure that you complete the entire test. Using our timed online practice tests will help you pace yourself appropriately.

Extended-response questions are scored according to how well the response fulfills the following performance characteristics:

1. Purpose: addressing the assignment in relation to relevant CSET subject matter and/or content specifications.

2. Subject matter knowledge: displaying and applying knowledge of subject matter accurately.

3. Support: using appropriate, quality supporting evidence.

4. Depth and breadth of understanding: demonstrating a wide familiarity with and a deep understanding of the relevant CSET subject matter requirements.

Short-response questions are only scored on the first three performance characteristics listed above.

When Should the CSET: English Test Be Taken?

Teacher preparation programs usually determine when their candidates take the various tests required for teacher certification. These programs will also clear you to take the necessary examinations and make final recommendations for certification to the Commission on Teacher Credentialing. Those seeking certification right out of school take the CSET: English test just before graduation. Passing each of the CSET: English Subtests is a requirement to teach English in California.

The CSET: English test is administered by appointment year round, Monday through Saturday (except for some holidays). Information about CSET: English registration and locations can be found at *www.ctcexams.nesinc.com*.

Is There a Registration Fee?

You must pay a registration fee to take the CSET: English exam. All fees must be paid in full by personal check, cashier's check, or money order. All payments must be made in U.S. dollars. Cash will not be accepted. If you register via the Internet or phone during the emergency registration period, payment must be made by VISA or MasterCard. As of this printing, fees are $72 for Subtest I and $75 per test for Subtests II, III, and IV. The fee for taking all four subtests together is $297.

SCORING THE EXAM

To pass the CSET: English exam, you must earn a passing score on each of the examination's required subtests. Each CSET: English subtest is scored separately. For each subtest, an individual's performance is evaluated against an established standard.

The credentialing commission sets a passing score for each subtest based on the professional judgments and recommendations of California educators. Passing scores are determined on the basis of total subtest performance. The total subtest score is based on the number of raw score points earned on each section (multiple-choice and/or constructed-response), the weighting of each section, and the scaling of that score. Raw scores are converted to a scale of 100 to 300. The minimum passing score for each subtest is 220.

You may choose to register for and take only some of the subtests for CSET: English in one session. Once you pass a subtest, you do not have to take that subtest again as long as you use the score to earn certification within five years of the test date.

Answers to CSET: English multiple-choice questions are scored electronically as either correct or incorrect. Your performance on multiple-choice questions is based strictly on the number of test questions answered correctly. There is no penalty for guessing. Each multiple-choice question counts the same toward the total score.

The constructed-response items are scored by qualified California educators using focused holistic scoring. Two sets of performance characteristics and two scoring scales are used to score the constructed-response items. Scorers will judge the overall effectiveness of your responses while focusing on the appropriate performance characteristics that are considered important for this exam. Each response is assigned a score based on an approved scoring scale. Sample scoring scales are found at the beginning of each practice test for Subtests III and IV.

How Will I Receive My Score Report and What Will It Look Like?

After you have taken the CSET, you will receive a score report for your records. Your results will also be sent to the CCTC and any institutions you indicated when you registered. Test results are released electronically on the score report dates listed for the CSET: English test at *www.ctcexams.nesinc.com.*

The score reports will be available for 45 days as PDF documents, which you may view, print, and save for your records. Candidates who register online can sign up to receive their score report by email.

For each subtest you take, your score report will include your passing status and, if you do not pass, your total subtest score. The reverse side of the score report contains diagnostic information about your performance. More information on scoring the subtests and score report results can be found online at *www.ctcexams.nesinc.com.*

Should I Take All Four Subtests at Once?

Most candidates prefer to take the entire CSET: English exam at once. However, you should remember that the timeframe of 6 hours makes for an exhausting session. Be realistic as you evaluate your capabilities. Perhaps you would perform better if you took the last test at another time, when you are rested and refreshed.

Can I Retake the Test?

Don't panic if you don't do well on one of the CSET: English subtests. You can take any subtest again—many candidates do. However, you must wait 45 calendar days from the original date you took the test to retake the test or subtest.

Can I Obtain Alternative Testing Arrangements?

Candidates who need alternative testing arrangements should complete the required documentation prior to registering. Most testing facilities can accommodate those with special requirements due to physical or learning disabilities, or those whose religious practices do not allow them to take tests on Saturdays. Check to see that such special arrangements are available at the testing location you select.

6-WEEK STUDY PLAN

Although our study plan is designed to be used in the six weeks before the exam, it can be condensed or expanded to suit your needs and schedule. Be sure to set aside enough time to study—at least two hours each day. The more time you spend studying, the more prepared and confident you will be on test day.

Whatever approach you take, stick to your plan. A disciplined study procedure will lead to success. You might want to study with others who are taking the exam. If so, consider organizing a study group with regularly scheduled meetings.

A sample 6-week study plan might look like the following:

Week	
1	At the REA Study Center, take Practice Test 1 for each subtest to determine your strengths and weaknesses. Your detailed score report will identify topics you most need to review. Read all the answers and explanations to Practice Test 1 carefully.
2–3	Study the review chapters. Use your score reports from Practice Test 1 to focus your study. Useful study techniques include highlighting key terms and information, taking notes as you review the book's sections, and making note cards with new terms and information.
4	Reread all your note cards, refresh your understanding of the exam's competencies and skills, and review your college textbooks and class notes. You should also examine any supplementary materials that will help you prepare for the test, particularly in your weaker areas.
5	Condense your notes. Make a structured list of important facts and concepts, based on your note cards and this book's review of domains. Again, review the answers and explanations for all missed questions on Practice Test I.
6	Take Practice Test 2 for each subtest at the REA Study Center. Check to see how much your score has improved. If you still get a few questions wrong, go back to the review and study the topics for those questions.

TEST-TAKING TIPS

Here are a few additional tips to improve your performance on the CSET: English exam.

Become comfortable with the format of the test. Stay calm and pace yourself as you take the practice tests in this book. Be prepared for the number of multiple-choice questions in each subtest and the types of constructed-response questions to expect. Simulating the test will boost your chances of doing well and enable you to take the actual CSET: English exam with great confidence.

Familiarize yourself with the directions on the test. Knowing what to expect will save you time and help you avoid anxiety on test day.

Read all of the possible answers on the multiple-choice questions. Just because you think you have quickly found the correct choice, do not assume it is the best answer. Read through all the choices to make sure you are not making a mistake by jumping to conclusions.

Use the process of elimination. Look at the answer choices and eliminate the ones you know are wrong, including answers that are partially wrong. Each answer choice you eliminate gives you a better chance of choosing the correct answer. There is no penalty for guessing, so **never** leave an answer blank.

Work at a steady pace and avoid focusing too long on any one question. Taking the timed practice tests at the REA Study Center will help you manage your time more efficiently.

Check that you have marked each answer correctly. Be sure that you mark your answers in correct sequence. The multiple-choice sections of the test are graded by computer and one mistake can throw off the entire section.

THE DAY OF THE TEST

On test day make sure to dress comfortably so that you are not distracted by being too hot or too cold. If possible, practice driving to the test center a few days before the test so that you are familiar with the area. Plan to arrive at the test center early. This will allow you to collect your thoughts and relax. It will also spare you the anxiety that comes with being late.

Check your CSET: English registration information to find out what time to arrive at the testing center. The day before the test, return to your testing account and review your admission ticket for any changes. If there is a change, you will have to print out a new ticket.

Before you leave for the test center, make sure you have your admission ticket and two forms of identification, one of which must contain a recent and recognizable photograph, your name, and your signature (e.g., a driver's license). All documents must be originals—not copies. You will not be admitted to the test center and you will forfeit your test fees if you do not have proper identification.

Unauthorized aids or printed materials are not allowed in the test center. These include dictionaries, textbooks, notebooks, calculators, briefcases, backpacks, or bags. Do not bring cell phones or other electronic or photographic devices into the test center.

Drinking, smoking, and eating are prohibited, as are visitors such as relatives, children, or friends. Personal items such as jewelry, watches, wallets, and purses must be stored in a locker outside of the testing room while you take the test.

Good luck on the CSET: English test!

Reading Literature and Informational Texts

2

On the CSET: English Subtest I, you will have 1 hour and 30 minutes to answer 40 multiple-choice questions in the following areas of Reading Literature and Informational Texts.

- **Reading Literature** will test your knowledge of American, British, and world literature, including major literary movements throughout history, literature for young adults, and major works by representative writers. It will also test your critical thinking and analytic skills for close reading of literary texts.

- **Craft and Structure of Literature** will address different genres and their salient features, basic elements of literature (plot, setting, character, theme, etc.), and the forms and purposes of dramatic literature. It also will test your ability to analyze an author's use of structure, tone, word choice, and point of view to create meaning and aesthetic impact.

- **Reading Informational Texts** will test your ability to analyze, interpret, and summarize informational texts such as literary nonfiction, historical texts, scientific articles and treatises, and technical writing. You will evaluate the structure and content of workplace, consumer, and public documents. You will also compare various features of print and non-print media, including film, television, and the Internet.

- **Craft and Structure of Informational Texts** will test your ability to analyze an author's use of figurative and connotative language in an informational text. You will also evaluate the effectiveness of an author's use of structure and point of view in making a clear and convincing argument. You will demonstrate knowledge of how text features, such as graphics, captions, and annotations, are used in public documents.

- **Integration of Knowledge and Ideas in Informational Texts** will test your ability to integrate and evaluate multiple information sources in different media and formats in order to address an issue or solve a problem. You will also evaluate the reasoning in seminal United States texts as well as their themes, purposes, and rhetorical features.

- **Text Complexity** will test your ability to use quantitative and qualitative tools to evaluate the complexity of texts and identify levels of text complexity within grade band ranges.

Subtest I will also include 10 questions on Composition and Rhetoric, which is covered in Chapter 4 of this book.

The questions on analyzing literature and informational texts in Subtest I call for a general knowledge of literature, literary movements, literary genres and devices, and types of informational text. You can review facts about literature and literary genres in surveys of world and English literature. It is not necessary to have a specialist's knowledge of any particular area to do well on the CSET: English test. Individual writers and works will generally be referenced for the ways they represent larger movements and traditions in literature, history, or critical theory. For example, you probably will not be asked, "What year was Mary Shelley's *Frankenstein* published?" However, you might see this question: "Mary Shelley's *Frankenstein* shares what important elements with other works of Romantic literature?" In the same way, you might be asked to compare authors or works from different periods: "What literary traits does Laurence Sterne's novel *Tristram Shandy* have in common with works of postmodernism?"

For further research on reading literature and informational texts, a teaching candidate for CSET: English should become familiar with all the selections in a secondary-level literature textbook. Literature survey books often include samples of informational texts in the form of essays, letters, autobiographical and biographical writings, and journalism. You should also consider examples of informational texts encountered in everyday life, including advertisements, instruction manuals, political tracts, brochures, contracts, and workplace posters. Teaching candidates should be guided by the literature and textual analysis standards in the California Common Core State Standards, which are available online. Websites with additional material will be included here where appropriate. In addition, you might consult the following sources:

> *Literature for Today's Young Adults* by Alleen Pace Nilsen, James Blasingame, Kenneth L. Donelson, and Don L.F. Nilsen (2012)

> *The Penguin Dictionary of Literary Terms and Literary Theory* by J.A. Cuddon and M.A.R. Habib (2014)

> *The Reading/Writing Connection: Strategies for Teaching and Learning in the Secondary Classroom* by Carol Booth Olson (2010)

> *Recommended Literature: Prekindergarten Through Grade Twelve,* a searchable database provided by the California Department of Education (2012)

READING LITERATURE

1.1 Reading Literature

a. Recognize, compare, and analyze works from different literary traditions to include:

- American (including works that represent cultural pluralism)

- British (including works that represent cultural pluralism)

- World literature and literature in translation (including cross-cultural literature)

- Mythology and oral tradition from a broad range of cultures

b. Trace development of major literary movements in historical periods (e.g., Homeric Greece, medieval, neoclassic, romantic, modern)

c. Describe the salient features of adolescent/young adult literature

d. Demonstrate critical thinking and analytic skills through close reading of texts

e. Cite strong and thorough textual evidence to support analysis of what a literary text says explicitly as well as inferences drawn from the text

f.   Determine themes or central ideas of a literary text and analyze their development over the course of the text

g.   Analyze and interpret major literary works in historical, aesthetic, political, and philosophical contexts

(*California Common Core State Standards for English Language Arts, RL.6–12.1–3*)

ANCIENT LITERATURE

The world's oldest literature dates to the Bronze Age, around the twenty-seventh century BCE, with the first system of recordkeeping and writing. The earliest literature is based on traditions of oral storytelling. Most of these stories concern mankind's relationship to the gods and nature. One of the first works to be preserved in writing is ***The Epic of Gilgamesh*** (c. 700 BCE), a long poem that originated in ancient Babylon. It tells the story of the Sumerian King Gilgamesh who is half-human half-god. At first Gilgamesh is young and headstrong, angering his people with his willful ways. The god Anu presents the king with a new friend and guide, the rough-hewn Enkidu, and the pair embark on a journey to the edge of the world in search of immortality and life's true meaning. Along the way, Gilgamesh learns about the inevitability of change and death and becomes a wiser ruler. Many works of ancient literature include this theme of an epic quest.

Probably the most influential works of ancient literature are Homer's epic poems ***The Iliad*** and ***The Odyssey*** (both c. 700 BCE). These blend the myths of Greek gods with the history of ancient Greek wars into unforgettable tales of heroism, betrayal, and revenge. *The Iliad* describes the Trojan War between the cities of Sparta and Troy, and includes characters such as the warriors Achilles and Hector; the Spartan king, Agamemnon; and the Trojan prince, Paris, who sparked the war by stealing Helen from her husband, Menelaus. *The Odyssey* relates the adventures of Odysseus, a general returning home from the war. On his voyage he encounters such creatures as the one-eyed Cyclops, the enchantress Circe, and the sweet-singing Sirens:

> Next, you will come to the Sirens
> Who beguile all men who encounter them.
> Whoever shall approach them unawares
> And listen to their sweet, enchanting voices
> Will never know the joy of reaching home
> And the greetings of a loving wife and children!

These works have influenced countless writers throughout history. Shakespeare's play *Troilus and Cressida* employs characters from the *Iliad,* while the poet Tennyson and the novelist James Joyce both based works on the *Odyssey.*

Another classic of Greek literature that is based on oral tradition is **Aesop's Fables** (500 BCE). These brief stories teach lessons about life and often include animals that act like people. Among the most famous of these are "Androcles and the Lion" and "The Ant and the Grasshopper." (*http://aesopfables.com/*) *gratitude is the sign of noble souls* *It is best to prepare for the days of necessity*

Most secondary-school literature courses explore **Greek mythology** and the following characters and tales:

- Zeus, the ruler of the gods

- Hera, the wife of Zeus and goddess of women and childbirth

- Athena, the goddess of wisdom and the arts, who sprang from the forehead of Zeus

- Hercules, the god of strength, who performed a set of near-impossible "Herculean" tasks

- Aphrodite, the goddess of love and beauty

- Hades, the god of the underworld and ruler of the dead

- Poseidon, the god of the sea

- Hermes, the fleet messenger of the gods

- "Daedalus and Icarus," in which Icarus, the son of the inventor Daedalus, flies on manmade wings too close to the sun

- "King Midas," in which a gold-loving ruler gains the ability to turn anything to gold at his touch

- "Pandora's Box," in which a young woman disobeys Zeus and opens a box releasing all the evils of the world

The Roman Empire produced three great poets with enormous influence on world literature: Virgil, Horace, and Ovid. Virgil's epic **The Aeneid** (c. 19 BCE) was modeled on Homer's epics and describes the adventures of Aeneas as he escapes from the sack of

Troy, voyages to Italy, and establishes a city that is the precursor of imperial Rome. Virgil also wrote masterful lyrics, such as his *Georgics* and *Eclogues* that describe nature and country life.

Horace was a lyric poet whose *Odes* (c. 23 BCE) addressed almost every aspect of Roman life, including the pomp of public ceremonies and celebrations of military success. He also wrote biting satires (*Epodes*, c. 30 BCE) meant to instruct the public in moral behavior. Horace's use of details from his own life in his work established a model for lyric poets through the ages.

Ovid's *Metamorphoses* (c. 8 BCE) is a long series of tales about the gods as well as human beings whose bodies are transformed into flowers, rocks, trees, and animals. It is one of the best sources for details about the mythology of the Greeks and Romans. Ovid also wrote *Ars Amatoria* ("The Art of Love," c. 2 BCE), which employed a sophisticated wit to describe the pleasures and pains of love and seduction. Passages like the following, which compares romantic conquest to a military operation, inspired Shakespeare and many later European poets:

> Love is a kind of warfare, and no mission for cowards.
> There are no faint hearts marching beneath this standard.
> Winter and darkness, endless roads and cruel sorrows,
> And toil of every kind fill love's campaigns.
> You'll endure the rain pouring from heavenly clouds,
> And often lie there frozen on the naked earth. . . .
> If you're denied a road that is safe and level,
> And the door is barred against you with a bolt,
> Focus your wits, slip down through an open skylight
> Or clamber inside by way of a high, secret window.
> She'll be thrilled, seeing you brave the risk of the chase:
> The surest proof to the lady of your love.

MEDIEVAL AND RENAISSANCE LITERATURE

The Middle Ages or Medieval period in literature extends from the fall of the Roman Empire (c. 500 CE) to the beginning of the Renaissance (c. 1485 CE). Much great literature continued to be produced in Latin, the language of the Roman Catholic Church, but other languages developed, including Anglo-Saxon or Old English. *Beowulf* (c. 800–1100 CE), the oldest surviving epic in Old English, tells the story of Beowulf, a warrior and eventual king who wins three epic battles over Grendel, a monstrous troll, Grendel's mother, and a powerful dragon. In the final battle, Beowulf dies from his wounds. The name of the poet who wrote *Beowulf* has not survived, a not uncommon feature of Medieval literature.

The Divine Comedy (1321 CE) by Dante Alighieri is an epic allegory in Italian. Its three parts (*Inferno, Purgatorio, Paradiso*) narrate Dante's journey through hell, purgatory, and heaven with first the poet Virgil and then the lovely Beatrice as his guides. The poem begins with Dante in a dark wood that represents a sinful state, and follows his progress upward through the levels, or "circles," of the dead. It concludes with the poet reaching a vision of heaven in which his soul is aligned with God. The work, which employs an intricate structure based on the number three, is written in *terza rima,* or rhymed stanzas of three lines:

> Midway in our life's journey, I went astray
> from the straight road and woke to find myself
> alone in a dark wood. How shall I say
>
> what wood that was! I never saw so drear,
> so rank, so arduous a wilderness!
> Its very memory gives a shape to fear.
>
> (John Ciardi translation)

Two other masterpieces of Medieval Italian literature are Petrarch's ***Canzoniere*** ("Songbook," c. 1350 CE) and Boccaccio's ***Decameron*** (1371 CE). Most of Petrarch's poems are love sonnets to a young woman named Laura, whom he glimpsed one day in a cathedral and idolized for the rest of his life. The *Decameron* presents one hundred tales told by ten refugees from the plague-ridden city of Florence. Their stories, based on oral sources and folklore, describe a wide variety of quick-witted merchants, jealous lovers, and superstitious villagers.

Geoffrey Chaucer's ***Canterbury Tales*** (c. 1380 CE) also is a cycle of stories. Chaucer frames his work as a story-telling contest by pilgrims on the road to Canterbury Cathedral. Writing in Middle English verse, Chaucer uses every resource of rhetoric and style to give each narrator an individual voice suited to his or her background. Among the most famous of the Canterbury Tales are:

- "The Knight's Tale," in which two young knights, Arcite and Palamon, battle for the hand of a duke's beautiful sister-in-law. The knight's tale explores his ideals of chivalry, loyalty, valor, and courtly love.

- "The Miller's Tale," in which a penniless student seduces the wife of his landlord, then convinces the landlord that a great flood is coming, whereupon the landlord spends the night hanging from the ceiling in a tub. The tale, told by the drunken miller, is filled with the bawdy humor he loves.

- "The Wife of Bath's Tale," in which a young knight who has raped a maiden is sentenced to discover what women really want. He meets a repulsive old woman who reveals that women want control of their husbands and their own lives. She tells the knight that she could be either ugly and faithful, or beautiful and unfaithful. When he allows her to choose, he is rewarded by her transformation into a lovely young woman. The tale, narrated by the down-to-earth Wife of Bath, reflects her knowledge of the world and view of the conflict between the sexes. Chaucer's Wife of Bath is one of the first great characters in English literature.

→ Characters personify moral qualities or abstractions

Drama in the Middle Ages took the form of mystery plays and morality plays written to teach Christian stories and values through the use of allegory and symbolism. The best known medieval morality play is ***The Summoning of Everyman*** (or simply ***Everyman***), an anonymous work from the late fifteenth century. It portrays God's accounting of the good and evil deeds in the life of Everyman, who represents all mankind. Its allegorical characters include Death, who is God's messenger, Fellowship, and Knowledge.

One of the first great works of the English Renaissance (1550–1660) is Edmund Spenser's epic poem ***The Faerie Queene*** (1596). One of the longest poems in the English language, it presents a many-leveled allegory that includes praise of Queen Elizabeth.

The greatest writer of the period, and perhaps of any period, is William Shakespeare. His poems and plays display a truly extraordinary wit, verbal inventiveness, and knowledge of human psychology. Shakespeare wrote comedies, histories, and tragedies with equal facility, and created unforgettable characters, from the sharp-tongued and witty Rosalinde (*As You Like It*) to the villainous Iago (*Othello*). The critic Harold Bloom has said that Shakespeare virtually invented the modern idea of personality by giving his characters such a variety of traits and emotions. His writings, while expressing the age-old truths of human personality and fate, also reflect the beliefs of his own time, such as the rigorous political and social hierarchy of feudalism, in which each person, from a courtier to a shopkeeper, has his or her ordained station in life. Among his works are:

Hamlet (c. 1600), is the story of a Danish prince who is charged by the ghost of his murdered father to avenge his death. Hamlet discovers that his uncle, Claudius, has murdered his father, taken his crown, and married his widow, Hamlet's mother. Despite this knowledge, Hamlet hesitates to take his revenge until the very end. Instead he feigns madness and vividly describes his divided feelings in famous soliloquies, or speeches to himself that are overheard by the audience:

> How all occasions do inform against me,
> And spur my dull revenge! What is a man,
> If his chief good and market of his time
> Be but to sleep and feed? A beast, no more.
> Sure, he that made us with such large discourse,
> Looking before and after, gave us not
> That capability and god-like reason
> To fust in us unused. Now, whether it be
> Bestial oblivion, or some craven scruple
> Of thinking too precisely on the event,
> A thought which, quarter'd, hath but one part wisdom
> And ever three parts coward, I do not know
> Why yet I live to say "This thing's to do;"
> Sith I have cause and will and strength and means
> To do't.

Romeo and Juliet (c. 1595), the story of doomed young lovers caught in the wake of their families' blood feud. The balcony scene between Romeo and Juliet is one of the great examples of love poetry in the English language.

A Midsummer Night's Dream (c. 1596), a play about quarreling kings and queens, young lovers, fairies, and a lowly but self-confident weaver named Bottom. While lost in the forest one night, Bottom is given the head of an ass by Puck, the playful servant of the fairy king. Puck also uses his magic to cause the queen of the fairies to fall in love with Bottom, and to complicate the relationships among the lovers in the forest.

Henry IV, *Parts 1 and 2* (c. 1597–1598), which describe the progress of Prince Hal from tavern roustabout to victorious warrior to king of England. Hal's lowlife companions include Falstaff, the fat, cowardly knight with a razor-sharp wit — one of the greatest comic characters in literature.

Julius Caesar (c. 1599), the story of Brutus, the noble Roman who leads a conspiracy to assassinate the tyrant Caesar and ends by paying with his life. The play includes a famous speech to the populace by Mark Antony ("Friends, Romans, countrymen, lend me your ears.").

King Lear (c. 1606), a play about an aging king who divides his kingdom between two daughters who pretend love for him, while rejecting the third, who genuinely loves him but feels it is unseemly to make a show of it. *Lear* portrays the terrors of age, betrayal, and isolation in scenes of matchless power and beauty.

Shakespeare's Sonnets (c. 1593–1600), a collection of poems about love, time, pride, loss, and regret that come closest to revealing details about Shakespeare's own life and emotions. They are filled with memorable lines and images, as in Sonnet 73:

> That time of year thou mayst in me behold
> When yellow leaves, or none, or few, do hang
> Upon those boughs which shake against the cold,
> Bare ruin'd choirs, where late the sweet birds sang.
> In me thou seest the twilight of such day
> As after sunset fadeth in the west,
> Which by and by black night doth take away
> Death's second self, that seals up all in rest.
> In me thou see'st the glowing of such fire
> That on the ashes of his youth doth lie,
> As the death-bed whereon it must expire,
> Consum'd with that which it was nourish'd by.
> This thou perceivest, which makes thy love more strong,
> To love that well which thou must leave ere long.

Elizabethan and Jacobean drama featured many other extraordinary playwrights, among whom were Christopher Marlowe, Thomas Middleton, John Webster, and Ben Jonson. Marlowe's *Tamburlaine*, *Doctor Faustus*, and *Edward II* are often cited as influences on Shakespeare. Jonson was known for satirical plays such as ***Bartholomew Fair*** and ***Every Man in His Humour***.

Middleton's ***The Changeling***, written with William Rowley, tells the story of Deflores, a troll-like henchman, who commits a murder for Beatrice, a lady at court, then demands her love as payment for the deed. It represents a category of drama called Jacobean revenge tragedy. These plays, the best of which contain verse that compares favorably in imaginative power to that of Shakespearean tragedy, are dark explorations of human psychology, with a crowd-pleasing penchant for violence and sex. This sample is from Act III:

Beatrice: Why, 'tis impossible thou canst be so wicked,
                 Or shelter such a cunning cruelty,
                 To make his death the murderer of my honour.
                 Thy language is so bold and vicious,
                 I cannot see which way I can forgive it
                 With any modesty.

Deflores: Push, you forget your self —
                 A woman dipt in blood, and talk of modesty?

Beatrice: O misery of sin! Would I had been bound
                 Perpetually unto my living hate
                 In that Piracquo, than to hear these words.
                 Think but upon the distance that Creation
                 Set 'twixt thy blood and mine, and keep thee there.

Deflores: Look but into your conscience, read me there,
                 "Tis a true book, you'll find me there your equal:
                 Push, fly not to your birth, but settle you
                 In what the act has made you . . .

The metaphysical poets of the early to mid-1600s included John Donne, George Herbert, and Andrew Marvell among others. These poets used outrageous metaphors, extended comparisons, and subtle wit to explore the fundamental nature of reality and humanity's place in it. Their imagination and obscurity made them favorites of the modernist poets of the twentieth century. A typical metaphysical lyric is Donne's "**The Flea**," in which the narrator insists that since a flea has bitten both him and the woman he seeks to seduce, then their blood is already mingled:

Mark but this flea, and mark in this,
How little that which thou deniest me is;
It suck'd me first, and now sucks thee,
And in this flea our two bloods mingled be.
Thou know'st that this cannot be said
A sin, nor shame, nor loss of maidenhead;
 Yet this enjoys before it woo,
 And pamper'd swells with one blood made of two;
 And this, alas! is more than we would do.

Around 1605, the Spaniard Miguel de Cervantes published the first of two volumes of ***Don Quixote***, his classic story of a man whose reading of novels about chivalry leads him to set out on his own knightly quests. Accompanied by a poor but sensible farmer named Sancho Panza, Quixote speaks in high-flown words and refuses to let go of his delusions despite being stymied time and again by the real world.

In 1667, the English poet John Milton published the ten books of ***Paradise Lost***, his long poem on the theme of mankind's fall from grace and God's banishment of Satan from heaven. Milton's stated purpose for the work was to "justify the ways of God to man." In the poem, he employs a powerful blank verse, as in this passage where Satan surveys hell:

Is this the Region, this the Soil, the Clime,
Said then the lost Arch-Angel, this the seat
That we must change for Heav'n, this mournful gloom
For that celestial light? Be it so, since he
Who now is sovereign can dispose and bid
What shall be right: farthest from him is best
Whom reason hath equal'd, force hath made supreme
Above his equals. Farewell happy fields
Where joy for ever dwells: Hail horrors, hail
Infernal world, and thou profoundest Hell
Receive thy new Possessor: One who brings
A mind not to be chang'd by Place or Time.

Pilgrim's Progress (1678) by John Bunyan is a Christian allegory of mankind's journey from the City of Destruction to the Celestial City. On the way, the pilgrim discovers the joys and challenges of a Christian believer's spiritual quest.

THE NEOCLASSICAL PERIOD

The period from the latter part of the 1600s to 1798 is the age of the Restoration in England, and is also called **the Neoclassical Period** and the age of enlightenment for its emphasis on reason and progress. While European writers such as Voltaire and Rousseau mocked the supremacy of the Catholic Church and believed in the ability to remake the world on a more rational basis, English writers such as Jonathan Swift, Alexander Pope, and Samuel Johnson used their wit and learning to satirize the follies of mankind. In this passage from Swift's *A Tale of a Tub* he satirizes what he sees as his era's excessive faith in rationalism:

> For great turns are not always given by strong hands, but by lucky adaption, and at proper seasons; and it is of no import where the fire was kindled, if the vapor has once got up into the brain. For the upper region of man is furnished like the middle region of the air; the materials are formed from causes of the widest difference, yet produce at last the same substance and effect. Mists arise from the earth, steams from dunghills, exhalations from the sea, and smoke from fire; yet all clouds are the same in composition as well as consequences, and the fumes issuing from a jakes[1] will furnish as comely and useful a vapor as incense from an altar. Thus far, I suppose, will easily be granted me; and then it will follow, that as the face of nature never produces rain but when it is overcast and disturbed, so human understanding, seated in the brain, must be troubled and overspread by vapors, ascending from the lower faculties to water the invention and render it fruitful.

Swift also wrote *Gulliver's Travels,* a satirical account of an imaginary journey to three lands inhabited by, respectively, six-inch-tall people, giants, and intelligent horse-like creatures. Daniel Defoe's **Robinson Crusoe**, a more realistic tale of a shipwrecked traveler, tells the story of how Crusoe struggles to survive on an island and eventually meets and befriends a frightened native named Friday. It is one of the early classics of the novel form.

---

1   latrine

Pope's essays and satires in heroic couplets included the mock-epic *Rape of the Lock*, *An Essay on Man*, *Epistle to Dr. Arbuthnot*, and one of the landmark satires in English literature, *The Dunciad*. In witty, aphoristic couplets, the poem ridicules those who pretend to have wit, culture, or knowledge but achieve only dullness. It concludes with "Dullness" sowing chaos everywhere:

> Thus at her [Dullness's] felt approach, and secret might,
> Art after Art goes out, and all is Night.
> See skulking Truth to her old Cavern fled,
> Mountains of Casuistry heap'd o'er her head!
> Philosophy, that lean'd on Heav'n before,
> Shrinks to her second cause, and is no more. . . .
> Lo! thy dread Empire, CHAOS! is restor'd;
> Light dies before thy uncreating word:
> Thy hand, great Anarch! lets the curtain fall;
> And Universal Darkness buries All.

Samuel Johnson, one of the great literary figures of the time, not only wrote essays, fiction, and poetry, but also compiled *A Dictionary of the English Language*. John Dryden, another master of heroic couplets, excelled in drama, poetry, and translation.

The Irish-born English novelist Laurence Sterne brought a sly wit and playfulness to his novel *Tristram Shandy*. Sterne allowed his narrator to leave aside what little plot there was in favor of digressions on all sorts of topics—from names to noses to warfare. In this he was the forerunner of many postmodern writers, who self-consciously tinker with the novel's form. Here Tristram Shandy insists that his digressions have an artful purpose:

> For in this long digression which I was accidentally led into, as in all
> my digressions (one only excepted) there is a master-stroke of digres-
> sive skill, the merit of which has all along, I fear, been overlooked by
> my reader, — not for want of penetration in him, — but because 'tis
> an excellence seldom looked for, or expected indeed, in a digression;
> — and it is this: That tho' my digressions are all fair, as you observe,
> — and that I fly off from what I am about, as far and as often too as
> any writer in *Great Britain;* yet I constantly take care to order affairs
> so, that my main business does not stand still in my absence.

In France, the Neoclassical Period abounded in writers who looked to Greek and Roman models for their inspiration. Pierre Corneille, the leading French dramatist of the mid-1600s, drew on Aristotle's ideas of unity in drama: unity of action (focus on events that occur during the running time of the play and are logically linked), unity of time (events compressed into an imaginary 24- or 30-hour period), and unity of place (events occurring in a limited area, such as within a palace or a single city — a non-Aristotelian idea that Corneille saw as following necessarily from unity of action and time). While Corneille respected the "three unities," he refused to follow them slavishly, which brought the scorn of French critics.

In plays such as *El Cid*, in which a Spanish knight is torn between his love for a girl and his self-imposed duty to take revenge on her father, Corneille successfully put his dramatic theories into practice. Another French dramatist inspired by classical authors was Jean Racine, whose plays *Phédre*, *Andromaque*, and *Athalie* were written in alexandrine verse (twelve-syllable lines) of great precision, grace, and emotional force.

Molière (the stage name of the actor/playwright Jean-Baptiste Poquelin) penned sparkling verse comedies such as *Tartuffe*, *The Misanthrope*, and *The Imaginary Invalid* that satirized the hypocrisy of French moralists and religious leaders. The French poet Jean de La Fontaine wrote fables in verse that were based on the oral tradition of fabulists such as the Greek Aesop (who may, in fact, be apochryphal) and the Roman Phaedrus. Like Aesop's fables, La Fontaine's featured animal characters that acted out brief tales exemplifying truths about life, fate, and human nature. Typical is his **"The Sun and the Frogs"**:

> The day the tyrant Sun was wed
> His subjects drank and cheered and fed.
> But only Aesop could divine
> How wrong they were to feel so fine.
> This Sun, said he, with hints of dread,
> Has plans beyond the marriage bed.
> At once, as one, near and beyond,
> The frogs cried out from every pond,
> Wailing with woe to contemplate
> The tyrant's offspring — awful fate!
> One sun, they said, is hard to take,
> But five or six? They'd dry each lake,
> Empty the seas, wipe out our race!
> Swimming the Styx is what we face.
> For a poor and unschooled animal,
> The Frog, I think, thinks fairly well.

THE ROMANTIC PERIOD

Dating from the late 1700s to the mid-nineteenth century, Romanticism was a reaction against an overemphasis on reason in favor of imagination and creativity. Romantic writers examined their own feelings and emotions with unprecedented curiosity and found inspiration not only in the beauties of nature but also in unusual sources, such as obscure writings of the Middle Ages and the evocative ruins of past societies. Many also opposed the dehumanizing effects of the Industrial Revolution, which led them to radical political ideas as well as a focus on individual imagination. Much of the best Romantic literature is in lyric poetry, but this was also the period when the novel came into its own.

The first great work of English Romanticism was a joint work by William Wordsworth and Samuel Taylor Coleridge: *Lyrical Ballads* (1798). The poets rejected rigid conventions in favor of the language that ordinary people used every day. Wordsworth's best poems express his ecstatic reaction to nature:

> And I have felt
> A presence that disturbs me with the joy
> Of Elevated thoughts; a sense sublime
> Of something far more deeply interfused,
> Whose dwelling is the light of setting suns,
> And the round ocean and the living air,
> And the blue sky, and in the mind of man:
> A motion and a spirit, that impels
> All thinking things, all objects of all thought,
> And rolls through all things.

For his part, Coleridge included *The Rime of the Ancient Mariner*, a long poem that consists of an old sailor's account of a cursed sea voyage that ends in tragedy. The poem includes many chilling elements, as the sailor describes being forced by the ship's crew to wear a dead albatross around his neck, and then watching the crew members die one by one from lack of fresh water ("Water, water, every where:/ Nor any drop to drink").

Other great Romantic poets included Percy Bysshe Shelley, John Keats, and George Gordon, Lord Byron. Shelley captured the Romantic spirit with **"Ozymandias,"** a lyric about the vanity of ancient kings whose monuments to themselves decay to dust. Although he died very young, Keats produced some of the most beautiful and profound odes in English, including "**Ode on a Grecian Urn**" and "**Ode to a Nightingale**." Byron wrote gloomy Romantic lyrics, but perhaps his greatest work is the long poem *Don Juan*, which is a comic satire more like those of the Neoclassical Age.

The Romantic infatuation with the ruins of the past led to Gothic novels — horror stories set in crumbling castles and old monasteries. Mary Shelley's *Frankenstein*, about a man of science who brings to life a stitched-together corpse, combines Gothic horror with questions about the limits of science in the modern world. Ann Radcliffe's *The Mysteries of Udolpho* describes a young woman who is imprisoned in an old Italian castle.

Writing somewhat against the Romantic grain, Jane Austen produced novels about sensible young women who strive to keep questions of romance and money in perspective. *Sense and Sensibility* and *Pride and Prejudice* display a casual wit and psychological penetration that were new in novels of the time.

Bridging the gap from Romanticism to Modernism in England was the Victorian period, which saw a further development in the English novel. Charles Dickens wrote *bildungsromans,* or novels that describe the development of a young person from childhood to maturity, such as *David Copperfield* and *Great Expectations*. (Other examples of the form in world literature include Gustave Flaubert's *Sentimental Education* [1869] and Thomas Mann's *The Magic Mountain* [1924]).

Dickens created a swarm of distinctive characters with a facility that rivaled Shakespeare's. Dickens is also important for his focus on social problems of the nineteenth century. Having himself worked at a blacking factory as a boy, he sympathized with the plight of children and orphans in the teeming slums of London, as in this passage from *Oliver Twist*:

> Although Oliver had enough to occupy his attention in keeping sight of his leader, he could not help bestowing a few hasty glances on either side of the way, as he passed along. A dirtier or more wretched place he had never seen. The street was very narrow and muddy, and the air was impregnated with filthy odours. There were a good many small shops; but the only stock in trade appeared to be heaps of children, who, even at that time of night, were crawling in and out at the doors, or screaming from inside.

At about the same time, Elizabeth Gaskell produced novels such as *Mary Barton* (1848) about social problems caused by industrialism in England.

Other great novelists of the period traced the adventures of long-suffering heroines, as in Thomas Hardy's *Tess of the D'Urbervilles*, Charlotte Brontë's *Jane Eyre*, and Emily Brontë's *Wuthering Heights*. Classic novels with female protagonists also appeared in other literatures during the nineteenth century. France's Gustave Flaubert traced the fall of a provincial wife with romantic longings in *Madame Bovary*. Russia's Leo Tolstoy presented the tragic consequences of a married woman's affair in *Anna Karenina*.

Thrill-seeking Victorian readers enjoyed detective stories and novels, such as Arthur Conan Doyle's works featuring Sherlock Holmes, and horror stories, such as Robert Louis Stevenson's *Dr. Jekyll and Mr. Hyde* and Bram Stoker's *Dracula*. In poetry, Robert Browning and Alfred, Lord Tennyson wrote long, novelistic poems and dramatic monologues that explored human psychology.

A poetic movement in France called Symbolism emerged to dominate the final two decades of the nineteenth century. It was a reaction against the Parnassian school of poets, who wrote verse that emphasized metrical form and restricted emotion. The stylistic, thematic, and philosophic tenets of Symbolism were established in such works as Charles Baudelaire's *The Flowers of Evil*, Arthur Rimbaud's *Illuminations*, and the poems of Paul Verlaine and Stéphane Mallarmé.

Symbolism focused on moods and transient sensations instead of lucid statements and logical descriptions. It embodied a desire to apprehend a transcendental realm of being, where the essence of life could be expressed subjectively in exotic, sometimes morbid terms. The freedom of association and arcane language of the style can be seen in these stanzas from Rimbaud's "**The Drunken Boat**":

> The storm made bliss of my sea-borne awakenings.
> Lighter than a cork, I danced on the waves
> Which men call eternal rollers of victims,
> For ten nights, without once missing the foolish eye of the harbor lights!

> Sweeter than the flesh of sour apples to children,
> The green water penetrated my pinewood hull

> And washed me clean of the bluish wine-stains and the splashes of sick-
> ness,
> Carrying away both rudder and anchor.

MODERNISM AND POSTMODERNISM

Modernism in literature arose as a feeling of disillusionment with modern culture and society, shock and a sense of waste after World War I, and a new urge to reject past forms and experiment with new ones. A key work of modernism is American expatriate T.S. Eliot's poem *The Waste Land* (1922). It uses dozens of allusions to myth, legend, and past literature to suggest mankind's restless search for spiritual meaning. Like some other modernist writers, Eliot describes the most ordinary daily routines and events in terms of mythical quests and literary forebears:

> At the violet hour, when the eyes and back
> Turn upward from the desk, when the human engine waits
> Like a taxi throbbing waiting,
> I Tiresias, though blind, throbbing between two lives,
> Old man with wrinkled female breasts, can see
> At the violet hour, the evening hour that strives
> Homeward, and brings the sailor home from sea,
> The typist home at teatime, clears her breakfast, lights
> Her stove, and lays out food in tins.

In his earlier "**Love Song of J. Alfred Prufrock**," Eliot used dramatic monologue to depict a frustrated, indecisive man at large in a modern city. Around the same time, Irish novelist James Joyce published *Ulysses*, which includes an elaborate analogy between the events in the life of an advertising salesman, Leonard Bloom, on one summer day in Dublin and the adventures of Odysseus in Homer's *Odyssey*. Joyce uses every tool at his disposal to tell his story, including parody, allusion, documentary-style reporting, and even stream of consciousness (the unfiltered thoughts of a character presented in words), as in this excerpt from Molly Bloom's soliloquy:

> ...I love flowers I'd love to have the whole place swimming in roses God
> of heaven there's nothing like nature the wild mountains then the sea and
> the waves rushing then the beautiful country with fields of oats and wheat

and all kinds of things and all the fine cattle going about that would do your heart good to see rivers and lakes and flowers all sorts of shapes and smells and colours springing up even out of the ditches primroses and violets nature it is as for them saying there's no God I wouldn't give a snap of my two fingers for all their learning why don't they go and create something I often asked him . . .

The Irish poet William Butler Yeats embraced modernism in powerful, allusive poems such as "**The Second Coming**" and "**Among School Children.**" Another literary modernist was Virginia Woolf, whose novels, including *To the Lighthouse* and *Mrs. Dalloway*, also experimented with stream-of-consciousness and psychological portraits.

The French novelist Marcel Proust's masterpiece, *In Search of Lost Time*, explores in fascinating detail the impressions and memories of a sensitive narrator in aristocratic Parisian circles. In Czechoslovakia, Franz Kafka wrote modernist classics that presented the absurdity and tragedy of mankind's situation in the world. In "**The Metamorphosis**," a man wakes up one morning to find himself transformed into a giant dung beetle. In his novels *The Trial* and *The Castle*, Kafka depicts protagonists caught in webs of bureaucracy and inexplicable guilt that mirror the difficulties of modern life.

Sensing the dangers of totalitarian political systems, some mid-twentieth Century novelists wrote dystopian fiction to portray what they saw as the opposite of "utopian" dreams. George Orwell's *1984* depicted an England enslaved by a dictatorial Big Brother and assailed by "doublespeak" slogans such "War Is Peace, Freedom Is Slavery, and Ignorance Is Strength." In *Brave New World*, Aldous Huxley invented a future in which a world government conditions the people to buy products and relieve their frustrations with drugs. Both books were inspired by *We*, an earlier dystopian novel by the Russian writer Yevgeny Zamyatin.

Postmodernism as a literary movement presented a fragmented view of reality that drew on parody, pastiche, unreliable narrators, irony, black humor, and a general feeling of cultural exhaustion. Postmodern protagonists often create their own versions of reality to compete with or replace the reality of everyday experience. The Argentine writer Jorge Luis Borges, for example, wrote tales about an infinite library, a universe created by a team of authors, and a man who can't forget anything he's ever seen or heard.

Vladimir Nabokov, a Russian writer who emigrated to the United States, created novels such as ***Lolita*** and ***Pale Fire*** that are as intricate and ingenious as puzzle boxes or a hall of mirrors. Gabriel García Márquez, Salman Rushdie, Margaret Atwood, Umberto Eco, and Jeannette Winterson have all written novels that include aspects of postmodernism. In novels such as *Money* and *London Fields,* Martin Amis presents a postmodernist version of today's media-driven world, in which people indulge their own fantasies to replace the frustrations of everyday reality.

Multicultural and postcolonial literature in the twentieth century has described and expressed emotions about the many human effects of imperialism and its final decline. Writers such as the Nigerians Wole Soyinka and Chinua Achebe, South Africa's Athol Fugard, and India's R.K. Narayan and Arundhati Roy have chronicled the struggles of their societies against Western and European dominance both economically and culturally. This passage from Achebe's ***Things Fall Apart*** expresses the people's distress and anger at the cultural imperialism in which whites try to change African customs and beliefs:

"Does the white man understand our custom about land?"

"How can he when he does not even speak our tongue? But he says that our customs are bad; and our own brothers who have taken up his religion also say that our customs are bad. How do you think we can fight when our own brothers have turned against us? The white man is very clever. He came quietly and peaceably with his religion. We were amused at his foolishness and allowed him to stay. Now he has won our brothers, and our clan can no longer act like one. He has put a knife on the things that held us together and we have fallen apart."

AMERICAN LITERATURE

The first American literature was Native American oral myths explaining how the world was created, describing how mankind and culture emerged, and relating the adventures of mythic heroes and tricksters. In trickster tales, the hero, usually an anthropomorphized animal, often is involved in mischief, deception, or treachery. The trickster may be able to change shapes or perform magic to cheat or deceive gods, humans, or other animals. Many indigenous myths also described the first encounters between Native Americans and white Europeans.

In one tale from the Brule Sioux, the trickster Spider Man goes from village to village warning his people about the coming of "the White Long-legs" who will change everything — as Native American life indeed did change with the coming of European settlers. This would become a common theme of Native American writers in the future: the dangers inherent in surrendering indigenous cultural values and traditions as a result of contact with European civilization.

Among the first written literature in America was the poetry of Anne Bradstreet (1612–1672), a Puritan who lived with her family in Massachusetts. Her best poems, such as "**To My Dear and Loving Husband**," describe family life, personal loss, and hopes for the future with the intimacy of a living voice. In general, however, literature had an uncertain start in the American colonies; Cotton Mather thought poetry almost a sickness and Benjamin Franklin dismissed it as not immediately useful to the colonies. The best writing was in political documents and tracts, such as the Federalist Papers and the Declaration of Independence, and Franklin's own *Poor Richard's Almanac* and *Autobiography*.

One poet who did break new ground was Phillis Wheatley. Born in Gambia, in Africa, she was sold into slavery at age seven. Yet she received an education in Boston and eventually published her *Poems* in 1773 — the first poetry published by an African American. In 1789 appeared *The Interesting Narrative of the Life of Olaudah Equiano, or Gustavus Vassa, the African*, a narrative of an African American's capture in Africa and voyage to America. Equiano's account of how he and his sister were seized while out playing and transported to a slave ship for the voyage across the ocean was harrowing and increased the efforts of abolitionists who were working to end slavery.

In the early part of the nineteenth century, Washington Irving became the first American writer to achieve international fame, with stories and tall tales such as "*Rip Van Winkle,*" about a man who falls asleep for twenty years, and "*The Legend of Sleepy Hollow,*" about the superstitious Ichabod Crane and his encounter with the headless horseman. James Fenimore Cooper helped create the mythic American West in his *Leatherstocking Tales* such as *The Last of the Mohicans* (1826), with its trapper hero, Hawkeye — the first of a long line of rugged individualists in American literature:

> . . .The hardy colonist, and the trained European who fought at his side, frequently expended months in struggling against the rapids of the streams, or in effecting the rugged passes of the mountains, in quest of an opportunity to exhibit their courage in a more martial conflict. But,

emulating the patience and self-denial of the practiced native warriors, they learned to overcome every difficulty; and it would seem that, in time, there was no recess of the woods so dark, nor any secret place so lovely, that it might claim exemption from the inroads of those who had pledged their blood to satiate their vengeance, or to uphold the cold and selfish policy of the distant monarchs of Europe.

Influenced by English Romanticism, Edgar Allan Poe created his own style of Gothic literature in poems about love and death such as *"Annabel Lee"* and *"The Raven."* Poe wrote with a distinctive style of rhythm and repetition:

> And the raven, never flitting, still is sitting, still is sitting
> On the pallid bust of Pallas just above my chamber door;
> And his eyes have all the seeming of a demon's that is dreaming,
> And the lamp-light o'er him streaming throws his shadow on the floor;
> And my soul from out that shadow that lies floating on the floor
> Shall be lifted — nevermore!

Poe also wrote short fiction, such as *"The Murders in the Rue Morgue"* (often cited as the first modern detective story), *"The Pit and the Pendulum,"* and *"The Telltale Heart."* The latter two are examples of Poe's emphasis on psychological horror. Poe also wrote essays about literary craftsmanship that were influential among French writers such as Baudelaire.

Transcendentalism was a New England movement whose members believed people have knowledge about themselves and the world that transcends the evidence of their senses. The transcendentalists favored imagination and intuition over logic. The poet and essayist Ralph Waldo Emerson, one of the movement's leaders, sought "an original relation to the universe" and the natural world through self-reliance, self-respect, and the tireless pursuit of truth. He is best known for essays such as *"Self-Reliance"* and *"Nature."*

Henry David Thoreau's *Walden* describes his attempt to put transcendentalism into practice by living a simpler life close to nature. The novelist Nathaniel Hawthorne and the poet Henry Wadsworth Longfellow also were associated with transcendentalism.

Although Emily Dickinson led a secluded life, she was one of the greatest American poets of the nineteenth century. Her unusual imagery and strong rhythms made her poetry instantly memorable, as in this example:

> Because I could not stop for Death
> He kindly stopped for me;
> The carriage held but just ourselves
> And Immortality.

The poet John Greenleaf Whittier claimed that he placed a higher value having his name on an Anti-Slavery Declaration than on the title page of a book. Whittier wrote many powerful poems against slavery, including *"The Slave Ship"* (1846), in which captured Africans who've been blinded by sickness are thrown overboard as useless for sale.

Walt Whitman's *Leaves of Grass*, one of the greatest books of poetry in American history, celebrated ordinary working people and the common experiences of life in America in long lines and repetitive cadences drawn from biblical verses, as in *"Crossing Brooklyn Ferry"*:

> Crowds of men and women attired in the usual costumes! How curious
>   you are to me!
> On the ferry-boats, the hundreds and hundreds that cross, returning home,
>   are more
> curious to me than you suppose, . . .
> Just as you feel when you look on the river and sky, so I felt,
> Just as any of you is one of a living crowd, I was one of a crowd,
> Just as you are refreshed by the gladness of the river, and the bright flow,
>   I was refreshed.

Herman Melville wrote novels of the sea, including *Moby Dick*, in which the sea captain Ahab obsessively pursues the white whale that wounded him in the past. Many of Mark Twain's novels and stories were based on his experiences as a riverboat captain on the Mississippi. *The Adventures of Huckleberry Finn*, his greatest book, is narrated in the rustic voice of Huck, a homeless boy who befriends Jim, a runaway slave. Despite being surrounded by racist attitudes, Huck recognizes Jim's humanity and the foolishness of racism.

Another classic book on racism and freedom was the *Narrative of the Life of Frederick Douglass*. It belongs to a genre called the slave narrative. In it, Douglass, a former slave and erudite speaker for the cause of abolition, describes his escape from bondage and the dehumanizing effects of slavery:

Every tone [of a hymn] was a testimony against slavery, and a prayer to God for deliverance from chains. The hearing of those wild notes always depressed my spirit, and filled me with ineffable sadness. I have frequently found myself in tears while hearing them. The mere recurrence to those songs, even now, afflicts me; and while I am writing these lines, an expression of feeling has already found its way down my cheek. To those songs I trace my first glimmering conception of the dehumanizing character of slavery. I can never get rid of that conception. Those songs still follow me, to deepen my hatred of slavery, and quicken my sympathies for my brethren in bonds.

Many important regional novelists appeared in the later nineteenth century with stories about American life away from the major cities. These included Willa Cather, who wrote about life on the Nebraska prairie; Kate Chopin, whose novel *The Awakening* was an early feminist novel set in her native New Orleans; and Sarah Orne Jewett, who captured the flavor of community life in New England in *The Country of the Pointed Firs*. Henry James's main subject in his many novels and stories, such as "Daisy Miller," *The American*, and *Portrait of a Lady*, was the innocent American abroad in a corrupt and sophisticated Europe. Stephen Crane's Civil War novel *The Red Badge of Courage* was a penetrating look at the reality of war from the point of view of a Union private.

American modernism in the first half of the twentieth century brought a variety of fresh approaches in poetry and prose. Ezra Pound, Amy Lowell, H. D. (Hilda Doolittle), and others helped found the Imagist movement, which featured free-verse poems phrased in common speech that addressed a wide variety of subject matter and conveyed meaning through clear, precisely described images. Some Imagist poems were based on European and Asian models, such as Pound's haiku-like **"In a Station of the Metro"**:

> The apparition of these faces in the crowd;
> Petals on a wet, black bough.

The poetry of Edwin Arlington Robinson and Robert Frost used traditional forms to present scenes from nature and explore tragic lives. Frost wrote about the New England countryside and its staunch, laconic people in poems such as *"Mending Wall," "Home Burial,"* and *"Stopping by Woods on a Snowy Evening."* William Carlos Williams's poems used his experiences as a country doctor to present free-verse portraits of his native New Jersey. The work of these poets inspired later Americans such as Robert Lowell, Elizabeth Bishop, and Sylvia Plath.

Novelists such as F. Scott Fitzgerald, Ernest Hemingway, and William Faulkner explored new techniques in prose, particularly in Hemingway's flat, minimalist style and Faulkner's stream-of-consciousness passages. Fitzgerald's *The Great Gatsby* focused on a romantic cipher of a hero to present an ironic version of the American Dream. Faulkner's novels, such as *The Sound and the Fury*, presented portraits of the American South and its tormented inhabitants, as did the novels and stories of Eudora Welty. The effects of the Great Depression on migrant farmers formed the subject of John Steinbeck's *The Grapes of Wrath*.

As modernism was replaced by the fragmentation of post-modernism, more American novelists and playwrights wrote about the illusions and disappointments of American life after World War II. Arthur Miller's play *The Death of a Salesman* depicted a man whose failures made him feel like an outcast. John Updike's *Rabbit Run* and other novels present characters who are spiritually adrift and unfulfilled. Kurt Vonnegut (*Slaughterhouse Five*) and Thomas Pynchon (*Gravity's Rainbow*) used fresh techniques, from comic science fiction to satires of science and nuclear war, to explore modern American life.

Many powerful multicultural voices emerged in the United States in the twentieth century. The Harlem Renaissance in New York's Harlem area produced poets such as Langston Hughes and James Weldon Johnson. African American writers such as Ralph Ellison, Richard Wright (*Native Son*), Zora Neale Hurston (*Their Eyes Were Watching God*), and James Baldwin, along with later novelists Alice Walker (*The Color Purple*) and Toni Morrison (*Song of Solomon*, *Beloved*), brought a new depth and realism to the depiction of African American life. Ellison's groundbreaking *Invisible Man* conveyed the sense of alienation from society felt by the main character:

> Or again, you often doubt if you really exist. You wonder whether you aren't simply a phantom in other people's minds. Say, a figure in a nightmare which the sleeper tries with all his strength to destroy. It's when you feel like this that, out of resentment, you begin to bump people back.

Native American experience found expression in the novels and poems of N. Scott Momaday, Louise Ehrdrich's novels, and poetry by Joy Harjo. Momaday won the Pulitzer Prize in 1969 for *House Made of Dawn*, a novel that draws on Kiowa and Pueblo storytelling traditions to present a story of a Native American's journey from a childhood pueblo to war in Europe and back to the United States.

Hispanic writers also emerged in twentieth century America, describing the tug of ancestral loyalties amid the bustle of modern life. ***Bless Me, Ultima*** by Rudolfo Anaya is a novel rich in Mexican folklore as it tells the story of a man who must find a synthesis of the old and new. In ***The House on Mango Street***, Sandra Cisneros addresses the same issues from a woman's perspective. Much poetry from Hispanic Americans also expresses this tension between cultures, as in Angela de Hoyos' *"To Walt Whitman"*:

> here's a guitar for you
> a chicana guitar so
> you can spill out a song
> for the open road
> big enough for my people . . .
> that I can't seem to find
> in your poems.

Novelists such as the Chinese Americans Amy Tan, Maxine Hong Kingston, and Gish Jen brought an Asian perspective to stories of immigrant life in America, such as Tan's ***The Joy Luck Club*** and Kingston's ***The Woman Warrior***, which is subtitled *Memoirs of a Girlhood Among Ghosts*. Novelists, poets, and playwrights of various cultural backgrounds have expressed a common struggle with feelings of inferiority or exclusion from the larger society.

Recent novels also have explored the immigrant experience and the sensation of being suspended between two cultures. Jean Kwok's ***Girl in Translation*** tells the story of a girl and her mother who emigrate from Hong Kong to a squalid tenement in Brooklyn, New York. In ***The Namesake***, Jhumpa Lahiri describes the cultural and generational gap faced by members of an Indian family living in the United States. In ***The Brief Wondrous Life of Oscar Wao***, Junot Diaz uses wild humor to present the story of an overweight nerd from the Dominican Republic who dreams of becoming a great fantasy writer in his adopted land of America. The popular success of these works, along with many other multicultural stories and immigrant tales, ensures that American literature will continue to be enriched by a wide variety of voices.

YOUNG ADULT LITERATURE

Most fiction for young adults, whether novels or short stories, feature adolescent characters who are trying to negotiate the problems and emotions of leaving childhood for the adult world. For this reason, literature for young adults is often called problem novels or coming of age fiction. These stories range from an historical setting to contemporary life to science fiction, but they have in common a focus on the protagonist's inner struggles with coming of age in whatever society is depicted.

Novels for young adults tend to be short (150 pages or less) with a focus on a main character's thoughts and actions in a plot that occurs over a relatively brief period of time. Authors tend to aim for immediacy, brisk action, simple, uncluttered prose, and problems that are familiar to teenagers everywhere.

Sometimes teachers of secondary English can find young adult fiction that mirrors the topic or setting of a more difficult adult work that the class is studying, to give struggling readers an aid to understanding. For example, S.E. Hinton's *The Outsiders*, about the rivalries between two social groups, might serve as an introduction to an important theme of Shakespeare's *Romeo and Juliet*. M.H. Herlong's *The Great Wide Sea*, with its story of a boy whose father is missing at sea and who must face a dangerous storm with his younger brother, might help students get into *The Rime of the Ancient Mariner* or one of Melville's sea stories.

Other notable titles in young adult literature include:

- *Emma* by Jane Austen (1816)

- *The Call of the Wild* by Jack London (1903)

- *A Tree Grows in Brooklyn* by Betty Smith (1943)

- *The Catcher in the Rye* by J.D. Salinger (1951)

- *The Pigman* by Paul Zindel (1968)

- *I Know Why the Caged Bird Sings* by Maya Angelou (1969)

- *Bless the Beasts and Children* by Glendon Swarthout (1970)

- *Are You There God? It's Me, Margaret* by Judy Blume (1970)

- *Hatchet* by Gary Paulsen (1987)

- *The Giver* by Lois Lowry (1992)

- *The Princess Diaries* by Meg Cabot (2000)

- *The Absolutely True Diary of a Part-time Indian* by Alexie Sherman (2007)

- *The Hunger Games* by Suzanne Collins (2008)

- *One Crazy Summer* by Rita Williams-Garcia (2010)

- *Moon over Manifest* by Clare Vanderpool (2010)

- *Paperboy* by Vince Vawter (2013)

- *The Crossover* by Kwame Alexander (2014)

ELEMENTS OF LITERATURE

1.2 Craft and Structure of Literature

a. Distinguish salient features of genres (e.g., short story, drama, poetry, novel, creative nonfiction)

b. Define and analyze basic elements of literature (e.g., plot, setting, character, point of view, theme, narrative structure, figurative language, tone, diction, style)

c. Analyze the impact of the author's choices regarding how to develop and relate elements of a story or drama (e.g., where a story is set, how the action is ordered, how the characters/archetypes are introduced and developed)

d. Articulate the relationship between the expressed purposes and the characteristics of different forms of dramatic literature (e.g., comedy, tragedy)

e. Determine the meaning of words and phrases as they are used in a text, including figurative and connotative meanings

f. Analyze the impact of an author's specific word choices on meaning and tone, including words with multiple meanings

g. Analyze how an author's choices concerning how to structure specific parts of a text (e.g., the choice of where to begin or end a story, the use of flashbacks) contribute to its overall structure and meaning as well as its aesthetic impact

h. Analyze point of view, including how authors develop and contrast points of view of different characters or narrators and particular points of view or cultural experiences reflected in works of world literature

(California Common Core State Standards for English Language Arts, RL.6–12.2–7, RL.6–12.9)

LITERARY GENRES

Literary genres are the different modes of literary creation developed over the centuries — you might think of genres as the different ways that literature is packaged and presented. As a teacher of secondary English, the most important points you will convey about literary works are their insights into life and the human condition. However, it is also important to be familiar with the array of literary genres, their particular characteristics, and when they were most in use. The following is a list of genres.

Absurdist fiction is a novel or play that presents humanity's plight as meaningless and without purpose. This genre arose in the twentieth century and often reflects a reaction against war, society, and the stresses of modern life. Examples include Samuel Beckett's play *Waiting for Godot* and Joseph Heller's novel *Catch-22*.

An **allegory** is a fictional narrative that contains a second, symbolic meaning in addition to its overt story. In this type of story, characters represent human qualities such as virtues and vices or abstract concepts such as death. John Bunyan's *Pilgrim's Progress* is an allegory of a Christian's journey to faith and redemption. C.S. Lewis's *The Lion, the Witch, and the Wardrobe* is also a Christian allegory. George Orwell's novel *Animal Farm* is an allegory of the Stalinist regime in the Soviet Union, using animal characters.

A **ballad** is a songlike poem that tells a story and often has a refrain, or repeated line or lines. Many ballads are in iambic form with alternating lines of four stresses and three stresses. Ballads were popular in Europe from the Middle Ages down to the nineteenth century. They often were lurid accounts of murders, revenge, and violence. Rudyard Kipling was a master of the ballad in cockney vernacular:

> "What are the bugles blowin' for?" said Files-on-Parade.
> "To turn you out, to turn you out", the Colour-Sergeant said.
> "What makes you look so white, so white?" said Files-on-Parade.
> "I'm dreadin' what I've got to watch," the Colour-Sergeant said.
>> "For they're hangin' Danny Deever, you can hear the Dead March play,
>> The regiment's in 'ollow square—they're hangin' him to-day;

They've taken of his buttons off an' cut his stripes away,
An' they're hangin' Danny Deever in the mornin'."

The **comic novel** is a feature of British and American literature. Like a dramatic comedy, it seeks to amuse the reader with larger-than-life characters and outlandish events. The English writers Evelyn Waugh and P.G. Wodehouse were masters of the comic novel, while Mark Twain excelled in the form in America.

A **dystopia**, or dystopian novel, is a narrative that depicts an anti-utopia, a world where ordinary people live regimented lives at the whim of a totalitarian government. Examples of dystopian fiction are Aldous Huxley's *Brave New World,* Yevgeny Zamyatin's *We,* and George Orwell's *1984.*

The **epic** is a long narrative poetic work in a formal or elevated style that features a heroic lead character who often must undertake a journey or a great trial to overcome a powerful foe. Many of the oldest epics survived as oral tales until they were finally written down. Epics include the *Ramayana* (written in Sanskrit), *The Iliad* and *The Odyssey* by Homer, and *The Aeneid* by Virgil.

An **epistolary novel** is written in the form of letters, diaries, and journal entries. Samuel Richardson's *Clarissa*, Bram Stoker's *Dracula,* and Alice Walker's *The Color Purple* are all epistolary novels. *The Antagonist* by Lynn Coady is a modern novel consisting of unanswered email messages.

An **essay** is a prose work written in the first-person expressing strong opinions about some topic or life experience.

A **fable** is a tale that provides a moral lesson and features animals with human characteristics. *Aesop's Fables,* from ancient Greece, include such famous tales as "The Tortoise and the Hare." The French writer La Fontaine wrote fables in verse, such as "The Cicada and the Ant."

A **fairy tale** is a story that features fantasy characters from folklore and usually ends happily. Often, a fairy tale begins with the words "Once upon a time —." The Brothers Grimm collected fairy tales (such as "Cinderella" and "Hansel and Gretel") from old Germanic sources, while the Danish writer Hans Christian Andersen penned most of his tales (such as "The Ugly Duckling") as original stories with fairy tale trappings.

Fantasy is a genre that blends historical material, such as Viking warriors or British knights, with invented elements such as wizards with magical powers and mythical creatures such as dragons and unicorns. This genre is sometimes called "sword and sorcery." J.R.R. Tolkien's *Lord of the Rings* is a fantasy classic.

A **farce** is a comic play that employs stock situations and characters and exaggerated emotions. Many critics consider farce, with its many clichés, to be the lowest form of dramatic comedy.

A **legend** is a traditional story that has become part of the collective experience of a nation, ethnic group, or culture. It features characters that are not historical but seem to have existed at some time in the distant past. An example is the story of King Arthur and the sword in the stone; another is the Spanish legend of the fountain of youth.

A **lyric poem** is a brief work in verse that addresses the reader directly and expresses the poet's feelings and perceptions.

A **myth** is an ancient story that presents the exploits of gods or heroes to explain some aspect of life or nature. The Greek myth of Persephone, for example, explained the cycle of the seasons and the rebirth of spring. Many Native American myths address the origins of the world.

The **novel** is a long work of prose fiction that is often realistic and tends to address the concerns of the society in which it is produced. As a form of storytelling, however, it has proven endlessly adaptable, incorporating elements of fantasy, history, and philosophy. Among the great novels of the nineteenth century are *Sense and Sensibility* by Jane Austen, *David Copperfield* by Charles Dickens, and *War and Peace* by Leo Tolstoy. The twentieth century saw such influential novels as *The Great Gatsby* by F. Scott Fitzgerald, *One Hundred Years of Solitude* by Gabriel García Márquez, and *The Color Purple* by Alice Walker.

A **parody** is a work written in imitation of an author's style or of a genre in order to make fun of it and mock its conventions. For example, the English author Max Beerbohm wrote a famous parody titled "The Mote in the Middle Distance" that imitated Henry James's ornate writing style.

A **poem** is a literary work that is generally written in rhythmic lines of various lengths that may be divided into groups called stanzas. Poems may be as long as novels or as brief as two lines, and they can address any subject from first love to nuclear war. Before the twentieth century, poems in English generally were written in formal verse, with regular metered rhythm and a pattern of rhymes. Since then, most poems are written in free verse, which dispenses with patterns of rhythm and rhyme. Poems may be written in a variety of forms, including:

- **elegy**   A poem in a solemn or melancholic tone, especially one that mourns the death of a person or group.

- **haiku**   A Japanese poetic form consisting of three lines with 5, 7, and 5 syllables. A haiku in English typically includes a seasonal word or image as part of a comparison of two things.

- **limerick**   A comic five-line poem (rhyme scheme AABBA) that seems to have originated in England in the early 1700s.

- **ode**   A meditative poem written in praise of someone or about a serious subject. Ancient Greek odes were performed to music, and had a precise three-part structure. Modern odes, such as those by the English poet John Keats, have an irregular form with lines of different length and intermittent rhymes. The end of Keats's "Ode on a Grecian Urn" is famously cryptic:

> When old age shall this generation waste,
> Thou [e.g., the urn] shalt remain, in midst of other woe
> Than ours, a friend to man, to whom thou say'st
> "Beauty is truth, truth beauty," — that is all
> Ye know on earth, and all ye need to know.

- **pastoral**   A poem that depicts rural life or the life of shepherds in an idealized form, often for urban audiences. An example is Christopher Marlowe's "The Passionate Shepherd to His Love":

> Come live with me and be my Love,
> And we will all the pleasures prove
> That hills and valleys, dale and field,
> And all the craggy mountains yield.

There will we sit upon the rocks
And see the shepherds feed their flocks,
By shallow rivers, to whose falls
Melodious birds sing madrigals.

- **sonnet** A fourteen-line poetic form that originated in Italy and later became popular in Shakespeare's England. The Italian or Petrarchan sonnet consists of two quatrains (four-line stanzas rhymed ABBA) and six lines variously rhymed in pairs. Here is a translation from Petrarch's Italian:

It was the day when the sun's rays turned white
Out of the pity it felt for its sire,
When I was caught and taken by desire,
For your fair eyes, my lady, held me quite.

It did not seem to me a time to mind
The blows of Love; therefore I went along
Fearless, without suspicion, and my wrong
Began with the grief common to mankind.

Love found me weak, completely without arms,
With the way clear from the eyes to the heart,
For they are doors of fears and halls of harms.

Hence to my mind it was no glorious part
For him to wound me when I was so low,
And not to you even display his bow.

The Shakespearian sonnet has three quatrains (rhymed ABAB) and a closing couplet (two rhymed lines). An example of the form is Robert Frost's "A Silken Tent":

She is as in a field a silken tent
At noonday when a sunny summer breeze
Has dried the dew and all its ropes relent
So that in guys it gently sways at ease,
And its supporting central cedar pole,
That is its pinnacle to heavenward

And signifies the sureness of the soul,
Seems to owe naught to any single cord,
But strictly held by none, is loosely bound
By countless silken ties of love and thought
To everything on earth the compass round,
And only by one's going slightly taut
In the capriciousness of summer air
Is of the slightest bondage made aware.

- **triolet**   An eight-line poetic form based on French models. A triolet's first, fourth, and seventh lines are identical, as are its second and final lines. Thomas Hardy's "How Great My Grief" is a good example:

How great my grief, my joys how few,
Since first it was my fate to know thee!
Have the slow years not brought to view
How great my grief, my joys how few,
Nor memory shaped old times anew,
Nor loving-kindness helped to show thee
How great my grief, my joys how few,
Since first it was my fate to know thee?

- **villanelle**   An intricate French poetic form with nineteen lines divided into five three-line stanzas (called tercets) and one final quatrain. A villanelle has only two rhyme sounds, so it is difficult to write one in English, which has a relative scarcity of rhymes. The first two stanzas of Elizabeth Bishop's "One Art" shows the wit and intricacy of a villanelle:

The art of losing isn't hard to master;
so many things seem filled with the intent
to be lost that their loss is no disaster.

Lose something every day. Accept the fluster
of lost door keys, the hour badly spent.
The art of losing isn't hard to master.

A **satire** is a work that ridicules the follies and vices of individuals and society, often through comic exaggeration. Some satires are gentle and light-hearted in their wit, while others constitute savage attacks. For example, C.S. Lewis's *The Screwtape Letters* is a witty satire of the difficulties and rewards of living a religious life through a series of letters to Satan from one of his agents in the field. On the other hand, Jonathan Swift's "A Modest Proposal" is darker, with its straight-faced proposal that Irish babies be eaten to solve problems of overpopulation and famine.

Science fiction depicts scientific and technological breakthroughs and their effects on future society. Sometimes an alternate universe is described in which history on earth unfolded differently. Classics of the genre include Ursula K. le Guin's *The Left Hand of Darkness,* Robert Heinlein's *Stranger in a Strange Land,* and Arthur C. Clarke's *Rendezvous with Rama.*

A **short story** is a brief work of prose fiction that often concentrates on a single incident and one or two main characters. Masters of the genre include Anton Chekhov, Edgar Allan Poe, Ernest Hemingway, Guy de Maupassant, Flannery O'Connor, and Raymond Carver.

A **utopian novel** depicts its author's ideas about what a perfectly ordered society would be like. The first such book was Sir Thomas More's *Utopia*, published in 1516. Later examples are Samuel Butler's *Erewhon* and Edward Bellamy's *Looking Backward.* The latter, published in 1887, has its hero wake up from hypnosis in the Boston of the year 2000, which has become a socialist paradise.

LITERARY DEVICES

Literary devices are the various tools of language and storytelling that writers use to convey meaning and create a personal style. As a teacher of secondary English, you should be able to isolate and identify these elements in a literary work and explain how they help support the theme of the work or add to its effect or meaning. Your students should already be familiar with the basic literary elements, such as plot, setting, characterization, theme, tone, and point of view. However, it is important for you to go beyond these and point out additional elements and devices that contribute to the overall effect of a literary work.

Alliteration is the repeating of initial consonant sounds in a sentence, paragraph, or line of poetry. It can be used for a hypnotic effect or to emphasize certain words and phrases. At the beginning of *Lolita*, Vladimir Nabokov has the narrator describe how to pronounce the heroine's name:

> "Lo-lee-ta: the *t*ip of the *t*ongue *t*aking a trip of three *s*teps down the
> pala*te t*o *t*ap, at three, on the *t*eeth. Lo. Lee. Ta."

An **allusion** is a reference in a literary work to some famous person, place, event, artwork, or other literary work. Writers use allusion to enrich their work with shared cultural markers. In "The Waste Land," T.S. Eliot writes: "London bridge is falling down falling down falling down," an allusion to a well-known children's song. The allusion also emphasizes the poem's theme of decay and hopelessness.

An **anachronism** is a detail of a literary work that is not appropriate for its time setting. For example, having a woman in Victorian England make a call on a cell phone would be an anachronism.

An **analogy** is when a writer emphasizes the ways two apparently unlike things are actually similar. Here Emily Dickinson sets up an analogy between a church and her surroundings at home:

> Some keep the Sabbath going to Church –
> I keep it, staying at Home –
> With a Bobolink for a Chorister –
> And an Orchard, for a Dome –
>
> Some keep the Sabbath in Surplice –
> I, just wear my Wings –
> And instead of tolling the Bell, for Church,
> Our little Sexton – sings.
>
> God preaches, a noted Clergyman –
> And the sermon is never long,
> So instead of getting to Heaven, at last –
> I'm going, all along.

An **antagonist** is a person who opposes or is hostile to the protagonist, or central character in a story. The criminal mastermind Professor Moriarty is the antagonist to Sherlock Holmes.

An **antithesis** is a figure of speech that balances an idea with a contrasting one or its opposite. From Robert Frost: "Some say the world will end in fire,/Some say in ice."

Assonance is the repetition of vowel sounds in a sentence or line of poetry. Robert Louis Stevenson uses the long *o* sound here:

> From folk that sat on the terrace and drew out the even long
> Sudden crowings of laughter, monotonous drone of song;

A **character** is a person or humanlike animal in a story, poem, or play. Writers use characterization to reveal a character's personality through actions, gestures, mode of speech, thoughts, and reactions from other characters.

The **climax** of a narrative is the point of greatest dramatic tension. For example, the climax of *Romeo and Juliet* occurs when Romeo kills Juliet's cousin Tybalt and the lovers make plans to run away together.

Connotation is the use of precise words to give a positive or negative slant to a statement or passage. For example, the word *fragrance* has a positive connotation; *stench* has a negative one. Both words mean "smell."

Denotation is the literal meaning of a word, as found in a dictionary.

A writer creates the tone of a work through the use of **diction**, which is the choice of words and style of language used. A writer may use archaic, or old-fashioned, words such as *thee* and *thou*; dialect or regional speech patterns; colloquialisms, such as "I knew that idea would *blow up in our faces*"; and jargon and technical language, such as "If you take the vitals and the BP is too high, get the patient to a clinic stat!"

A **dramatic monologue** is a poetic form generally written in blank verse that presents the thoughts and emotions of a character in a particular situation. There is usually also an implied listener and setting, and often the speaker inadvertently reveals his or her true character in the course of the poem.

Enjambment is the continuation of a clause or sentence from one line of poetry to the next. Poets may use enjambment to subvert the reader's expectations about what the lines are saying. Enjambment can also create a faster pace or a change of rhythm.

en-jam-ment

continuation of a sentence w/out a pause beyond the end of a line, stanza or couplet

An **epigraph** is a quotation from another source that appears at the beginning of a literary work and suggests its theme.

Epilogue is a concluding section added to the end of a literary work.

Epiphany is a sudden, overwhelming realization about the meaning of something.

A **euphemism** is an inoffensive phrase used to replace a more direct or unpleasant expression. For example, the euphemism "She passed on" might be used for "She died."

A **figure of speech** is the use of words aside from their literal meaning. Often a figure of speech is used for an artistic or emotionally heightened effect. Types of figures of speech include simile, metaphor, hyperbole, personification, onomatopoeia, irony, oxymoron, metonymy, antithesis, and euphemism.

A **flashback** is a description or episode in a literary work that interrupts the main story to recount something that happened in the past.

Foreshadowing is when an author provides clues to what will happen later in a narrative. For example, the witches' speech at the beginning of *Macbeth* foreshadows the tragedy to come.

Heroic couplets are a form of English poetry with pairs of rhyming lines in iambic pentameter (five stresses to a line). This form was particularly important in the work of eighteenth century poets such as Alexander Pope, Samuel Johnson, and John Dryden. Here is a heroic couplet from Pope:

> Truth guards the poet, sanctifies the line
> And makes immortal, Verse as mean as mine.

Hyperbole is an absurdly exaggerated statement: "I am so thirsty I could drink the ocean dry."

Imagery is the use of descriptive language to enlist the senses in evoking a scene, situation, or state of mind. Here is an example from Edna St. Vincent Millay:

> But your voice, — never the rushing
> Of a river underground,

> Not the rising of the wind
> In the trees before the rain,
> Not the woodcock's watery call,
> Not the note the white-throat utters,
> Not the feet of children pushing
> Yellow leaves along the gutters
> In the blue and bitter fall,
> Shall content my musing mind
> For the beauty of that sound
> That in no new way at all
> Ever will be heard again.

Irony is a sudden discordance between the expected meaning of words or actions and what they actually mean. There are several kinds of irony in literary use. Useful examples are found in Shakespeare's *Hamlet*:

- Verbal irony is saying one thing and meaning something else. Hamlet mocks how hastily his mother married his uncle after his father's death: "Thrift, thrift, Horatio, the funeral baked meats did coldly furnish forth the wedding tables."

- Situational irony is when a situation is in reality much different than the character or characters think: For his final sword battle with Laertes, Hamlet is unaware that Laertes' sword has a deadly poison on its tip.

- Dramatic irony is when the audience is aware of something that the characters onstage (or in a story) do not know. In *Hamlet*, the audience knows that Hamlet is feigning madness to gain time, while the characters around him think he is genuinely mad.

A **malapropism** is a word mistaken for another word with a similar sound. Often it is used in the speeches of a comic character. The term gets its name from Mrs. Malaprop (from the French *mal a propos* or "ill-suited to the purpose"), a character in *The Rivals,* a play by Richard Brinsley Sheridan. For example, she says:

"I thought she had *persisted* from corresponding with him." (for *desisted*)

A **metaphor** is a figure of speech in which two unlike things are compared without the use of the words *like* or *as*, as in this poem by Emily Dickinson comparing hope to a bird:

Hope is the thing with feathers
That perches in the soul,
And sings the tune – without the words
And never stops at all,

And sweetest in the gale is heard;
And sore must be the storm
That could abash the little bird
That kept so many warm.

I've heard it in the chillest land,
And on the strangest sea;
Yet, never, in extremity,
It asked a crumb of me.

Meter is a way of measuring the rhythm in formal verse. Meter is shown by dividing a line of verse into feet, or units of two or three syllables. For example, each foot of an iambic meter has an unstressed syllable followed by a stressed syllable. A line of formal verse can have one foot (monometer), two (dimeter), three (trimeter), four (tetrameter), five (pentameter), or six (hexameter). Most formal English verse is in tetrameter or pentameter lines.

Here are the most common meters in English verse, with the slash marks denoting a stressed syllable:

- iambic (– /)
  Example: And miles to go before I sleep.

- trochaic (/ –)
  Example: Homeward goes the weary shepherd.

- anapestic (– – /)
  Example: The mysterious stranger appeared on the steps.

- dactylic (/ – –)
  Example: Feelings of sadness are calling me home.

Metonymy is a figure of speech in which a word is substituted for another word with which it is somehow linked or closely associated. For example, "The pen is mightier than the sword" means that the power of writing or literature is greater than military force.

Onomatopoeia is using words that imitate sounds, such as *crash, ring, clatter, buzz,* and *boom.*

An **oxymoron** is a phrase made up of words that seem contradictory when placed together but actually express a special meaning, such as "act naturally," "a deafening silence," and "passive aggressive."

A **paradox** is a statement whose two parts seems contradictory, yet upon further study convey a deeper truth. Here is an example in prose from George Orwell's *Animal Farm*: "All animals are equal, but some are more equal than others." And Frost's poem "The Tuft of Flowers" has "Men work together whether they work together or apart."

Personification is a figure of speech in which human characteristics are given to something nonhuman, such as an animal, object, or concept. The poet William Blake wrote:

> "Ah, William, we're weary of weather,"
> Said the sunflowers, shining with dew.
> "Our traveling habits have tired us.
> Can you give us a room with a view?"

Point of view is how a literary work is narrated.

- First-person point of view is when the main character tells the story in his or her own words: "I knew I was in danger from the beginning."

- Second-person point of view is when the author uses pronouns such as *you* to describe the main character. The effect is to include the reader as the main character: "You are walking down a dark street long past midnight."

- Third-person point of view is when a person outside the story is the narrator.

- Omniscient point of view, in which the narrator has knowledge of everything in the story including all the characters' thoughts and emotions, or limited om-

Limited omniscient niscient, in which the narrator knows the thoughts and inner emotions of one character.

A **plot** is the sequence of events in a narrative such as a short story, novel, or play. Most plots have five main sections:

- introduction or exposition, in which the characters and setting are introduced

- rising action, in which the main problem or conflict arises

- climax, in which a dramatic turn of events creates great tension

- falling action, in which the climax leads to an unwinding of the problem or conflict

- resolution, in which the problem or conflict is worked out in the end.

Prologue is the introductory section of a literary work.

The **protagonist** is the central character in a narrative, such as Hamlet, Huckleberry Finn, or Emma Bovary.

A **refrain** is a line or phrase that is repeated at regular intervals in a poem, usually at the end of a stanza. In his poem "The Raven," Edgar Allan Poe employs the refrain "Quoth the Raven, 'Nevermore.'"

Rhyme is the matching of end sounds in lines of verse. Here is an example from Sara Teasdale:

> I am the brown bird pining
> To leave the nest and fly —
> Oh, be the fresh cloud shining,
> Oh, be for me the sky!

Modern poets sometimes use slant rhymes or half rhymes instead of exact rhymes. These are words that are similar in their ending sounds but not exactly the same. From W. B. Yeats:

> When have I last looked on
> The round green eyes and the long wavering bodies

> Of the dark leopards of the moon?
> All the wild witches, those most noble ladies, . . .

Some poets also use internal rhyme, in which matching sounds are included within lines.

Rhythm is the arrangement of beats or stresses in verse or prose. In verse, rhythm is measured in meter.

Setting is the time and place in which a narrative unfolds. The time may be the historical past, the present, or thousands of years in the future. The location of the narrative may be a realistically described place that actually exists or an imaginary place such as another planet or another dimension.

A **simile** is the comparison of two unlike things using the words *like* or *as*. For example, in Elizabeth Bishop's "The Fish":

> Here and there
> His brown skin hung in strips
> Like ancient wallpaper,
> And its pattern of darker brown
> Was like wallpaper:
> Shapes like full-blown roses
> Stained and lost through age.

A **symbol** in literature is an object, place, action, or idea that an author uses to represent a larger meaning. For example, in Anton Chekhov's play *The Seagull,* a dead seagull is used as a symbol for a hapless young girl who is mistreated by another character in the drama.

Synecdoche is a figure of speech in which a part stands for the whole, as in referring to an old man as "a graybeard."

Si-nek-duh-kee

The **theme** of a literary work is the central idea about life or the human condition that it presents. For example, in "Mending Wall," Robert Frost addresses the theme of freedom versus security.

Tone is the manner in which a writer approaches his or her material and is expressed in style and pervading atmosphere. For example, the tone of Mark Twain's "The Celebrated Jumping Frog of Calaveras County" is light and playful owing to its casual style, while the tone of Mary Shelley's *Frankenstein* is dark, serious, and foreboding.

DRAMATIC LITERATURE

Drama is the performance of a narrative by actors onstage before an audience. The Greek city of Athens was the birthplace of drama. Greek plays served a ceremonial function in society, exploring human fate and the capriciousness of the gods. The Athenians held festivals of drama in which playwrights competed for a prize. *add notion or unpredictable change*

The Greek theater included tragedy, comedy, and satyr plays (comic burlesques on mythological subjects). Individual actors in masks portrayed the main characters, while a group called the chorus explained the plot to the audience and made comments on the action. It is believed that ancient Greek drama never used more than three actors on the stage at once.

For Greek playwrights, tragedy and comedy were always separate; there was nothing like Shakespeare's "comic relief" in a tragedy. The Greeks developed their own theatrical traditions, such as *deus ex machina* in which the gods intervene at a point of crisis to save the hero or change the course of events. One of the greatest Greek dramas is Sophocles' ***Oedipus the King***, in which a king learns that he has unwittingly killed his own father and married his mother.

Today the term *drama* usually refers to a realistic play that is neither a comedy nor a tragedy, such as Arthur Miller's *Death of a Salesman* and David Mamet's *Glengarry Glen Ross*.

A **tragedy** is a drama in which a protagonist who is heroic or well respected brings about his or her own downfall through a fatal character flaw. For example, in Shakespeare's *Macbeth*, a Scottish warrior succumbs to ambition and embarks on a series of murders to gain the throne. Most critics regard tragedy as the pinnacle of dramatic art.

A **comedy** is a play written to be amusing, and often features exaggerated characters and funny situations. The plot of Shakepeare's *A Comedy of Errors,* for example, turns on several cases of mistaken identity.

A **dramatic monologue** is a poetic form in which a character speaks in his or her own voice with an implied listener at hand. It is usually written in blank verse or rhymed couplets and was a favorite vehicle for Victorian poets such as Alfred, Lord Tennyson ("Ulysses") and Robert Browning ("My Last Duchess"):

> That's my last duchess painted on the wall,
> Looking as if she were alive. I call
> That piece a wonder, now: Fra Pandolf's hands
> Worked busily a day, and there she stands.
> Will't please you sit and look at her? . . .

A **soliloquy** is a dramatic speech in which a character talks to him- or herself, allowing the audience to overhear and judge the character's state of mind. It is an important element in the tragedies of Shakespeare and his contemporaries. In *Julius Caesar*, Brutus contemplates murdering Caesar lest he become an unstoppable tyrant:

> It must be by his death: and for my part,
> I know no personal cause to spurn at him,
> But for the general. He would be crown'd:
> How that might change his nature, there's the question.
> It is the bright day that brings forth the adder;
> And that craves wary walking. Crown him?— that;
> And then, I grant, we put a sting in him,
> That at his will he may do danger with.
> The abuse of greatness is, when it disjoins
> Remorse from power: and, to speak truth of Caesar,
> I have not known when his affections sway'd
> More than his reason. But 'tis a common proof,
> That lowliness is young ambition's ladder,
> Whereto the climber-upward turns his face;
> But when he once attains the upmost round,
> He then unto the ladder turns his back,
> Looks in the clouds, scorning the base degrees
> By which he did ascend. So Caesar may.
> Then, lest he may, prevent. And, since the quarrel
> Will bear no color for the thing he is,
> Fashion it thus: that what he is, augmented,

Would run to these and these extremities:

And therefore think him as a serpent's egg

Which, hatch'd, would, as his kind, grow mischievous,

And kill him in the shell.

The Theater of the Absurd is a late-twentieth century dramatic movement that sought to illustrate the essentially purposeless and illogical nature of mankind's condition. Characters in these plays use dislocated, repetitious, and clichéd speech to present a chaotic, senseless modern world. Among the plays associated with this genre are Samuel Beckett's *Waiting for Godot*, Tom Stoppard's *Rosencrantz and Guildenstern Are Dead*, and Eugene Ionesco's *Rhinoceros*.

CRITICAL THINKING AND ANALYTIC SKILLS

A teacher of secondary English must help students master the skills necessary to analyze a literary work and unlock its meaning. This requires students to make a close reading of each text, using tools such as the following.

- **Setting a Purpose for Reading:** Students should skim a text to help them decide their purpose for reading. They might want to solve a problem, find information, compare elements with another text, or verify predictions about the outcome. If a story is set in the present-day and is written in straightforward language, students might concentrate on the story's overall effect. If a story has an unusual historical setting or is written in old-fashioned prose, students may have to focus first on the details of setting, customs, and language in order to understand the plot. Setting an appropriate purpose for reading will also help students decide on the speed of their reading.

- **Analyzing Vocabulary:** Students should look for unfamiliar words and decode them by analyzing word parts (root, prefix, suffix), looking for context clues (the words and sentences around the unfamiliar word), and perhaps using a dictionary or online source for definitions. Students should also be aware of words that can be easily confused (*who's-whose, threw-through*), words borrowed from other languages (*baguette* is a French word for a small loaf of bread; *angst* is a German word for fear), and content-area words (*genetics* is the study of genes; *laptop* is a portable computer). Teachers should encourage students to keep a list of unfamiliar words they have found during the school year.

- **Developing Habits of Self-Monitoring in Reading:** Students should strive to be always aware of their thinking processes as they read (an approach also known as *metacognition*). This helps them monitor their level of engagement with the text, whether they understand what they are reading, and how they might use other strategies to improve their understanding. Owing to students' variety of cultural backgrounds and experiences, most will benefit greatly from the teacher previewing a text with a discussion, photos or artwork, film excerpts or music, and other aids. Students might also write questions to answer using information from the text.

During reading, students must focus on how well they understand the text and reread passages that are opaque. Students might write notes, make predictions, or summarize what they have read. The teacher can pause students at certain points in their reading and hold a group discussion of the text.

To encourage student involvement after reading, the teacher might ask students to map the plot, visualize the setting and characters, role-play a conflict between characters, or retell the story in their own words. Students can use graphic organizers to compare characters or show how the story is organized. A teacher should minister to the varying levels of comprehension among students by preparing a variety of questions and activities about the text. Simpler questions might ask about plot points or how the story was resolved. More difficult activities might urge students to compare the story with another book or film, decide how a character might have acted differently, or write a short poem about the moral principle involved in the text.

LITERARY CRITICISM

As a teacher of secondary English, you need not be a literary critic. However, you should be able to locate and apply criticism of important texts and authors using print or electronic resources. You should also be familiar with major approaches to literary criticism.

The types of literary criticism are as various as the number of critics, but several major areas can be described. Ideas from critical articles and books might prove helpful as a starting point in class discussions of a poem, story, or play. As a teacher, you might choose which type of critical ideas to use with the class based on the particular literary work being discussed.

Structuralist: This theory holds that certain underlying patterns and symmetries are common to the literatures of almost all societies and cultures. Structuralist theory draws many of its ideas from sociology and anthropology. Structuralists go beyond assessing the quality of a work in favor of placing it in a larger cultural context.

Formalist: This approach is concerned purely with how a text's literary elements contribute to a coherent whole. It prefers to address questions of style, word choice, and use of conventions instead of biographical or historical sources.

New Criticism: A critical movement akin to formalism that focused mainly on lyric poems and examined them as verbal objects without reference to the author's biography or outside influences. New critics looked closely at a poem's diction, imagery, and underlying meaning.

Historical: Historical critics focus on a work's context in history and how its allusions, style, and point of view fit (or defy) the conventions of its period. An historical critic might also examine the effect a novel such as the anti-slavery *Uncle Tom's Cabin* had on the social views and politics of its time.

New Historicism: The new historicism critics aim simultaneously to understand a text through its historical context and influences as well as to interpret cultural and intellectual history through the study of relevant literary and sub-literary texts. For example, a new historicist approach to Shakespeare would see him not as an autonomous genius working alone, but as a product of the Renaissance theatre world and all its cultural and social influences.

Biographical: This approach focuses on how details of the writer's life and the period she or he lived in are reflected in the work and explain how it was produced. This is also called traditional criticism.

Postcolonial: Postcolonial critics examine literary works as examples of Western colonialism and imperialism and try to show how these works helped further ideas of racial and cultural inequality. For example, a postcolonial critic of Shakespeare's *The Tempest* might focus on the character of Caliban and how he represents a culture that has been colonized and oppressed by western Europeans as represented by Prospero.

Psychoanalytic: This school of criticism combs the language and plots of literary works for examples of Freudian concepts such as repressed consciousness, the struggles of the superego, the Oedipus complex, etc. For example, when Virginia Woolf describes a character as being "full of locked drawers," a psychoanalytic critic would see evidence of repressed thoughts. Similarly, the Jungian school explains the meaning of literary works using examples of archetypes from mythology or native cultures.

Reader-Response: These critics focus on the reader's role in responding to, and, in effect, "creating" a piece of literature. The idea is that each reader brings to a work his or her own experiences, biases, and expectations, which in turn causes each reading to be different. For example, a reader's response to John Steinbeck's "The Red Pony" might focus on how the final image of the dead animal summons feelings of sympathy, horror, or outrage in the reader.

Marxist: This school of criticism views literature through a political lens, as in how a work depicts or glosses over the exploitation of workers by wealthy or powerful interests.

Feminist: This approach emphasizes the role of women in literature, either as authors and poets or as characters in a narrative. A feminist critic might examine how Emily Brontë displayed a uniquely feminine viewpoint toward her heroine in her novel *Wuthering Heights*.

Deconstructionist: This approach, which is linked to postmodernism, insists that a literary work is primarily a construction of words and its possible meanings are not limited to what its author intends. Deconstructionist critics question traditional assumptions about truth and certainty. They seek to deconstruct a text to show its ideological biases related to gender, race, class, culture, and economic condition.

Philosophical: These critics look at the ethical or religious questions raised by a work of literature, and seek to bring out the author's own ideas about what is ethical and how life should be lived.

RESEARCHING SOURCES OF LITERARY CRITICISM

Public and university libraries are a good source for books of literary criticism. *The Johns Hopkins Guide to Literary Theory and Criticism* offers an index to major critical works and articles. The best work of individual critics is often published in book form, such as T.S. Eliot's *The Sacred Wood,* Randall Jarrell's *Poetry and the Age,* Harold Bloom's *The Western Canon,* and Susan Sontag's *Against Interpretation.* Of course, current critical essays and reviews can be found in publications such as *The New York Review of Books, The Times Literary Supplement, The New York Times Book Review,* and *The New Republic.*

Certain online sites, such as the ipl2 Literary Criticism Collection (*www.ipl.org/div/litcrit/*), provide search engines for locating criticism by author's last name, title, or literary period. They can help you quickly review some critical approaches to great works. One advantage of using an online database for literary research is the ability to search texts for key names, terms or phrases.

INFORMATIONAL TEXTS

1.3 Reading Informational Texts

a. Cite strong and thorough textual evidence to support analysis of what an informational text (e.g., literary nonfiction, historical, scientific, technical texts) says explicitly as well as inferences drawn from the text

b. Determine central ideas of an informational text and analyze their development over the course of the text, including how they interact and build on one another to provide a complex analysis

c. Provide an objective summary of an informational text

d. Analyze a complex set of ideas or sequence of events in an informational text and explain how specific individuals, ideas, or events interact and develop over the course of the text

e. Compare various features of print and nonprint media (e.g., film, television, Internet)

f. Evaluate the structure and content of a variety of consumer, workplace, and public documents

g. Interpret individual informational texts in their cultural, social, and political contexts

(California Common Core State Standards for English Language Arts, RI.6–12.1–3)

The CSET: English exam places a new emphasis on analyzing and interpreting informational texts. In today's curriculum students begin as early as the primary grades to read and analyze informational texts. They often are required to answer questions strictly by referring to the assigned text, without drawing on prior knowledge. This requires close analysis of an author's argument and evidence, as well as knowledge of the rhetorical tools she or he uses to present that argument.

On the CSET: English exam you will read and analyze excerpts from informational texts. These are chosen from many different categories of nonfiction writing. The following list will give you a good idea of the types of informational texts you might see on the test.

Essays are short pieces of nonfiction writing that can be formal or informal and address any topic. Writers use the essay form to make an argument, explore a moral, political, or aesthetic issue, or recount a personal experience. On the test you might encounter excerpts from essays like the following:

- "On Friendship" by Michel de Montaigne

- "Self-Reliance" by Ralph Waldo Emerson

- "A Room of One's Own" by Virginia Woolf

- "Politics and the English Language" by George Orwell

- "The Paranoid Style in American Politics" by Richard J. Hofstadter

- "Notes on 'Camp'" by Susan Sontag

- "Mau-Mauing the Flak Catchers" by Tom Wolfe

- "Living Like Weasels" by Annie Dillard

- "The Ugly Tourist" by Jamaica Kincaid

- "Thirteen Ways of Looking at a Black Man" by Henry Louis Gates

- "The Hole in Our Collective Memory: How Copyright Made Mid-Century Books Vanish" by Rebecca J. Rosen

- "The Future of College?" by Graeme Wood

Autobiography is the story of a person's life written by that person. Autobiographies may be written by professional authors, artists, performers, politicians, businesspeople, scientists, and celebrities. Some examples of autobiography include the following:

- *Confessions* by St. Augustine

- *The Autobiography of Benjamin Franklin*

- *Up from Slavery* by Booker T. Washington

- *Testament of Youth* by Vera Brittain

- *Speak, Memory* by Vladimir Nabokov

- *The Double Helix: The Discovery of the Structure of DNA* by James Watson

- *I Know Why the Caged Bird Sings* by Maya Angelou

- *Wild Swans* by Jung Chang

- *A Heartbreaking Work of Staggering Genius* by Dave Eggers

- *Dreams of My Father* by Barack Obama

- *Infidel: My Life* by Ayaan Hirsi Ali

Biography is the story of a person's life written by another person. Some examples of biography include the following:

- *Lives of the Most Excellent Painters, Sculptors, and Architects* by Giorgio Vasari

- *The Life of Samuel Johnson* by James Boswell

- *Eminent Victorians* by Lytton Strachey

- *Seeing Mary Plain: A Life of Mary McCarthy* by Frances Kiernan

- *Baseball's Great Experiment: Jackie Robinson and His Legacy* by Jules Tygiel

- *Lincoln* by David Herbert Donald

- *Steve Jobs* by Walter Isaacson

Personal documents include letters, diaries, journals, and notebooks that reveal personal information about the writer and his or her opinions, culture, and historical period. Some examples of personal documents include the following:

- The Diary of Samuel Pepys

- The Journals of Lewis and Clark

- The Adams-Jefferson Letters

- *Charles Darwin's Beagle Diary*

- *The Diary of a Young Girl* by Anne Frank

- Journals of Sylvia Plath

- *Dear Scott, Dearest Zelda: The Love Letters of F. Scott and Zelda Fitzgerald*

Historical and political writings range from official government documents to speeches and articles written for political purposes. Examples of these include the following:

- The Federalist Papers

- The Declaration of Independence

- The Constitution of the United States of America

- The Gettysburg Address

- Franklin D. Roosevelt's first inaugural address

- *Brown v. Board of Education of Topeka* (Supreme Court decision)

Features of Print and Visual Media

While print media remain important in today's culture, people increasingly are turning to visual media for news and entertainment. Print media include books, newspapers, magazines, journals, pamphlets, fliers, and other printed materials. Readership of newspapers and magazines has been in decline for many years, mainly due to the competition from broadcast media and newer media such as Internet sites.

Television news remains an important source of information for most Americans, but increasingly consumers turn to the Internet for up-to-the-minute reports. Print sources such as newspapers still provide the most detailed coverage of news; a newspaper article almost always contains much more information than a TV news story on the same topic. *The New York Times, The Washington Post,* and other large newspapers now have their own websites that can be updated quickly with breaking news to compete with other sources.

Other types of visual and broadcast media include feature films (both fictional and documentary), television drama, talk radio, Internet radio, websites, and weblogs or "blogs."

This variety of print and visual media gives a teacher of secondary English the chance to present materials in several different ways. For example, to enrich a reading of Harper Lee's *To Kill a Mockingbird,* a teacher could show the class the film version from 1962 and hold a discussion comparing it to the novel; suggest websites that contain oral-history interviews about the struggle for civil rights in the United States; and copy and distribute old newspaper articles and editorials about cases involving racial discrimination in the South.

Consumer, Workplace, and Public Documents

On the CSET: English exam you should be prepared to analyze a variety of documents one might encounter in everyday life or in work situations. These include the following:

- Job application: an application for employment that includes personal information, work history, and qualifications

- License application: an application for a license to do something legally, such as operate a motor vehicle

- Insurance form: an application for insurance or a statement of a claim on an existing insurance policy

- Safety regulations chart: a workplace document explaining safety procedures and specifying certain hazards and unsafe actions

- Instruction manual: a step-by-step guide to assembling or using an item

- Warranty: a contract stating that a manufacturer will repair or replace a defective product during a certain period after the product is purchased

- Service contract: an agreement to have service or repairs performed during a certain period for a specified fee

- Tax return: a form that must be filled out annually with correct information about a person's employment, income, and taxes owed

For example, you might go over the following workplace poster with students:

Job Safety and Health

It's the law!

Employees:

- You have the right to notify your employer or OSHA about workplace hazards. You may ask OSHA (Occupational Safety and Health Administration) to keep your name confidential.
- You have the right to request an OSHA inspection if you believe that there are unsafe and unhealthful conditions in your workplace. You or your representative may participate in that inspection.
- You can file a complaint with OSHA within 30 days of retaliation or discrimination by your employer for making safety and health complaints or for exercising your rights under the *OSH Act*.
- You have the right to see OSHA citations issued to your employer. Your employer must post the citations at or near the place of the alleged violations.
- Your employer must correct workplace hazards by the date indicated on the citation and must certify that these hazards have been reduced or eliminated.
- You have the right to copies of your medical records and records of your exposures to toxic and harmful substances or conditions.
- Your employer must post this notice in your workplace.
- You must comply with all occupational safety and health standards issued under the *OSH Act* that apply to your own actions and conduct on the job.

Employers:

- You must furnish your employees a place of employment free from recognized hazards.
- You must comply with the occupational safety and health standards issued under the *OSH Act*.

In discussing this poster with students, you might ask what is the main purpose of the document (to explain policies for employees to address problems of workplace safety) and why the document is organized with bulleted points (to help the reader quickly and easily scan the document to find out the rights and responsibilities of employees and employers).

ANALYZING INFORMATIONAL TEXTS

1.4 Craft and Structure of Informational Texts

a. Determine the meaning of words and phrases as they are used in an informational text, including figurative, connotative, and technical meanings, and analyze how an author uses and refines the meaning of a key term or terms over the course of a text

b. Analyze and evaluate the effectiveness of the structure an author uses in his or her exposition or argument, including whether the structure makes points clear, convincing, and engaging

c. Analyze the use of text features (e.g., graphics, headers, captions) in public documents

d. Determine an author's point of view and/or purpose in an informational text and analyze how style and content advance that point of view and/or purpose, including how effective rhetoric and content contribute to the power, persuasiveness, or aesthetics of the text

(*California Common Core State Standards for English Language Arts, RI.6–12.4–6*)

1.5 Integration of Knowledge and Ideas in Informational Texts

a. Integrate and evaluate multiple sources of information presented in different media or formats (e.g., visually, quantitatively, spoken, performed, written) in order to address a question or solve a problem

b. Delineate and evaluate the reasoning in seminal U.S. texts, including the application of constitutional principles and use of legal reasoning and the premises, purposes, and arguments in works of public advocacy

c. Analyze seventeenth-, eighteenth-, and nineteenth-century foundational U.S. documents of historical and literary significance for their themes, purposes, and rhetorical features

(*California Common Core State Standards for English Language Arts, RI.6–12.7–9*)

On the CSET: English exam, you will be required to analyze excerpts from various kinds of informational texts. You might identify the author's point of view or purpose in writing. You might also analyze how effectively the author uses literary tools to present his or her point of view or to accomplish a certain purpose. Elements to look for in analyzing an informational text include the following:

- **Text structure, or how the material is organized**. Text structures include cause/effect, problem/solution, hypothesis/support, compare/contrast, topic/illustration, point/counterpoint, chronological order, sequential steps, and classification.

- **Language usage**. This includes examples of figurative language, connotative language, and technical terms. It can also include the use of style, tone, humor, and irony.

- **Methods of persuasion**. These include an appeal to reason or logic; an appeal to emotion, such as fear, anger, or pity; and an appeal to morality or shared values.

- **Use of text features**. These include items such as graphics (photos, illustrations, charts, tables, maps), captions, headings, and annotations.

EVALUATING TEXT COMPLEXITY

1.6 Text Complexity

a. Evaluate text complexity using quantitative tools and measures, as well as knowledge of qualitative dimensions such as levels of meaning, structure, language conventionality and clarity, and background knowledge demands

b. Identify levels of text complexity within grade band ranges

c. Apply knowledge of reader variables such as language, motivation, background knowledge, skill levels, and experiences, as well as task variables such as purpose and complexity when matching readers to a text and task

(*California Common Core State Standards for English Language Arts, RL.6–12.10, RI.6–12.10, Appendix A: Reading*)

Note: *Content from SMR 1.6 Text Complexity is featured only in Subtest I.*

On the CSET: English exam you will see questions about evaluating text complexity and identifying appropriate levels of text complexity for students within certain grade ranges. Text complexity is measured using three factors:

- **Qualitative evaluation of the text** involves levels of meaning, structure, conventionality and clarity of language, and demands on background knowledge.

- **Quantitative evaluation of the text** involves readability measures and similar methods of scoring complexity.

- **Matching the reader to text and task** involves finding the right level of text complexity according to a reader's own variables, such as motivation, background knowledge, and skill level, and also according to the task variables, such as the purpose of the assignment and the difficulty of the task and questions that are posed.

For grades K–5, the range of text complexity includes the following:

Literature

- Stories include children's adventure stories, folktales, myths, legends, fables, fantasy tales, and realistic fiction.

- Dramas include plays with staged dialogue and brief, familiar scenes.

- Poetry includes nursery rhymes, narrative poems, limericks, and free verse poems.

Informational Text

- Nonfiction texts include biographies, autobiographies, and books about history, social studies, and science.

- Technical texts include directions, forms, and information presented in graphs, charts, and maps.

- Texts can also include digital sources on a variety of topics.

For grades 6–12, the range of text complexity includes the following:

Literature

- Stories include adventure stories, historical fiction, mysteries, myths, realistic fiction, science fiction, allegories, parodies, satire, and graphic novels.

- Dramas include one-act and multi-act plays, both in written form and on film.

- Poetry includes narrative poems, epics, ballads, lyrical poems, odes, sonnets, and free verse poems.

Informational Text

- Nonfiction texts include personal essays, speeches, opinion pieces, essays on art and literature, biographies, memoirs, and journalism.

- Technical texts include scientific, technical, economic, and historical accounts written for a broad audience.

- Texts can also include digital sources on a variety of topics.

For example, on the CSET: English exam you might be presented with an excerpt from *David Copperfield* by Charles Dickens and asked which of four qualitative measurements of text complexity would be most likely to increase the difficulty level of the excerpt for a class of eleventh graders. The answer choices might include sentence structure, conventions of language, demands on background knowledge, and layers of meaning. You would then analyze the excerpt to find which of the choices contributes most to text complexity for students.

Language, Linguistics, and Literacy

CHAPTER 3

On the CSET: English Subtest II, you will have 1 hour to answer 50 multiple-choice questions in three main areas: Language, Linguistics, and Literacy.

- **Human Language Structures** will test your knowledge of the following: the nature of human language, the differences among languages, the universality of linguistic structures, and changes to languages across time, locale, and communities; word analysis, including sound patterns (phonology) and inflection, derivation, compounds, roots, and affixes (morphology); sentence structure (syntax), word and sentence meanings (semantics), and the function of language in context (pragmatics).

- **Acquisition and Development of Language and Literacy** will require you to explain the influences of various factors on language acquisition and development; explain the influence of a first language on second language development; and describe methods for developing academic literacy. You should demonstrate the ability to consult general and specialized reference materials, including dictionaries, glossaries, and thesauruses, both print and digital, to find the pronunciation or precise meaning of a word.

You should be able to apply knowledge of general academic and domain-specific words and phrases. You should be able to use knowledge of Greek, Latin, and Anglo-

Saxon roots and affixes to draw inferences about scientific and mathematical terms. You also should be familiar with the cognitive elements of reading and writing processes, and be able to explain metacognitive strategies for making sense of text, including pre-reading strategies, predicting, questioning, word analysis, and concept formation.

- **Grammatical Structures of English** will test your ability to identify methods of sentence construction, to analyze parts of speech and their distinctive structures and functions, to describe the forms and functions of the English verb system, and to recognize conventions of English orthography and changes in word meaning and pronunciation.

Subtest II does not include any constructed-response questions.

The questions in Subtest II require teacher candidates to demonstrate knowledge of the foundations and contexts of language, linguistics, and literacy found in the *California Common Core State Standards: English Language Arts and Literacy in History/Social Studies, Science, and Technical Subjects* (2013). Candidates should have both a broad and deep conceptual grasp of the subject matter.

Coming as they do from a variety of linguistic and sociocultural backgrounds, California students can face challenges in mastering the English language. The diversity of the student population requires teacher candidates to have a broad theoretical knowledge of the principles of language acquisition and development, including the influence of a first language on acquiring a second. You should also have knowledge of the nature of language and historical and cultural perspectives on the development of English, and a subtle understanding of how English literacy develops among both native and non-native speakers.

Questions on Subtest II will require a certain amount of special knowledge in the areas of language, linguistics, and literacy. For example, you might be asked to identify the smallest unit of meaning in a language or to choose which topic is part of the study of pragmatics.

As with the literary information in Chapter 2, the following descriptions are meant to provide a general idea of what is featured on the CSET English Subtest II. For further research, you should consult the following sources:

- *Developing Readers and Writers in the Content Areas K–12* by David W. Moore, Sharon Arthur Moore, Patricia M. Cunningham, and James W. Cunningham (2010)

- *The Development of Language* by Jean Berko Gleason and Nan Bernstein Ratner (2012)

- *How Languages Are Learned* by Patsy M. Lightblown and Nina Spada (2013)

- *Language Development* by Erika Hoff (2013)

- *Literacy: Helping Children to Construct Meaning* by J. David Cooper, Michael D. Robinson, Jill Ann Slansky, and Nancy D. Kiger (2014)

- *Literature-Based Reading Activities* by Ruth Helen Yopp and Hallie Kay Yopp (2009)

- *The Reading/Writing Connection: Strategies for Teaching and Learning in the Secondary Classroom* by Carol Booth Olson (2010)

HUMAN LANGUAGE STRUCTURES

2.1 Human Language Structures

a. Demonstrate knowledge of the nature of human language, differences among languages, the universality of linguistic structures, and language change across time, locale, and communities

b. Demonstrate knowledge of word analysis, including sound patterns (phonology) and inflection, derivation, compounding, roots and affixes (morphology)

c. Demonstrate knowledge of sentence structures (syntax), word and sentence meanings (semantics), and language function in communicative context (pragmatics)

(California Common Core State Standards for English Language Arts, L.6–12.3–4)

History of the English Language

The English language is part of the Germanic branch of the Indo-European family of languages, which includes Danish, Dutch, and German among others. Originally confined to Britain, English is now spoken throughout the world. Its historical development typically is divided into three periods: Old English (including Anglo-Saxon), Middle English, and Modern English. Scholars generally divide the last period further into Early Modern English and Late Modern English.

The prehistory of English (before 600 CE) is mostly hypothetical and has been pieced together from later documents in English and earlier ones in related Indo-European languages. In fact, most scholars see the origins of English in a now-lost language they call Indo-European, which probably originated in northeastern Europe or around the Black Sea between 3000 and 2000 BCE.

Traces of this original language can be discerned in the similarities between, for example, the English word *daughter* and the German *Tochter,* the Armenian *dushtr,* and the Sanskrit *duhitár.* Soon after 2000 BCE, Indo-European seems to have split into several languages due to migration and normal linguistic changes. One of these offshoots, often called Primitive Germanic, also left no written evidence of itself but apparently spread to what is now Scandinavia and northern Germany. A further series of migrations seeded the language throughout northern Europe. This Germanic language included a smaller eastern branch, called Gothic, and a much larger western branch that eventually became English, Dutch, and German.

Old English

Old English or Anglo-Saxon developed from the Germanic dialects spoken by tribes migrating from northern Europe about 500 CE. By about 730 CE, the Venerable Bede, an early historian, was referring to invaders from the north as Angles, Saxons, and Jutes. Their language developed regionally into four major dialects of Old English:

- Northumbrian in the north

- Mercian in the Midlands

- West Saxon in the south and west

- Kentish in the southeast

The West Saxon dialect eventually became the literary standard, making it the basis for modern studies of Old English. To modern eyes, Old English looks stranger than a page of French or Italian because of the use of certain characters that no longer appear in our alphabet. Old English was first written in runic characters, but when the Anglo-Saxons converted to Christianity their scribes began writing in a Latin alphabet that combined runes and Latin letters. While Old English never rivaled Latin as a day-to-day administrative language, it does survive as a means of literary expression, as in the oldest preserved English epic, *Beowulf*.

With the Viking invasions of the ninth century, Old Norse and Danish shared many words with Old English, to the extent that the two language groups were mutually intelligible—and often almost interchangeable. Much of the everyday language of English has roots in Old Norse, which shows the close contact between the Danish invaders and the indigenous people. Old Norse also had a profound influence on Northern English and Scottish dialects.

Middle English

The whole course of the English language changed with the Norman Conquest of 1066. The advent of Middle English is dated from this period. William the Conqueror's victory at Hastings brought a new French influence to all facets of English life, not least its language. The conquerors and the new aristocracy spoke a dialect of Old French called Anglo-Norman, while yeoman farmers and commoners held to the Germanic-based dialect.

During the 300 years from the Norman Conquest to Chaucer, the English language changed more radically than at any comparable period. It is often pointed out that English readers today can make it through Chaucer's language of 600 years ago with some success, while Chaucer himself would have understood almost nothing of the Old English in use 300 years before he wrote.

Structurally, the elaborate system of cases, genders, and numbers disappeared from articles and adjectives, became greatly simplified in noun usage, and remained much the same only with personal pronouns. Modals such as *shall* and *will* became common as a way of referring to the future. Many more dialects sprung up than had been the case with Old English, and unregulated spelling shows the influx of these variant forms.

Large changes in English vocabulary did not begin until about 1250 — quite some time after the Norman Conquest. This coincided with the period of greatest influence regarding the French language and English. As Norman nobles settled into the English court, they brought with them many French words such as *bouquet* and *chandelier*. As Middle English became established among the merchant classes, it began to replace Anglo-Norman forms and also incorporated increasing numbers of French words. As a result, some 10,000 French words were adopted into Middle English. This influence finally began to wane in about 1400, but by then the English language had been permanently changed from a Germanic-based one to a combination Germanic-Romance language hybrid.

In 1362, the Statute of Pleading made English the official language of legal proceedings in England. Yet in the field of law, French-based words were predominant and included such familiar terms as *attorney, petition, inquest, felon, evidence,* and *arrest.* When, near the end of the 1300s, Chaucer used the East Midland dialect of London for his *Canterbury Tales,* this compromise of dialects, with its heavy French influence, had become a sort of Standard English.

Modern English

Early Modern English dates from the 1500 to 1800, or roughly from the era of the English Renaissance to Wordsworth. Several factors combined to bring large changes to the English language in these years. The influence of the Renaissance, with its emphasis on Greek and Latin literature, resulted in many Greek and Latin words being imported into English. While the "revival of learning" in this period mainly used Latin as a common language, educated people throughout Europe increasingly employed the vernaculars, or common languages, in their everyday writing. English attained an established position as a vehicle for popular literature.

In the late 1500s, English pamphleteers and playwrights chided each other for introducing "inkhorn terms," or fancy Latinate words, into English. Shakespeare coined words frequently, including such now-familiar words as *indistinguishable, profitless, submerge,* and *unimpaired* (and some, like *unhair* or *mislike,* that didn't catch on). Scholars estimate that more than 26,000 new words entered the English language between 1500 and 1660.

Another major revolution in English came with the Great Vowel Shift, which began with late Middle English and continued into the Renaissance era. This brought changes in the phonology, or sound patterns, of the English language that resulted in vowel phonemes that eventually approximated to the patterns we use today. In other words, the Great Vowel Shift changed the way long vowels were pronounced, and marked a major change from Middle English to Modern English. In general, the long vowels came to be pronounced with the tongue higher in the mouth and the letter *e* at the end of words became silent. For example, Chaucer's *Lyf,* pronounced /leef/, became the modern word *life.*

The Middle English *name* was pronounced /nam-a/ and *down* was /doon/. Shakespeare pronounced *clean* to rhyme with *lane,* while now it rhymes with *bean.*

In linguistic terms, the Great Vowel Shift happened suddenly—in the course of a single century—and its shortening of vowel sounds continues today (but without such rapid change). Of course, the Great Vowel Shift is also responsible for the unorthodox and sometimes apparently random use of vowels in the spelling of English words, as the common spellings of many words no longer corresponded to their sounds.

Finally, there was the influence of printed books. Around 1476, William Caxton introduced into England the process of printing from movable type. This development saw a huge increase in the number of books printed in English, brought cheaper books within the reach of ordinary people for the first time, and helped promote a standard, uniform version of the language. Milestones in this process were the appearance of the King James version of the Bible in 1611 and the First Folio of Shakespeare's plays in 1623. With printers and publishing houses centered in London, the London dialect of English became dominant.

The Late Modern English period extends from around 1800 to the present and has seen a further expansion of the English vocabulary due to several factors. The Industrial Revolution and the rise of new technologies helped introduce many new scientific words into English, most of them adapted from Greek and Latin roots, including such words as *oxygen, protein,* and *vaccine.* Other technological terms, such as *horsepower* and *typewriter,* combined English roots.

English naval dominance and the rise of global trade brought an influx of foreign words into English, such as *pundit* (Hindi), *sauna* (Finnish), and *tycoon* (Japanese). Military excursions served to introduce new words such as *camouflage, radar, grenade,* and *nosedive.*

From the seventeenth century on, American English increasingly diverted from the British version in pronunciation, spelling, and vocabulary. Many words were borrowed or adapted from Native American languages, such as *hickory, canoe,* and *barbecue.* Spanish also provided many now-standard English words, including *stampede, canyon,* and *vigilante.* In fact, Modern English has added words from languages throughout the world, including Russian, Hebrew, and Chinese. Even today, computer science and other technologies continue to add words such as *byte, blog, digitize,* and *cyberspace* to the English language.

Dialects

A variation of a language that is spoken by inhabitants of a particular geographical area is called a **dialect**. A dialect can have its own grammar and vocabulary. Dialects spoken by large groups of people may even have their own subdialects. Certain dialects in English are so well established that they have institutional support; these include Southern American English, African American English, Hawaiian English, Appalachian English, and Spanglish.

English and American literary works confront students with various dialects, from the Cockney speech of some of Charles Dickens' characters to the Southern American dialect Mark Twain employs for his narrator in *The Adventures of Huckleberry Finn*. An array of dialects can also be heard in dialogue of modern films and plays and in the lyrics of popular songs.

Pidgin and Creolization

Pidgin is another name for a contact language made up of two or more languages. Such makeshift languages were originally employed by traders, plantation workers and overseers, and Europeans in their contacts with various indigenous peoples. The term *pidgin* apparently came from the Chinese word for "business." Despite its negative connotation, Pidgin English and Pidgin forms of other languages have helped bridge the gap between people with no common language. Pidgin English is characterized by a small vocabulary and simple grammatical structures.

Another way that two or more different languages can merge into a common language is called **creolization**. This process takes place when a simple code like pidgin continues to develop over time and acquires native speakers. New vocabulary is added to the code and it adopts new, more complicated linguistic principles until finally it has a complexity similar to other languages. In Louisiana, a Creole developed from the merging of French and African languages.

Linguistics

Linguistics is the systematic study of language in order to find general principles and structures that link human languages. Linguistics includes a number of branches, divided mainly between the study of language form, language meaning, and language in context.

Sub-fields of linguistic study include:

- morphology, or the composition of words

- syntax, or the composition of sentences

- phonology, or the sound patterns of words and phrases

- phonetics, or the actual properties of speech sounds and non-speech sounds

- semantics, or the meaning of words

- pragmatics, or language usage in context

- sociolinguistics, or language and society

Morphology, syntax, and phonology are all part of the **grammar** of a language.

In the 1800s, most linguists thought of language as a collection of speech sounds, words, and grammatical endings. This approach was called **atomistic**. In the early years of the twentieth century, a Swiss linguist named Ferdinand de Saussure revolutionized the field with his **structuralist** view of language as a system in which each element of sound and meaning is mainly defined by how it relates to other elements.

Saussure's work, however, was overtaken in mid-century by that of the American Noam Chomsky, the key figure in modern linguistics. Chomsky developed an influential theory of **generative grammar**. He emphasized that people share an innate and universal set of linguistic structures, which accounts for why young children can learn a new language so easily. Chomsky also insisted that people have a genetic predisposition to language.

Chomsky developed the concept of **Universal Grammar**, a set of principles that apply to all languages and are unconsciously accessible to every human language user. Universal Grammar includes the fundamental qualities shared by all languages. Similarities between languages may be due to common aspects of human experience, such as the need for water and thus for a word meaning "water." Similarities may also be due to common patterns of descent. For example, the Spanish and Italian languages both descended from Latin and therefore share qualities because of this common ancestry.

Similarities also come about from contact between cultures and the borrowing of words and sentence structures. Much of modern linguistics attempts to account for language similarities and differences throughout the world. Chomsky later elaborated his theories into the idea of **transformational grammar**, which saw languages as having a shared deep structure and a variable surface structure.

Word Analysis

The CSET: English Subtest II will test the candidate's knowledge of **word analysis**, including sound patterns (phonology) and inflection, derivation, compounding, and roots and affixes (morphology).

Phonology

The study of how sounds are organized and used in languages is called **phonology**. It seeks to make an inventory of sounds and their features, as well as provide rules specifying how sounds in a language interact with each other. The smallest unit of speech sound is the **phoneme**. It combines with other units of speech sound to form a word. For example, the word *tray* contains three phonemes: /t/, /r/, and /a/. The word *thrill* contains four phonemes: /th/, /r/, /i/, and /l/. (As you can see from these examples, a phoneme is *not* the same as a syllable.) The equivalent of a phoneme in written language is a **grapheme**, a letter or number of letters that represent a phoneme or sound.

An important part of phonology is determining which phonetic sounds in a language are distinctive and significant. It also tries to determine how users of the language interpret the various sounds.

Related to phonology is **phonetics**, or the study of how speech sounds are made and understood. Dictionaries include phonetic spellings for words to show the correct pronunciations. For example, the phonetic spelling of *explicit* is /ik SPLI sit/.

Morphology

Morphology is the branch of linguistics that deals with the internal structure and forms of words. It is concerned with the rules for the use of **morphemes**, or the smallest units of meaning, in a language. For example, the morphology of English allows its speakers to know that plural endings depend on the last sound of the word stem: *spatula/ spatulas*; *patch/patches*.

Methods of Word Analysis

Vocabulary skills are one of the most important tools in effective reading. A student must be taught to use several different methods to decode unfamiliar words. One method is to use **context clues** to find a word's meaning. Context clues are the words and sentences around the unfamiliar word that often provide clues to its meaning. For example, notice how the underlined words in the following sentence help you understand the meaning of the italicized word:

> Mr. Peachtree could be *irascible* in the morning before he'd had his coffee, but later in the day <u>his sunny disposition tended to re-emerge.</u>

You can tell from the context clues that *irascible* means "irritable or crabby."

Another way to decode an unfamiliar word is to use **morphemic analysis** to identify the parts of the word. Students should learn to recognize prefixes, roots, and suffixes and know their meanings. (Prefixes and suffixes are also called affixes.) For example, the word *hypertension* contains the prefix *hyper* (over or excess) and the root word *tension,* and it means "high blood pressure." Many prefixes and suffixes come from Latin and Greek and have specific meanings. The words *illustrate, illustrious,* and *lustrous* come from the Latin root *lustrare* for "purify, polish, or make bright." Sometimes words contain letters that look like a prefix or suffix but actually are not. For example, the words *reapply* and *trilateral* contain the prefixes *re-* and *tri-,* respectively. However, the words *relinquish* and *tribunal* do not contain prefixes.

Students can also analyze an unfamiliar word as part of a **word family,** or a category of words built around the same word part. For example, the words *anachronism, chronicle, chronometer,* and *chronological* all include the word part *chron-,* which comes from the Greek word for "time."

Compound words are words made up of two or more smaller words. Students can decode compounds by noticing the meanings of the smaller words, as in *sailboat* (a boat with a sail) or *curveball* (a pitched ball that curves).

Students should also be aware of **borrowed words,** or words imported from other languages, such as *taboo* (from the Tongan word *tabu* for a forbidden act), *avant-garde* (from the French word for an advanced artistic work or movement), *angst* (from the German word for fear), and *ad infinitum* (from the Latin words meaning "to infinity").

Students should recognize **inflectional affixes**. These are word endings that serve various grammatical purposes but don't change the meaning of a word:

-s, -es	plural: balls, switches
-'s	possessive: Jane's
-s	verb, present-tense third-person singular: thrives
-ing	verb, present-participle/gerund: going
-ed	verb, simple past tense: wandered
-en	verb, past perfect participle: tighten
-er	adjective, comparative: harder
-est	adjective, superlative: fewest

Students should also recognize **derivational affixes**, which alter the meaning of a word by building on a base.

Prefixes	
anti-	against: antiaircraft
de-	undo: deactivate
ex-	former: ex-president
mis-	in a faulty manner: misinterpret
re-	do again: reestablish

Suffixes	
-ly	characteristic of: cautiously
-er, -or	person or profession: plumber, actor
-ion, -tion, -ation, -ition, -sion	process or action: occupation, explosion, attention
-ible, -able	ability to do something: fixable, combustible
-al, -ial, -ical	with characteristics of: natural, cranial, ecclesiastical
-y	characterized by: leafy
-ness	condition or state of: happiness
-ty, -ity	state of or quality of: safety, creativity
-ment	action or process: establishment

Suffixes *(continued)*	
-ic -ous, -eous	having characteristics of: artistic
-ious	having the qualities of: clamorous, courteous, curious
-en	made of or like: leaden
-ive, -ative, -itive	adjective form of a verb: inquisitive, talkative, active
-ful	full of: joyful
-less	lacking or without: pointless

Sentence Structure

Sentence structure can be analyzed by using **syntax**, or the rules and principles for constructing sentences in a language. An English sentence can be diagramed to show how the various parts of speech fit together to form the whole. The diagram below represents the structure of the sentence "The man in the pickup works on a farm."

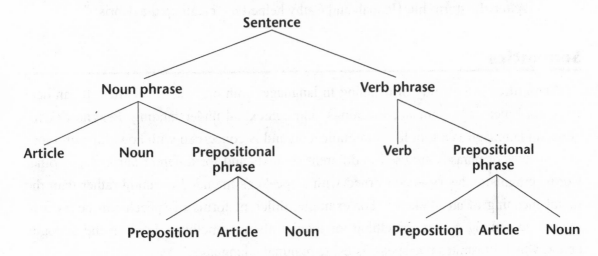

Sentences can be simple, compound, or complex. A **simple sentence** or independent clause contains a subject and a verb and expresses a complete thought. The subject, the verb, or both may be compound in a simple sentence.

Many people browse in the corner bookstore on Saturday mornings.

Apples and pears make a refreshing snack on hot days.

Linda goes to the school library and studies hard every day.

A **compound sentence** contains two independent clauses joined by a coordinator, such as *for, and, nor, but, or, yet, so.*

I hoped to finish first or second, **but** Joel won the race.

Our team scored fourteen runs, **yet** we still lost the game!

We can eat before the movie, **or** we can cook out at home afterward.

A **complex sentence** has an independent clause joined by one or more dependent clauses. A complex sentence always has a subordinator such as *since, because, after, although,* or *when* or a relative pronoun such as *who, which,* or *that.*

When I saw the dark clouds massed in the west, I knew a storm was on its way.

People are stocking up on bottled water and canned food **because** the predicted storm could knock out power lines.

After the storm hit, Hannah and Cathy helped me clean up the debris.

Semantics

Semantics is the study of meaning in language, both oral and contextual. It can deal with word meanings, sentence meanings, and contextual understanding. **Pragmatics** focuses on language as a tool for communication and is concerned with how different types of sentences or phrases are used in different contexts and for different purposes. In other words, pragmatic theory is concerned with a speaker's intended meaning rather than the literal meaning of an utterance. For example, different forms of speech can be used to request something, assert something, or inquire about something. Look at the dialogue below, which illustrates two speakers using pragmatic language.

Nelda: It's so hot outside!

Richard: I think it's hotter *inside* right now.

Nelda: I'll turn up the air-conditioning.

Richard: And it's so dark in here that I can barely see the pages of my book.

Nelda: Is your arm broken?

To someone who lacks a pragmatic knowledge of American English, Nelda's last utterance might be puzzling. However, Nelda knows that Richard is asking her to turn on a light without actually making the request. When she asks "Is your arm broken?" she is telling him to turn on the light himself.

A reader or listener shows **pragmatic competence** when he or she understands the true meaning of a passage or utterance. For example, in Shakespeare's *Julius Caesar,* when Mark Antony claims repeatedly that Brutus is "an honorable man," the reader knows that Antony means just the opposite. Likewise, in the sentence "Mr. Groves asked his students to submit their term papers on Thursday," it is understood that the word *asked* functions as a synonym for *ordered.*

Students should also be aware that new expressions can be generated from long-established words with fresh meanings. The expression "browse a new site on the web" contains the familiar words *browse* (which dates to the fifteenth century) and *web,* yet the expression refers to the latest computer technology. Other changes in usage may be due to cultural factors. For example, in American English, the old term *postman* has been replaced by *mail carrier* to reflect modern attitudes toward gender-neutral language in the workplace.

Etymology

In a dictionary, the **etymology** or word origin appears in square brackets after the pronunciation and part of speech of the word. Here is a sample etymology for the word *diction:*

L *diction-, dictio* speaking, style, fr. *dicere* to say; akin to OE *te*[long e]*on* to accuse, *dicare* to proclaim, dedicate, GK *deiknynai* to show, *dike* [long e] judgment, right.

Notice that this word origin entry traces the lineage of the word *diction* back to Old English, Latin, and Greek.

In learning etymologies, students should be aware of "word families," or words that share a common etymology. For example, *diction* shares an etymology with *dictate, dictionary,* and *dictum.*

Print sources for etymologies include:

- *The Oxford Guide to Etymology* by Philip Durkin

- *Concise Dictionary of English Etymology* by Walter W. Skeat

- *Barnhart Concise Dictionary of Etymology* by Robert K. Barnhart

Online sources for etymologies include:

- Online Etymology Dictionary: *www.etymonline.com*

- Resources about languages: *www.wordorigins.org/index.php/resources/*

- English Etymology Resources at LearningNerd: *learningnerd.wordpress.com/2006/08/27/English-etymology/*

Orthography

Orthography is a standardized system for writing words with the proper letters according to accepted rules of usage. It includes the spelling rules for a language. For example, one of the main spelling rules in English is "*i* before *e* except after *c*, or when sounded as *ay*, as in *neighbor* and *weigh*." The word *conscience* (with *ie* after *c*) is an exception to this rule.

Difficulties in spelling words are generally due to unpredictable sound-symbol correspondences. For example, the word *hotel* is pronounced just as its letters would suggest. Yet *faction* contains the digraph *ti* pronounced as /sh/ and *knot* contains the digraph *kn* pronounced as /n/—making both less predictable in sound-symbol correspondence. Also, as previously mentioned, the Great Vowel Shift in the Middle English period made English a particularly difficult language to spell. Spellings that originally matched up with sounds lost that relation when vowel sounds changed over the course of a single century.

American spellings differ from English spellings for many words. This came about when New England settlers adopted Noah Webster's rules for spelling. American spelling does not use *u* in many words ending in: *-our,* such as *honor/honour* and *succor/succour*. It also tends not to have double consonants in second syllables, as in *traveler/traveller*. American spelling employs *–ize* in place of *–ise* in certain words, such as *organize/organise*.

ACQUISITION AND DEVELOPMENT OF LANGUAGE AND LITERACY

2.2 Acquisition and Development of Language and Literacy

a. Explain the influences of cognitive, affective, and sociocultural factors on language acquisition and development

b. Explain the influence of a first language on the acquisition of a subsequent language

c. Describe methods and techniques for developing academic literacy (e.g., tapping prior knowledge through semantic mapping, word analogies, cohesion analysis)

d. Demonstrate the ability to consult general and specialized reference materials (e.g., college-level dictionaries, rhyming dictionaries, bilingual dictionaries, glossaries, thesauruses), both print and digital, to find the pronunciation of words and/or determine or clarify their precise meaning, part of speech, etymology, and/or standard usage

e. Apply knowledge of general academic and domain-specific words and phrases

f. Apply knowledge of Greek, Latin, and Anglo-Saxon roots and affixes to draw inferences concerning the meaning of scientific and mathematical terminology

g. Describe and explain cognitive elements of reading and writing processes (e.g., decoding and encoding, constructing meaning, recognizing and using text conventions of different genres)

h. Explain metacognitive strategies for making sense of text (e.g., pre-reading activities, predicting, questioning, word analysis, concept formation)

(California Common Core State Standards for English Language Arts, W.6–12.4–5, L.6–12.3–4)

Language Acquisition

The process by which people acquire the ability to understand and use words is called **language acquisition**. Toddlers move quickly—in fact, in a matter of months—from forming single words to speaking in complete sentences. Noam Chomsky explained this capacity for acquiring language skills with his theory of **Universal Grammar** or the

Language Acquisition Device. He reasoned that while many rules of grammar are too complex for young children to figure out, they still manage to use language grammatically. Thus, for Chomsky, this capacity must be genetically endowed or innate, since it can't have been learned in the ordinary way.

Theorists differ about the exact stages and details of language acquisition, but the basic outline is widely acknowledged. Children acquire language in a series of imitative stages that are roughly the same but far from identical and that overlap in sequence with possible regressions along the way. Most children begin babbling around age two, and are likely to have a vocabulary of about fifty words. This vocabulary will then increase to more than 200 words, after which the rate of word learning proceeds very rapidly, with the child increasingly using prepositions and articles.

By the preschool years, the child is using fairly sophisticated sentence patterns and vocabulary, including terms that relate things according to size, location, time, and quantity. Generally by the age of four to six, the child has mastered basic sentence grammar and proceeds to use language more efficiently and creatively, including in narratives and conversations. While there are certainly differences in the rate of development in these stages, the sequence is standard within and across the stages.

Language Development

The question of which factors affect language development most closely follows the familiar academic debate of "nature versus nurture." Certainly a combination of biological and environmental factors is important to developing language skills. These include:

- **Genetic Predisposition or Innate Capacity**. This refers to Chomsky's theory of a Universal Grammar that is programmed into every human brain and facilitates language development.

- **Social Interaction**. Some experts believe that a child's social environment is crucial to language development. They maintain that adults play an important role by giving children examples of correct usage to imitate. There is also evidence that children who are surrounded with more examples of complex vocabulary and sentence structure tend to develop language skills more quickly and effectively. Some researchers also emphasize the importance of actually using language, rather than just hearing others use it. Research indicates, for example, that a second-language learner who wants to integrate into the culture in which the second language is spoken is more likely to be successful in learning the second language.

- **Sociocultural Factors**. Research indicates that social class has a major effect on how children use language, and that different social classes employ different language codes. Thus, a child's sociocultural circumstance may determine to a large degree his or her language usage and skills. For example, English-speaking children from different sociocultural backgrounds have been found to differ also in the style and structure of their spoken narratives, with some focusing on open-ended stories developed through free association and others on stories with a central topic or conclusion. Also, some sociocultural situations may feature discrimination against gender groups or ethnic groups, which can in turn affect language development. These factors certainly can have a bearing on children learning a second language.

- **Affective Factors**. These are personal qualities such as empathy, self-esteem, extroversion, lack of inhibition or anxiety (i.e., the willingness to risk embarrassment), ability to imitate, and overall outlook that would positively affect the acquisition of language skills. At the same time, lack of these qualities can have negative consequences. Since language usage is such a pervasive feature of school life and home life, these factors clearly are crucial to a child's development and especially to his or her ability to learn a second language.

Learning a Second Language

Acquiring a second language includes all the variables of learning a first language with the addition of other factors that complicate the process. Some schools in the United States promote **bilingualism**, a system in which students are taught in their native language. Others use a **transitional** system that allows students to speak their own language until they have learned enough English to participate in English-only classes. There are also schools that follow a system of **total immersion**, in which students must immediately take part in English-only classes with no transitional period. (This is sometimes referred to as the "sink or swim" approach.)

It is the goal of American educators to teach all students to use Standard English effectively. Research shows that use of Standard English can be a reliable indicator of academic and economic success in society. Students who speak with a dialect that differs from standard patterns of English speech in vocabulary, grammar, or pronunciation may face lowered expectations from teachers. Therefore, teachers should strive to avoid embarrassing or demeaning students who speak in a dialect or with an accent, while still working to enhance these students' abilities to speak Standard English.

Krashen's Theory of Second Language Acquisition

An American named Stephen Krashen is a leading expert in linguistics and language acquisition studies. **Krashen's Theory of Second Language Acquisition** consists of the following five hypotheses:

1. **The Acquisition-Learning hypothesis** is the most fundamental of Krashen's ideas. For him, there are two independent systems for learning a second language: the acquired system and the learned system. The acquired system uses a subconscious process much like the one that children go through in learning a first language. It depends on natural, meaningful communication in the target language, so that the speaker is concentrating mainly on communicating instead of on forming sentences. The learning system, on the other hand, is the traditional process of formal instruction in a language. Krashen insists that "acquisition" is significantly more important than "learning."

2. **The Monitor hypothesis** explains that acquisition and learning are related, with the former being the initiator of an utterance and the latter being its "monitor" or editor. Krashen believes that the role of the monitor is (or should be) minor, useful only in correcting deviations from standard speech and giving speech a more polished look. The monitor function is also used only when certain conditions are met; i.e., the learner of a second language must have time to monitor, focus on form or correctness, and a knowledge of the rule to be monitored.

3. **The Natural Order hypothesis**, based on research findings, declares that acquiring grammatical structures in a second language always follows a "natural order," regardless of the student's age, first language background, and conditions of exposure to the second language.

4. **The Input hypothesis**, concerned with acquisition not learning, posits that a second language learner makes progress along the "natural order" of development each time he or she receives an input from the second language that is one step beyond his or her current level of competence in the language.

5. **The Affective Filter hypothesis** includes Krashen's idea that a number of "affective variables," such as motivation, self-confidence, and anxiety, play an important "facilitative but non-causal" role in language acquisition. Low motivation, lack of

self-esteem, and high levels of anxiety act as filters that form a mental block, preventing the student from using comprehensible input for acquisition.

An example of an affective factor that influences second-language acquisition is the businessperson who is unwilling to risk embarrassment when speaking in the second language among clients and tries to avoid mistakes by using known vocabulary and forming sentences mentally before speaking them.

The Influence of a First Language on Second Language Development

A major source of syntactic errors in a student's use of a second language is the student's first language. For example, a native Spanish speaker learning English might say "shirt blue" instead of "the blue shirt." Many errors are caused by a speaker trying to apply the syntactical rules of his or her first language to the second language.

When the languages are fairly close in syntactical rules, as English and Spanish are, there are fewer such errors than when the languages diverge more radically, as English does from German. In effect, a second-language learner internalizes a systematic set of rules to use in speaking and understanding the second language, thus creating his or her own "interlanguage." This interlanguage serves as an intermediate step in acquiring the target language.

Besides the linguistic distance between languages, there are other factors that affect second language development. The student's level of proficiency in the first language certainly affects acquisition of a second language. A student who is more academically sophisticated in his or her first language will find learning a second language much easier. For example, foreign exchange students tend to find success in American high school classes due to their proficiency in their native language.

Students' prior knowledge of the second language also helps the process. Some students may enter American classrooms with prior skills in English ranging from conversational fluency to formal knowledge of the language.

Students may need to learn a dialect and a formal speech register that differ from those they know in daily life. This forces them to acquire speech patterns that are very different from those they are familiar with in their social group. This also raises the question of the relative prestige of the student's first language versus the second language.

Students whose first language has a perceived lower status compared to the second may give up their own linguistic and cultural background in order to join the more "prestigious" group associated with the second language.

Teachers should recognize that learning a second language does not mean abandoning one's first language or dialect. Instead, it means adding a new language to a student's repertoire. Nevertheless, it is also important to remember that second-language learners who want to integrate more fully into the culture in which the second language is spoken tend to be more successful at acquiring the second language. This would explain the success of the immigrant who moves to a city or country where he or she feels accepted by the speakers of the language to be acquired.

Teachers should also be aware of such factors as peer group pressure, role models, and home support in second language development. Teenagers heavily influenced by their peer groups may feel pressured *not* to speak the target language too proficiently or like a native speaker in order not to feel estranged from the peer groups.

Students can benefit from positive role models who have negotiated the difficulties of learning a second language. Discussions with role models can help students better understand the daily challenges of second language acquisition. Support from home is also important, whether parents speak the second language to the student at home or communicate in both the native language and the second language for comfort.

The age of the language learner also plays a role. **The critical period hypothesis** affirms that a person's ability to learn language peaks during early childhood. Research indicates that second-language learners under the age of fifteen tend to achieve greater proficiency in grammar, pronunciation, vocabulary, and comprehension than adult learners. One reason for this difference may be that the brain's language faculty either shuts down or becomes less accessible after a certain age. Thus an adult must use other cognitive mechanisms to learn a second language.

Research also suggests that there is a limited period during which infants can discriminate between all the phonemes in human speech. This would explain why second-language learners have difficulty recognizing certain phonemes in a second language. It also accounts for the fact that older students or adults learning a second language tend to retain an accent, meaning that they are still employing many of the phonemes from their first language.

Developing Academic Literacy

Teaching students who speak nonstandard English or English as a second language requires new strategies and approaches. The teacher should always focus on understanding the students and accepting their form of speech, regardless of dialect or deficiencies, as a valid form of communication, while also modeling consistently in classroom instruction the rules of Standard English.

In dealing with dialects and non-proficient English speakers, teachers should be aware of the following types of linguistic behavior:

- **Transfer** is when a speaker uses his or her second language in a way that is semantically or syntactically appropriate for the first or native language but not for the second.

- **Negative transfer** is when a speaker uses skills from a previously learned behavior or topic but applies them incorrectly to a new topic. For example, a student who recalls that the past tense of *fake* is *faked* and then assumes that the past tense of *take* is *taked* is employing negative transfer.

- **Hypercorrection** is when a person who has been corrected for a mistake in usage makes further mistakes in trying to avoid the original error. For example, a student who has been corrected for saying "Me and him played soccer yesterday" tries to avoid using the objective case *me* altogether and incorrectly says, "The teacher gave he and I the assignment yesterday."

- **Borrowing** is when a speaker switches into his or her first language and borrows single words or entire phrases for which he or she knows no equivalent in the second language. The result can be a hybrid language such as Spanglish.

Reading Comprehension and Accessing Prior Knowledge

Teachers can use various methods to tap into students' prior knowledge of a subject and increase their reading comprehension skills. The following are some of the most effective approaches:

- **Semantic Mapping** is a method by which a teacher solicits responses to a word or phrase through a process of brainstorming or free association. The teacher might write a word or phrase on the blackboard and ask students to suggest other words they think of as a result. Graphic organizers such as Venn diagrams, clusters, or word trees can also be used.

- **Semantic Feature Analysis** is a reading comprehension activity for which students use a chart to organize information by categories, analyze ideas, compare concepts, and make inferences about a written text.

- **Repeated Oral Reading**, in which a student repeatedly reads aloud a short text, helps improve a student's fluency and reading rate regardless of reading level.

- **Note Taking** helps a reader to paraphrase what has been read and thus focus on meaning and interpretation.

- **Word Analogies** compare two or more things by analyzing how they are alike or different. A teacher might ask, "What features does this word share with other words you have seen?"

- **Visual Imaging Skills** are the student's ability to use personal images or experiences to comprehend a word's meaning. To activate these skills, a teacher might ask, "Can you describe an incident from your own life that reminded you of this word?"

- **Cohesion Analysis** is a method of analyzing how all the parts of a work come together to create an overall effect or convey a message. For example, a reader faced with a difficult passage might read ahead or review previous sections to see how the unfamiliar part fits into the whole.

Standard English

The form of English that is most widely accepted, employed, and understood in the English-speaking world is called Standard English. In its ideal form, it is free of regional and class differences and accomplishes a consensus of proper word order, punctuation, and spelling. While many scholars and theorists resist the idea of Standard English as being a myth or a practical impossibility, publishers, educators, writers, and public speakers find the concept useful as a guide to proper formal usage.

Researchers and educators agree that the ability to use Standard English is one of the most important predictors of success in school and in the commercial world. As a result, teachers should strive to help students who use nonstandard English for various social and cultural reasons to master Standard English.

Correct use of Standard English also includes knowing what kind of language to use in various academic and social situations. For example, the language used in an academic essay should be formal yet not stilted or obscure, with no slang or dialect. The best academic writing is clear, concise, and coherent. On the other hand, an email message to a teacher should be less formal yet direct and succinct.

A person with a good command of Standard English may be able to switch more easily between different modes of speaking or writing. **Code-switching** is when a person changes dialects or switches from formal to informal speech depending on which group he or she is interacting with. For example, a teacher might use Standard English when speaking to her class and use a more relaxed dialect with members of her family or social group.

Cognitive Elements of Reading and Writing

To read and write effectively, students must be taught to use a number of interrelated tools for comprehension. These tools include:

- Understanding the differences between formal and informal language (in academic essays, job applications, letters to the editor, etc.)

- Using explicit comprehension to understand the literal meaning of a text

- Using inferential comprehension to understand the inferred meaning of a text, or to "read between the lines"

- Understand the variety of genres (fiction, nonfiction, drama, poetry, etc.)

- Have an awareness of different authorial voices (first person, third person, omniscient)

- Recognize styles and purposes of writing (informative, persuasive, entertainment, etc.)

- Recognize organizational patterns of writing (time order, compare/contrast, problem/solution, enumeration and description, definition and example)

To show knowledge of organizational structures, for example, you might determine which one would be most appropriate for an essay written with the following thesis statement:

> Despite being separated by less than 80 years, Shakespeare's and Dryden's versions of the Antony and Cleopatra story showed vast differences of dramatic approach.

Since the thesis statement is focused on *differences,* the organizational pattern should be comparison/contrast.

Decoding

Another important tool for comprehension is the ability to decode language, or translate the symbols of letters and words into meaningful information. Students invariably find many unfamiliar words in their reading, and they must be prepared to decode these words in various ways. First of all, students should develop a strong base of **sight words**, or words such as *I, is, that, there,* and *am* that can be decoded on sight immediately. It is also helpful if students compile a list of words that do not follow the regular rules of English pronunciation.

Students should also be taught to use **language sounds** (phonics) and **the meanings of word parts** (morphemes) to analyze and decode unfamiliar words. They may also use context clues, or the words and sentences around an unfamiliar word, to decode the word. For example, how is the italicized word pronounced in this sentence?

Having built a large lead, the team was *content* to coast through the last innings.

Using context clues and the syntax of the sentence, a reader could determine that *content* here is used as an adjective and refers to a relaxing of intensity, and so is pronounced with the stress on the second syllable.

Construction of Linguistic Meaning

From a young age, children understand that language is made up of sounds that are combined into words that in turn are arranged in sentences to convey information and ideas. Each part of this process is governed by linguistic rules. To comprehend language, a person must have an implicit knowledge of these functions. It helps that people are born with an innate predilection for language and its structures.

- **Phonology:** The student must be able to hear, distinguish, and categorize speech sounds.

- **Syntax:** The student must implicitly understand the rules of how words fit together to make phrases and sentences and to convey ideas.

- **Semantics:** The student must develop an understanding of the meaning of words and sentences and how words fit together to create different meanings. This can also include inferred meanings and pragmatics.

Cognitive Approach to Writing

As in reading, writing also involves a cognitive process of using and understanding language. Before and during the writing process, student writers should think about the following elements:

- **Appropriate rhetorical strategy:** The writer should consider the audience, the purpose for writing, and the genre of the piece of writing. These considerations will determine the appropriate tone and style of rhetoric.

- **Nature of the writing process:** The writer should follow the steps for composition, including planning, drafting, writing, revision, editing, and sharing.

- **Interaction with other disciplines and communities:** The writer should consider how a piece of writing seeks to affect and is affected by different communities, including family, peers, and teachers, and what other disciplines it refers to or reflects.

- **Awareness of thought processes:** The writer should reflect on or be aware of his or her own thought processes in the course of writing.

- **Evaluation of effectiveness:** The writer should judge how well a piece of writing fulfills its original intention and meets the needs of its intended audience.

Metacognitive Strategies for Understanding Text

Metacognition, or self-awareness during the reading process, ensures that a student's mind is engaged while reading and that the student is ready to use a variety of tools and strategies to unlock the meaning of a text.

Prereading strategies help prepare a reader's comprehension by accessing prior knowledge of the subject or seeking information that enriches the subject. For example, a student preparing to read a Native American creation myth might review prior knowledge or readings of creation stories from other cultures and how they were structured. The student might also access background knowledge about Native American culture that might help with comprehension.

Predicting is a skill in which the reader makes predictions about the text before and during the reading. A reader might predict from the title or first paragraph what the piece will be about, or predict the ending of a story based on character analysis, story details, or genre expectations.

Questioning is when a reader asks and answers questions about a text all through the reading process. For example, a reader might ask: "Why is this character so reluctant to admit to the others that he has been in this position before?" Such questions provide a focus for the reading from start to finish.

Word analysis is the decoding of unfamiliar words or words used in an unfamiliar context throughout a text. Words can be decoded using context clues, syntactic clues, word structure, word families, and content-area information.

Concept formation is used during and after the reading to connect and categorize ideas and reflect on the material's overall meaning and effect.

Levels of Reading Comprehension

In general, students comprehend the material they read on three levels:

- **Literal comprehension** is the ability to obtain the basic facts and details of the story.

- **Inferential comprehension** is the ability to make inferences and draw conclusions about the story.

- **Applied comprehension** is the ability to move beyond the story to think critically and creatively about its implications and larger meaning.

Related to the levels of reading comprehension are the levels of higher-order thinking questions as based on **Bloom's Taxonomy**.

Knowledge Questions

- What happened after . . . ?

- Who was it that . . . ?

- Can you tell why . . . ?

- Which is true of false . . . ?

Comprehension Questions

- What was the main idea . . . ?

- Can you distinguish between . . . ?

- What do you think might happen next . . . ?

- Can you provide an example of . . . ?

Application Questions

- Could this have happened in . . . ?

- Can you group by characteristics such as . . . ?

- Can you apply this outcome to some experience of your own . . . ?

- Would this example be useful if you had a . . . ?

Analysis Questions

- Which events could have happened . . . ?

- If . . . had happened, what might the ending have been?

- What were some of the motives behind . . . ?

- What was the problem with . . . ?

Synthesis Questions

- If you had to compose a song about . . . ?

- What would happen if . . . ?

- If faced with the same problem as . . . , how would you . . . ?

- What proposal could you develop that would . . . ?

Evaluation Questions

- How would you judge the value of . . . ?

- What is a better solution to . . . ?

- How effective are . . . ?

- If you were reviewing . . . , what would you write?

GRAMMATICAL STRUCTURES OF ENGLISH

2.3 Grammatical Structures of English

a. Identify methods of sentence construction (e.g., sentence combining with coordinators and subordinators; sentence embedding and expanding with clausal and phrasal modifiers)

b. Analyze parts of speech and their distinctive structures and functions (e.g., noun phrases including count and noncount nouns and the determiner system; prepositions, adjectives, and adverbs; word transformations)

c. Describe the forms and functions of the English verb system (e.g., modals, verb complements, verbal phrases)

d. Recognize conventions of English orthography and changes in word meaning and pronunciation

(California Common Core State Standards for English Language Arts, L.6–12.1)

Methods of Sentence Construction

This section of the CSET English Subtest II will ask you about different methods of combining sentences. One method is to combine simple sentences (or independent clauses) with a coordinator to create a compound sentence. **Coordinating conjunctions** include *and, or, but, nor, for, yet,* and *so.*

Our team scored ten goals, **yet** we still lost the match.

Another method is to combine simple sentences with a subordinator to create a complex sentence with a dependent clause. **Subordinating conjunctions** include *after, although, as, as if, because, before, even though, if, since, unless, when, whenever, until, while,* etc. Notice that the dependent clause in a complex sentence contains the subordinating conjunction.

Although our team scored ten goals, we still lost the match.

Clausal and Phrasal Modifiers

A **clausal modifier** is a clause that acts like an adverb or adjective and adds detail to a sentence. An **adverb clause** is a phrase that begins with a subordinating conjunction and modifies a verb, adjective, or other adverb.

The ballerina left the stage **before the performance ended**.

Here, the word *before* serves as a subordinating conjunction, and the entire phrase "before the performance ended" is an adverb clause modifying the verb *left*.

An **adjective clause** is a clause that modifies a noun, pronoun, or other adjective.

Raymond, **who sang for us yesterday**, got a part in the school musical.

The clause "who sang for us yesterday" is an adjective clause modifying the noun *Raymond*.

A **phrasal modifier** is a phrase that functions as an adjective or adverb in a sentence. Look at these examples of prepositional phrases.

The sweet potatoes **in the bin** are no longer fresh. (adjective modifying *potatoes*)

Coach Brooks blew his whistle **at precisely four o'clock** to signal the end of practice. (adverb modifying *blew*)

Appositional Phrases

An **appositional phrase** identifies or describes a nearby noun. Such a phrase may be "embedded," which means that it is set within the body of the sentence instead of coming at the beginning or end.

Notice how the following two sentences can be combined using an embedded appositional phrase.

> Kevin Durant is my favorite basketball player. He was voted Most Valuable Player in the NBA last year.

> Kevin Durant, **my favorite basketball player**, was voted Most Valuable Player in the NBA last year.

Nouns and Noun Phrases

Nouns can be divided into count and noncount nouns. **Count nouns** refer to things that can be divided up into smaller units that are separate from one another: *chair, word, plate, teammate*. Count nouns may be preceded in indefinite constructions by modifiers such as *a* or *one*.

Noncount nouns refer to things that cannot be counted because they are regarded as wholes that are not divisible into parts, as a concept or substance. They often refer to abstractions and may have a collective meaning: *furniture, weather, progress, water*. In indefinite constructions, noncount nouns are preceded by modifying words such as *much* or *some*.

The **determiner system** is made up of modifying words called **determiners** that are always followed by a noun. The categories of determiners are as follows:

- articles: *a, an, the*

- possessive nouns: *Susan's, the building's, my uncle's*

- possessive pronouns: *your, my, his, whose*, etc.

- numbers: *one, two*, etc.

- indefinite pronouns: *few, more, every, each, either, all, both, some, any*, etc.

Some students of English as a second language have difficulties with choosing the correct determiner, particularly if their native language either has no articles or a different system of choosing articles and determiner words.

Identifying whether nouns are count or noncount helps with plurals. Count nouns are pluralized by adding a final -s, while noncount nouns cannot be pluralized.

A **noun phrase** functions as a noun in a sentence, as in this example:

To reach the finals of the competition is quite an accomplishment.

Word Transformations

An exercise in altering the syntax of a sentence yet employing or retaining a key word and the basic sentence meaning is called **word transformations**. Such exercises are helpful for students learning English as a second language.

Look at this sentence: It's the most beautiful statue I've ever seen.

Now transform this sentence using the word *seen* and the following frame:

I . . . beautiful statue.

Sample answer: I have never seen a more beautiful statue.

Modals, Verb Complements, and Verbal Phrases

Modals, or modal auxiliary verbs, are a set of English verbs that are used with other verbs to express capability, possibility, willingness, suggestion, or something similar. Modals include *can, could, may, might, must, ought, shall, should, will,* and *would*.

Use of Modal	Example
Ability to do something	I can play chess.
Permission to do something	Can I join the chess club?
Request	Can you give me a ride?
Offer	I can loan you my chess set.
Suggestion	Can we play chess this afternoon?
Possibility	The competition can get heated at the club.

A **verb complement** is the arrangement of one verb as the object of another verb. In English, this construction occurs in three ways:

With infinitives:

I told him **to begin**.

I wasn't ready **to begin**.

I waited for the woman **to close the door**.

With gerunds:

Juan considered **starting a new job**.

I regretted **his leaving his old job**.

He wavered about **leaving his old friends**.

With noun clauses:

Our boss requested **that we meet today**.

I wondered **why she requested a meeting**.

I didn't know **that the boss had taken another job**.

She told us **when she would leave**.

A **verbal phrase** is made up of a verbal (a verb that also functions as another part of speech) and all of its modifiers and objects. A verbal phrase can be a participial phrase, a gerund phrase, or an infinitive phrase. Verbal phrases can function in a sentence as various parts of speech.

> **Watching her favorite television show**, Alisha finally was able to relax. (The phrase in bold is a participial phrase that functions as an adjective modifying *Alisha*.)

> **Watching television** is Alisha's favorite way to relax. (The phrase in bold is a gerund phrase that functions as a noun and the subject of the sentence.)

> Alisha loves **to watch her favorite television show**. (The phrase in bold is an infinitive phrase that functions as a direct object in the sentence.)

Note: Further information about the structures of English grammar can be found in Chapter 4.

CHAPTER 4

Composition and Rhetoric

On the CSET: English Subtest III, you will answer two constructed-response questions—one based on one or more literary texts, the other on a nonliterary text. You will have 2 hours to write your essays. The essay responses will reflect your command of the following relevant knowledge and skills associated with Composition and Rhetoric.

- **Writing Processes (Individual and Collaborative)** include the ability to reflect on and describe your own writing processes. You should be able to develop and strengthen writing when necessary by such methods as freewriting, planning, revising, editing, rewriting, or trying a different approach by focusing on what is most significant for your specific purpose and audience. You should also be able to use strategies such as creating graphic organizers, outlines, notes, charts, and summaries to convey and/or clarify content.

- **Text Types and Purposes** require you to recognize and use a variety of writing applications, including argument, informative/explanatory text, narrative, and historical investigation. You should demonstrate an awareness of audience, purpose, and context in writing. You must demonstrate the ability to recognize and use various text structures for narrative and non-narrative texts. You must be able to apply a variety of methods to develop ideas in an essay, including analogy, cause and effect, and compare and contrast. In analyzing topics or texts, you must be able to use valid reasoning and relevant evidence to support claims. You must apply rhetorical techniques to develop arguments, including appeals to logic and emotion. You must demonstrate the ability to write informative/explanatory texts to examine and present complex ideas, concepts, and information. You must also use evidence from literary texts to support your analysis of literature.

- **Production and Distribution of Writing** will test your ability to employ precise and extensive vocabulary and effective diction. You must use various clause-joining techniques to express logical connections between ideas. You must be able to identify and use clausal and phrasal modifiers to control flow, pace, and emphasis. You must also identify and use devices such as active and passive voice, expletives, and transitional phrases to control focus in sentences and paragraphs. You should demonstrate the ability to use technology, including the Internet, to produce, publish, and update writing products.

- **Conventions of Oral and Written Language** will test your ability to apply knowledge of linguistic structure to use the conventions of Standard English. You must understand and use a range of conventions in spoken and written English, including effective sentence structure, preferred usage, and conventional forms of spelling, capitalization, and punctuation. You should also be able to adapt speech to a variety of contexts and tasks, demonstrating a command of formal English.

- **Research to Build and Present Knowledge** requires you to demonstrate knowledge of strategies for developing research questions and methods of inquiry and investigation. You must know how to gather relevant information from various authoritative print and digital sources and assess the strengths and limitations of each source. You must know how to interpret and apply information, integrating it into a written text while avoiding plagiarism and overreliance on any one source. You should know the professional conventions for citation and attribution, including footnotes and endnotes.

PREPARING FOR CSET: ENGLISH SUBTEST III

The CSET: English Subtest III asks you to respond in writing to two constructed-response questions. One question will deal with one or more literary texts and the other will address an informational text. Subtest III does not include any multiple-choice questions. However, 10 multiple-choice questions on Composition and Rhetoric are included in Subtest I.

For each constructed-response question in Subtest III, you should write a response of about 800–1,000 words. You may write longer responses if you prefer. Your responses will be assessed according to the subject-matter knowledge and skill they demonstrate, not writing ability. You should, however, write clearly enough to allow for a valid judgment of your knowledge and skills regarding the subject matter. You should write for an audience of educators in the field.

A typical constructed-response question on literary texts in Subtest III might require teacher candidates to read and analyze two (or more) texts and then identify a common theme, compare and contrast the authors' approach to the theme, including use of literary techniques, and draw a conclusion about how the techniques the authors used affected the ideas expressed. Be prepared to analyze the historical context for a literary text and the author's relationship to that context. For example, Mark Twain's novel *The Adventures of Huckleberry Finn* deals with race relations in America through the story of Huck, a poor Southern boy, and his friendship with Jim, a runaway slave. Twain's novel appeared just two decades after the Civil War had ended slavery, and it used humor and satire—hallmarks of Twain's genius—to address the problem of racism in a new way.

The constructed-response question on an informational text might require teacher candidates to read and analyze a nonfiction passage by summarizing the author's main argument, evaluating the author's reasoning, describing the author's use of rhetorical devices for a purpose such as persuasion, identifying the target audience, and evaluating the passage's success in accomplishing its purpose.

Your responses will be assessed based on the following:

Purpose: How well your response accomplishes the task set by the prompt in relation to relevant CSET: English subject matter requirements.

Subject Matter Knowledge: How well you apply accurate knowledge about CSET: English subject matter in your response.

Support: How well and how appropriately you use evidence from relevant CSET: English subject matter requirements in support of your response.

Depth and Breadth of Understanding: The degree to which your response shows a deep understanding of the relevant CSET: English subject matter requirements.

You will not use any reference materials in the testing session. All the necessary information will be included with the writing prompts. Read each prompt carefully and repeatedly to make sure you understand your task before you begin to write. Think about how to organize your responses to address each prompt completely. Check your work and make any changes needed to improve your responses.

Along with the writing standards listed below, Subtest III will also test your knowledge of Reading Literature (SMR 1.1) and Craft and Structure of Literature (SMR 1.2) for the literary text prompt, and your knowledge of Reading Informational Texts (SMR 1.3), Craft and Structure of Informational Texts (SMR 1.4), and Integration of Knowledge and Ideas in Informational Texts (SMR 1.5) for the informational text prompt. These standards are reviewed in Chapter 1.

REVIEWING THE WRITING PROCESS

The following sections on composition and rhetoric are meant to guide you in reviewing the writing process. The National Council of Teachers of English (NCTE) asserts that writing is a teachable skill, and that teachers can use a variety of methods to help students improve their writing skills. To be an effective teacher of writing, you must have command of all the stages of the writing process, from prewriting to presentation, writing activities that can improve students' writing skills, and research strategies that students can employ.

According to NCTE guidelines, "Developing writers require support. This support can best come through carefully designed writing instruction oriented toward acquiring new strategies and skills. Certainly, writers can benefit from teachers who simply support and give them time to write. However, instruction matters. Teachers of writing should be well-versed in composition theory and research, and they should know methods for turning that theory into practice. When writing teachers first walk into classrooms, they should already know and practice good composition. However, much as in doctoring, learning to teach well is a lifetime process, and lifetime development is the key to successful practice. Students deserve no less."

Below are some suggested resources to help you prepare for Subtest III and the ten multiple-choice questions on Composition and Rhetoric in Subtest I.

- *A Teaching Subject: Composition Since 1966* by Joseph Harris (1996)

- *Developing Readers and Writers in the Content Areas K–12* by David W. Moore, Sharon Arthur Moore, Patricia M. Cunningham, and James W. Cunningham (2010)

- *Imaginative Writing: The Elements of Craft* by Janet Burroway (2010)

- *The Little, Brown Handbook* by H. Ramsey Fowler and Jane E. Aaron (2011)

- *The Reading/Writing Connection: Strategies for Teaching and Learning in the Secondary Classroom* by Carol Booth Olson (2010)

- *Steps for Writers: Composing Essays,* Volume 2, by Philip Eggers (2012)

- *Writing Workshop: The Essential Guide* by Ralph Fletcher and Joann Portalupi (2001)

WRITING PROCESSES (INDIVIDUAL AND COLLABORATIVE)

3.1 Writing Processes (Individual and Collaborative)

a. Reflect on and describe their own writing processes

b. Develop and strengthen writing as needed by freewriting, planning, revising, editing, rewriting, or trying a new approach, focusing on what is most significant for a specific purpose and audience

c. Clarify and record meaning using strategies such as creating graphic organizers, outlines, notes, charts, summaries, or précis

(*California Common Core State Standards for English Language Arts, W.6–12.5–6*)

As with most skills, improvement in writing requires practice—lots of practice. And students should practice by actually writing, not merely by listening to advice about how to write or doing drills in freewriting, brainstorming, organizing ideas, or using grammar.

Student writers who write frequently learn more about their own processes of composition and develop methods that work best for them. Writing often and on a variety of topics and in a variety of ways gives students confidence about how to approach a writing task. As a result, confronting a blank sheet of paper and a writing prompt is no longer such a daunting prospect.

It is important for teachers to recognize that writing doesn't occur only within the walls of a classroom. Students write all the time in their personal lives—for example, by texting and emailing to family and friends, writing journals, blogging, and pursuing their own creative projects. Teachers should encourage this kind of "self-sponsored" writing while at the same time urging students to think about using and improving their writing skills in everything they write.

One way to encourage student writing is to organize the classroom as a writer's workshop and to present students with opportunities to write in frequent structured sessions. To set up a successful writer's workshop, a writing teacher might do the following:

- Set aside time for structured writing sessions.

- Begin some sessions with a freewriting exercise, in which students write nonstop for a set period (10–15 minutes) on whatever topic comes to mind. Tell students not to make corrections as they write, and not to make judgments on what they are writing. The object is to make students less self-conscious about the writing process. Freewriting can release inner tensions and help students tap into their own creativity.

- Begin some sessions with a brief lesson on some element of the writing process, such as brainstorming, grammar and mechanics, or rewriting.

- Give students a certain amount of free time to plan writing.

- Use writing time to also hold brief conferences with individual students when necessary.

- Encourage interaction among students to share ideas about how to plan, draft, and revise their work.

- Set aside time for students to share their writing with the group and get feedback.

- Have students keep writing portfolios to check the progress of their writing skills.

• Model the skills and metacognitive processes involved in successful writing.

WRITING TO RESPOND TO LITERATURE

One of the two writing prompts on the CSET: English Subtest III will direct you to respond to a literary text. The following are some exercises suitable for a student writing workshop that will give you practice in teaching and reviewing this skill.

- **Readings**. Students should have opportunities to read aloud examples of good writing they have discovered in novels, short stories, plays, or even magazines and websites. Students should also read their own work aloud to the group and let the audience critique the writing for style, clarity, and impact. Students should learn to make critical comments without getting personal. Everyone should realize that the point of the reading sessions is to improve each student's writing skills.

- **Recasting of genre**. A good exercise to explore how different genres require different styles of writing is to recast a piece of writing into another genre. For example, a student might take a poem he or she wrote and expand it into a short story with a plot and characters. Similarly, the main thrust of a passage from a novel or short story could be boiled down into a lyric poem.

A student might, for instance, write a haiku (a three-line poem with a five-syllable line, a seven-syllable line, and another five-syllable line) based on this paragraph from *Pnin* by Vladimir Nabokov:

> "The brook in the gully behind the garden, a trembling trickle most of the time, was tonight a loud torrent that tumbled over itself in its avid truckling to gravity, as it carried through corridors of beech and spruce last year's leaves, and some leafless twigs, and a brand-new, unwanted soccer ball that had recently rolled into the water from the sloping lawn after Pnin disposed of it by defenestration."

A possible haiku:

> Brook, gully, garden.
> Trickle now a torrent, loud.
> Leaves, twigs, a lost ball.

- **Focus on voice**. Successful writers develop their own **voice** or distinctive style. Students in a classroom workshop should keep their writing assignments in a portfolio so each of them can monitor the development of a unique writing voice. The teacher should point out that writing with the most impact tends to feature declarative sentences with precise subjects and verbs doing much of the work of each sentence. To develop a strong writing voice, students might practice rewriting weak or vague sentences to make them clearer and more forceful.

- **Perspective**. Another good workshop assignment is for students to rewrite a scene from a novel, short story, play, or film from the perspective of one of the characters in the scene. Students should try to imagine what the character is feeling and how the character might express his or her reactions to what is happening. An example of switching perspective to gain insight is the play *Wicked,* which is presented from the viewpoint of the Wicked Witch of the East, whose green skin has always made her an outcast.

- **Making stale writing fresh**. In workshop sessions, students should help each other avoid stale or ineffective writing, such as overuse of clichéd similes and metaphors (*free as a bird, proud as a peacock, the chance of a lifetime, a mountain of debt*), lack of variety in sentence length, vague words and phrases, overwriting and pretentious language, and weak transitions.

ADDITIONAL EXERCISES FOR RESPONDING TO LITERATURE

These exercises will help students read more carefully and think about literary texts in new ways.

- Write a diary entry that the main character might have written.

- Write a parody of a story by exaggerating the events of the plot or the characters' traits.

- Design a book jacket for a novel or play that expresses the main theme.

- Write a movie trailer for the imaginary movie version of a novel or story.

- Make a collage of clipped illustrations and photos that express aspects of a poem or short story.

- Hold a panel discussion about a novel or play and its impact on the reader or viewer.

- Compare and contrast two characters from different works of fiction.

- Write ten questions that you would like to ask an author in an interview.

- Write a ballad or song using the incidents in a novel or short story.

- Write a continuation of a short story or play in which you speculate on what the characters would do after the story has concluded.

- Write an editorial expressing your opinions about a controversial issue raised in a novel, play, television show, or movie.

THE WRITING PROCESS

Successful writers at any level learn to focus not only on the finished product but on the process necessary to achieve a polished, clear, coherent piece of writing. Approaching this process has two aspects. First, writers must develop through repeated practice a repertory of routines, strategies, and skills for composing, revising, and editing many different kinds of text. Second, they should also develop a sort of meta-awareness about their own individual processes, which will help them most when they get stuck in the planning stages or in the middle of creating a piece of writing. Here, a good writing teacher can help students by using established research, theory, and practice to guide them through problems and difficulties.

As you examine the writing process, remember that the process is not—and should not be—a formulaic series of rigid steps. Instead, the steps should be seen as overlapping and recursive; even the most experienced writers may have to rethink an approach or "go back to the drawing board" under certain circumstances. With this in mind, teachers of writing should present one or more alternate strategies for each step of the writing process, thereby providing students with opportunities to identify methods that work best for themselves in different writing situations.

A writing instructor should also remember that certain writing tasks in the workplace or other settings involve collaboration. Student writers should learn to work effectively with each other.

The following sections will review the steps of the writing process: prewriting, drafting, revising, editing, and sharing/publishing.

Prewriting: Clarifying the Task

The student writer should not begin writing until he or she is certain about what the prompt or assignment requires. Possible concerns include:

- **Purpose**. What is the reason for writing, or what is to be accomplished at the end? What audience are you addressing?

- **Preparation**. What actions should be taken before beginning, such as reading a passage or consulting a source?

- **Components**. What are the required elements in the assignment (outlines to follow, questions to answer, conclusions to draw)?

- **Evaluation**. What criteria will the grader or instructor use to determine if you have satisfied the prompt or completed the assignment?

Prewriting: Thinking and Planning

Once the task has been clarified, the student writer can think about possible approaches to take or topics to address. On a timed prompt, the writer must decide on an approach fairly rapidly. For a larger assignment like a term paper, the writer might do additional reading on several related topics while pondering the best course to take in planning and writing the paper.

Again, although the writing process is presented here as a series of orderly steps, it is not generally so tidy in execution. The steps are iterative—they influence each other and recur constantly. Students should be reminded that the original ideas or approach that they settle on may have to be revised after further research or even after the drafting process has begun. Or, once the editing has begun, the writer may notice that more information is needed or an argument needs to be bolstered with different examples. Student writers should be prepared for a process that may double back on itself before a polished finish product is achieved.

Prewriting: Determining the Purpose

To focus the purpose for writing, the student writer should write a **thesis statement** that lays out the overall point of view or argument that the writer wants to make about the topic. A thesis statement written in the planning stage may have to be revised during drafting. Nevertheless, it will serve as a guide for developing the essay or paper.

Before beginning to draft an essay or any piece of writing, the student writer might complete these statements:

My purpose in writing this is to . . .

My main points are . . .

And my conclusion is that . . .

Prewriting: Thinking About the Audience

Student writers should remember to direct their writing to a specific audience. In classroom writing, the audience might be the teacher and their classmates. On an essay test, the audience is the grader who will read and evaluate the writing. Students should imagine that they are presenting their information or making their argument to the grader face-to-face. They might even imagine a grader asking questions such as "What is your main point? How can you prove that? What sources support that? What conclusions can be drawn from this?"

To satisfy the expectations of an academic grader, students should remember the following:

- The grader will judge whether the response completely addresses the prompt.

- The grader will evaluate the writer's ability to articulate, sustain, and support an argument.

- The grader will examine the writer's use of appropriate examples from the reading passage and any other sources.

- The grader will evaluate the writing on its logic, structure, fluency, coherency, and use of the conventions of Standard English.

On assignments such as term papers, the teacher/grader will also look at the writer's ability to cite source material correctly.

Prewriting: Strategies for Generating Content

A student writer will find it much easier to draft an essay when he or she has a plan or outline to follow. The following strategies can be used to generate ideas before drafting:

- **Brainstorming**. The student writer should list ideas at random that could be of use in the essay. He or she should resist the urge to make corrections or straighten out the syntax. Any potentially relevant idea should be jotted down.

- **Making an outline**. The student writer can make a cursory outline of ideas, which will serve to organize the material into main ideas and supporting details.

- **Using a graphic organizer**. The student writer can use a variety of graphic organizers to generate ideas. For example, an essay with a compare/contrast structure could be organized around a T-chart or Venn diagram that lists how two characters or settings are alike and different. Visual thinkers could use a word web to connect supporting details to a main topic or idea. A flow chart could be used to show a logical or chronological flow of ideas from start to finish.

- **Making a K/W/L chart**. Ideas for a term paper or longer essay can be organized using a K/W/L chart. The first column of the chart lists What I **K**NOW, the second column What I **W**ANT to Learn, and third column What I **L**EARNED.

- **Writing a summary or précis**. For a term paper, the student writer might summarize sources such as articles, essays, or chapters so that he or she can quickly review the information they contain. A **précis** is a concise summary based on a complete reading of a work. It is made up of:

  (1) A sentence containing the author's name, the title of the work, and the date in parentheses followed by the work's major claim or thesis statement.

  (2) A brief description of how the author develops and supports the thesis statement.

  (3) A sentence setting out the author's main purpose in writing the work.

  (4) A sentence describing the intended audience for the work.

Drafting: Main Idea or Argument

The next stage of the writing process after prewriting is drafting or actually writing the essay. Having settled on what the task is, who the audience is, and what ideas he or she wants to present, the student writer should draft an opening sentence and paragraph that includes the **main idea**. This is a statement or brief paragraph that articulates the main argument or point to be made and briefly describes what the essay is about.

The student writer should remember that the opening of an essay must clearly announce the topic or the main point, as in the following:

> "This passage from the novel *Tristram Shandy* demonstrates how the author, Laurence Sterne, anticipated the self-reflexive, playful fiction of today's postmodernist writers. Like many of them, he ultimately was writing a novel about the difficulties of writing a novel."

If the prompt calls for the writer to take one side of an argument, this point of view should be included in the opening:

> "While social media such as email, text messaging, Twitter, and other forms seems to bring people together, its actual effect is to separate people by lessening the impulse and opportunity for them to interact face to face."

Drafting: Thinking about the Audience

As in the Prewriting stage, the student writer should think about the target audience during the Drafting stage. He or she should try to estimate how much the audience knows about the topic and fill in the gaps. The student writer should also anticipate questions, objections, or alternate viewpoints that the audience might have, and answer these in the course of the essay.

Drafting: Creating Paragraphs

The student writer should think of the first sentence of each paragraph as a sub-topic sentence or main idea. The sentences that follow it should then support the idea with examples, definitions, quotes, explanations, and other details. When the paragraphs of an essay are composed properly, the reader often can read only the first sentences of each paragraph to get a good idea of what the essay is about.

The student writer should also try to vary the length of paragraphs. An occasional short paragraph can be used effectively for emphasis. The writer should double-check a long paragraph to see that it does not include more than one main idea, which can be confusing to the reader.

Drafting: Logical Transitions

A successful piece of writing flows because one idea seems to lead seamlessly to the next. The student writer should always try to show the connections between ideas so that the argument doesn't "jump around" or seem disconnected. Some important reminders about logical transitions include:

- **Announce each sub-topic and then discuss it**. Don't bring up an idea and leave it hanging.

- **Use words that show the stages of your presentation or argument**. They may be numerical words, such as *first, second,* and *third*. They may also be words and phrases such as *at first, initially, then, next, finally,* and *in conclusion*.

- **Use words that connect ideas**. Words and phrases such as *because, therefore, however, in addition to, despite,* and *consequently* show strong connections between sentences and paragraphs and help the reader follow the main ideas or argument.

- **Use repetition for emphasis**. Repeating key words and phrases signals that they are important.

- **Use consistent word choice to prevent confusion**. The reader should not be thinking, "Does this term mean the same thing as that one?"

Drafting: A Strong Conclusion

A successful essay should culminate in a strong conclusion that wraps up the argument in a logical way. A good conclusion may also:

- Present a solution to a problem

- Call for a particular action

- List consequences

- Briefly expand on the main idea

There is no need for the student writer to rehash, word for word, the thesis statement or main idea of the essay in the conclusion. Likewise, major new ideas should not be introduced and left hanging in the last paragraph. Instead, the student writer should briefly review the main point or the main argument covered in the essay.

Occasionally, the writer may find that the main idea is presented more clearly in the conclusion than in the introduction. In such a case, he or she might decide that the new version should be moved to the beginning of the essay. A writer should compare his or her introduction and conclusion to ensure that they don't contradict each other and that they are not identical in wording.

Revising: What to Consider

The revising stage is when the student writer should "re-view" the entire essay to see if he or she has actually written what was planned or intended. In the classroom, a student writer can find out what needs to be revised by reading the draft aloud to the class and asking for questions or comments.

In a successful writing workshop environment, students should not feel defensive about criticism nor should they shy away from making critical remarks or suggestions. The important thing is to be honest while still maintaining a polite and respectful tone.

When working alone, the student writer should revise by looking at a paper as an outside critic would do, asking such questions as "Does this need to be cut? Does this statement need more support? Do the paragraphs or main point need to be reordered? Does something need to be restated more clearly?" Things to consider during revision include:

- Audience
- Structure
- Content
- Logic

- Coherence
- Voice
- Style
- Tone

Revising: Think of Your Audience

At the revising stage, as at the other stages of writing, the writer should consider who will be reading the essay and how much they know about the topic. The student writer should try to imagine a grader or another student coming to the essay with limited knowledge of the subject matter. In that case, does something need to be defined or explained? Are the explanations already in the essay clear enough? Are there sufficient supporting details? Is the main point stated clearly and concisely? Thinking about the audience first will make the revision process much easier.

Revising: Structure

In revising an essay or paper, the student writer should consider whether the structure includes a strong introduction, a clear sequence of main points and supporting details, and a strong conclusion. Could a reader easily fill in an outline of the main points in the essay or paper? Do the topic sentences of the paragraphs serve as a sort of skeleton of the essay? Are there sections or sentences that would be more effective if moved to another location?

Revising: Content and Flow

At the revising stage, the student writer should also examine the content and flow of the essay. Ideas should be presented clearly and accurately, in language that is consistent without being too repetitive. For example, if the subject has been referred to consistently as "the Civil War," it may be confusing to the reader if it is suddenly called "the War Between the States" or "the Great Rebellion." Look for synonyms and restatements that might cause problems with clarity.

When revising, the student writer should also look for logical connections of ideas. When ideas are presented in a logical order with connector words that emphasize how they are related, the essay flows for the reader. The writer should also look for unnecessary details that might be interesting in themselves but do not belong in the essay and are best eliminated.

Revising: Voice, Style, and Tone

The revising stage is also the time to consider how the writing sounds to the audience. A formal essay should be written in Standard English that is accurate and expressive without being ornate or florid. Again, problems with voice can often be detected by reading the essay aloud to the other students in the classroom. If the student writer can't imagine saying the words that he or she wrote in a normal conversation, then there might be a problem with overwriting. Student writers should try to write in a style that is formal without being pompous or pretentious.

Pretentious Writing:

> Lincoln, with the presentation of his historic oration at Gettysburg, attempted to effect the rededication of the Union and its supporters to the overall task of achieving victory in the Civil War and rekindling the vital spirit of liberty in the nation as a whole.

Effective Writing:

> In the Gettysburg Address, Lincoln sought to inspire Union troops and their supporters to win the war and bring about a rebirth of liberty in the nation.

The student writer should check the essay for a consistent voice and tone. The writing should not be too casual or too full of jargon. The writer should avoid slang words or colloquial language. While wit is desirable, sarcasm or cheap jokes are never appropriate.

Revising: Active Voice vs. Passive Voice

Active voice is when the emphasis is on a subject doing something, instead of something being done to it. Using the active voice tends to make writing sound more forceful and assured.

Passive Voice:

> The garage was cleaned by Stan and his friends.

Active Voice:

> Stan and his friends cleaned the garage.

While both versions say the same thing, the sentence with the active voice places the emphasis on Stan and his friends performing an action. Sometimes the writer may use the passive voice on purpose—as here, if the desired emphasis is on the garage being cleaned. However, in general, it is best to use active voice as much as possible.

Revising: Conciseness and Sentence Variety

Student writers should revise their work for conciseness by cutting out unnecessary words and phrases. Redundant phrases include words that can be eliminated without changing the meaning, such as *advance planning, commute back and forth,* and *end result.*

Often writers who are working quickly will include too many prepositional phrases and infinitives. By eliminating as many as possible, the writer can be more concise.

Too many prepositions:

> As **of** now, they are not **in** a position **to** make a decision **due to** the fact that there is a majority of the board members who are not **in** possession **of** the evidence.

More concise:

> They cannot make a decision because a majority of the board members do not have the evidence.

Another way to make writing more lively and interesting is to vary the length of sentences and paragraphs. Student writers might also insert an occasional question or exclamation for variety.

Editing: Spelling, Grammar, and Punctuation

The editing stage of the writing process is when the writer polishes the work and corrects mistakes. This is also called **proofreading**. Misspelled words, grammatical errors such as subject-verb disagreement or inconsistent verb tense, or punctuation errors such as misplaced commas not only make the final product look sloppy, they can also confuse the intended meaning. By editing to correct mistakes, the student writer demonstrates his or her commitment to the quality of the work.

Editing: Word Choice

The editing stage provides an opportunity for the student writer to check that he or she has used strong, accurate words, particularly nouns and verbs. The writer should also try to avoid sexist language by using gender-neutral terms.

> The wise *person* can *get* a large return on *his* money.
> Wise *investors* can *earn* a large return on *their* money.

Student writers should also replace slang, technical jargon, and padded phrases.

> To be successful, the young composer had to *work his tail off* every day.
> To be successful, the young composer had to *work very hard* every day.

> *By the age of two months,* the child *at the developmental median* will smile *upon visual contact* with his or her *female parent's* face.

> *At two months,* the *average* child will smile *at the sight* of his or her *mother's* face.

Editing: Attribution of Sources

During the editing stage, the student writer should also check that quotations in the essay are accurate and correctly attributed. In an essay based on a literary passage, the writer should include only brief quotations (inside quotation marks), since the grader is already familiar with the passage. In longer term papers, the writer should include the source in parentheses at the end of the paragraph or in a list at the end of the paper, depending on the style required.

Sharing/Publishing: The Student Writer

For the student writer, sharing/publishing involves presenting the finished product to the grader or teacher or to the intended audience. For an essay test, the response should be written clearly in ink, with as few cross-outs and corrections as possible. If there is time, the student should rewrite the essay so that there are no corrections.

For a classroom presentation, the student should practice reading the paper so that he or she doesn't stumble on any of the wording and can read it fluently. The student may also incorporate a variety of software applications, including databases, graphics, and spreadsheets, into a term paper. Each chart or graphic should be clearly labeled in the final document.

Sharing/Publishing: The Writing Teacher

For the writing teacher, the sharing/publishing stage of the writing process means evaluating and grading the finished product. **Holistic grading** is when the teacher grades the essay on the overall impression it makes. A **grading rubric** provides the overall criteria for each level of scoring. One weakness of the holistic approach is that it is generally very subjective.

Alternatively, the teacher may use an **analytical evaluation** approach, which involves checking every phase of the writing assignment and giving a point value to each separate skill. While this approach is more objective, it also analyzes the writing process in parts rather than as an interrelated whole.

Sharing/Publishing: Conferencing and Portfolios

The writing teacher should hold periodic conferences with students to discuss the success of their completed writing assignments and the skills they need to improve. This is one of the most valuable tools of the classroom writing workshop approach. Another helpful tool is the **student portfolio** of writing assignments. When students save their papers and compare their finished assignments, they can see how they have improved and where they can improve further. This self-evaluation process is vital for a writer at any level.

TEXT TYPES AND PURPOSES

3.2 Text Types and Purposes

a. Recognize and use a variety of writing applications (e.g., argument, informative/explanatory text, narrative, business and technical documents, historical investigation)

b. Demonstrate awareness of audience, purpose, and context

c. Recognize and use various text structures (e.g., narrative and non-narrative organizational patterns)

d. Apply a variety of methods to develop ideas within an essay (e.g., analogy, cause and effect, compare and contrast, definition, illustration, description, hypothesis)

e. Demonstrate the ability to write arguments to support claims in an analysis of substantive topics or texts, using valid reasoning and relevant and sufficient evidence

f. Apply rhetorical techniques to develop arguments, including appeals to logic through inductive/deductive reasoning and appeals to emotion or ethical belief

g. Demonstrate the ability to write informative/explanatory texts to examine and convey complex ideas, concepts, and information clearly and accurately through the effective selection, organization, and analysis of content

h. Use evidence from literary texts to support analysis and reflection and to compose creative and aesthetically compelling responses to literature

(*California Common Core State Standards for English Language Arts, W.6–12.1–3*)

WRITING APPLICATIONS

The writing teacher must be familiar with and able to teach a variety of **writing applications**. When students are aware of different literary genres and modes of writing, they are better able to compare them in analytical essays and write in those genres themselves.

- **Narrative writing** tells a story, and usually includes plot, characters, setting, chronological structure, and theme. Some narrative genres are novel, short story, play, myth, legend, and fable.

- **Descriptive writing** uses sensory language, rich detail, and figurative language such as simile, metaphor, and personification to portray people, places, or things. Good descriptive writing helps a reader visualize a scene or appeals to all of a reader's senses. This kind of writing may be used in fiction and nonfiction.

- **Expository writing** seeks to inform, explain, instruct, clarify, or define. It generally features a main topic, supporting details and facts, strong organization, and logical transitions. Genres for expository writing include newspaper and magazine articles, manuals, guidebooks, catalogues, instructions, reports, research papers, letters, and newsletters.

- **Persuasive writing** seeks to convince the reader to agree with a point of view or take a particular action. The writer states a position or opinion and supports it with facts and examples. Persuasive writing may appeal to logic or emotion. This kind of writing appears in editorials, letters to the editor, speeches, advertisements, pamphlets, and petitions.

- **Autobiographical and biographical writing** focuses on the facts of a person's life. In autobiography, a writer describes his or her own life in books or articles, letters, diaries, and journals. Biography is when a writer describes someone else's life, often that of an historical figure, politician, artist, or celebrity.

- **Business and technical documents** include various kinds of letters such as inquiries, complaints, orders, responses, and acknowledgments. Business documents are formal means of communication between two people, a person and a corporation, or two corporations. A business letter typically includes a salutation followed by a colon, a body of concise, un-indented paragraphs that are clear and straightforward, and a closing such as "Sincerely" or "Regards" followed by the sender's typed name, signature, and title.

- **Historical investigation** is writing about a certain historical period, event, trend, group, or individual. This kind of writing may include elements of narrative, descriptive, expository, and even persuasive writing. The historian identifies a topic, does research and gathers evidence from primary and secondary sources, develops a focused research question, and selects relevant evidence and examples that pertain to the research question.

TEXT STRUCTURES

The writing teacher should help students recognize and apply a variety of **text structures** to organize and develop ideas in their writing. Some of the most useful examples include:

- **Cause/Effect**. The writer shows how actions or events and their results are related.

- **Problem/Solution**. The writer describes a problem and proposes a solution.

- **Hypothesis/Support**. The writer presents a hypothesis or theory and provides details and examples to support it or refute it.

- **Compare/Contrast**. The writer shows how two or more people, things, or ideas are alike and different. The writer may also use analogy and metaphor to liken a situation to something familiar, as in comparing a political campaign to a military battle.

- **Definition/Description**. The writer defines a topic by describing it in detail. For example, stem cells could be described as immature cells that can develop into many different types of cells.

- **Illustration**. The writer presents a topic and then gives examples to explain it further.

- **Analogy**. The writer compares a topic to another thing or idea that is different from the topic but familiar to the reader. For example, a doctor's method of diagnosing disease could be compared to a detective using clues to solve a crime.

- **Chronological**. The writer presents facts or events in time order.

- **Directions**. The writer explains how something is done in sequential steps.

- **Classification**. The writer explains how concepts or terms are related.

METHODS OF PERSUASIVE WRITING

The writing teacher should help students apply critical-thinking skills to evaluate different persuasive techniques in writing. Three types of rhetorical strategies in persuasive writing include the following:

- **Appeal to reason**. The writer employs logic to make an argument. In **inductive reasoning**, the writer presents a specific case or example and then draws general conclusions from it. The evidence presented should be reliable and the conclusions drawn should apply to the specific case. Inductive arguments include the following types:

Part-to-whole: where the whole is assumed to be like individual parts only larger.

The simplified tax form has been a huge success in my state. Therefore, it should be used as a model for federal tax reform.

Extrapolation: where areas beyond the area of focus are assumed to be like the focused-on area.

In home entertainment, people have come to expect more choices about what TV programs to watch, what songs to listen to, and what games to play. Why not give them more choices with regard to their health care as well?

Prediction: where the future is assumed to be like the past.

In the twentieth century, the automobile changed living patterns by encouraging people to live in suburbs that were miles from their workplaces. Should more cities build light-rail systems today, people will once again see new options in where they live and work.

In **deductive reasoning**, the writer presents a generalization and then applies it to a specific case. The generalization should be based on reliable evidence.

Immunization has been one of the most successful public-health initiatives in American history. Today it can help us eliminate one of the most deadly childhood diseases.

A **syllogism** is a form of deductive reasoning with a major premise, a minor premise, and a conclusion.

Major premise:	All the players on the soccer team are A students.
Minor premise:	Jocasta is a player on the soccer team.
Conclusion:	Jocasta is an A student.

- **Appeal to emotion**. The writer employs an emotional argument designed to engage a reader's sympathies, values, and compassion. Emotional appeals often use sources such as personal interviews, anecdotes, testimony, and visual evidence to bolster an argument. For example, an argument favoring federal aid for small farms might include an interview with a farmer who is struggling to survive. An emotional appeal to fear may cause readers to feel that their own safety, security, or health is in danger.

- **Appeal to ethical belief**. The writer tries to gain support for an argument by linking it to a widely accepted value or ethical belief. For example, an essay that is against increases in military spending might appeal to religious values of peace and brotherhood or ethical beliefs about opposing violence and imperialism.

Types of Persuasive Speech

Writers also use three main types of persuasive speech strategies to frame an argument.

- **Proposition of fact**. In this type of argument, the writer tries to convince the reader that a proposition is true or false. An argument of this kind might be "Should Physical Education classes in school be compulsory?" or "Do school officials have the right to search students' lockers?"

- **Questions of value**. In this type of argument, the writer tries to convince the reader that an action or activity was right or wrong, moral or immoral, ethical or unethical, or better or worse than another action. For example: "Is it proper for a Supreme Court justice to make speeches on national issues that might come before the Court someday?"

- **Questions of policy**. In this type of argument, the writer tries to convince the reader that some action should or should not be taken. For example: "Should the federal government re-equip its vehicles to run on natural gas instead of gasoline?"

Logical Fallacies

Arguments that include common errors in reasoning or assumption are called logical fallacies. Student writers should avoid these errors in writing a persuasive essay. Recognizing logical fallacies can also be helpful in a debate.

- **Bandwagon appeal**. This argument taps into people's desire to be like the group or to belong. It argues that "everyone is doing this" or "everyone believes this."

- **Red herring**. This argument avoids the key issue by introducing another issue as a diversion. For example, in an article about policing the use of performance-enhancing drugs in professional cycling, the writer might say, "While some cyclists might use drugs to help their endurance, they are certainly not as bad as drug dealers who get innocent victims hooked on dangerous substances"—a point that is irrelevant to the main issue.

- **Straw man**. This argument creates a "straw man" by exaggerating, overstating, or over-simplifying an opposing point of view. For example, "My opponent would eliminate all government aid programs until children were left to starve and parents forced to take the most menial jobs just to survive."

- **Slippery slope**. This argument is based on the idea that if a first step is taken, then a second and third step will follow inevitably, until a disaster occurs like a person sliding on a slippery incline until he or she falls to the bottom. Example: "If our city council allows video cameras to be placed at intersections, soon they will put them in our neighborhoods. And next will come the camera in front of each house and then inside each house. We can't allow this intrusion into our privacy to stand."

- **Glittering generalities**. This argument uses "glad words" that sound important but actually have little or no real meaning. The words, such as *honest, fair,* and *decent,* are employed in general statements that can't be proved or disproved.

- **Begging the question**. This argument assumes as evidence the very conclusion it is trying to prove. For example, "Useless courses like Home Economics should be dropped from the curriculum at our school. Think how much money is wasted on useless courses each year." Yet the writer has not proved that the course is useless; it is just assumed to be so.

- **Ad hominem**. This argument is an attack on a person's character instead of on the person's ideas or opinions. Example: "Since college professors are all arrogant intellectual snobs, their notions of what an ordinary student would find most useful in his or her life and career is not likely to be very helpful."

- **Hasty generalization**. This argument is also called "jumping to conclusions." It bases its conclusion on too few samples to prove the point. Example: "Two people I know personally have never been vaccinated and neither has ever had a serious illness or physical condition. Therefore, vaccinations are largely unnecessary."

- **Either/or**. This argument falsely reduces an argument to two oversimplified alternatives. Example: "So it seems to me we can either content ourselves with cars exactly as they are or else abandon cars altogether and go back to horse-and-buggy days."

Classical Argument

In the fifth century BCE, Greeks developed the **Classical Argument**, a method for speakers and writers to argue a case logically to an open-minded audience. In simple form, it consists of these parts.

1. The **introduction** sets up a rapport with the reader or audience and announces the theme or thesis of the argument.

2. The **narration** summarizes background material relevant to the case and sets up what is at stake in the outcome.

3. The **confirmation** lays out in logical order, from strongest to weakest (or most obvious to most subtle), the claims that support the thesis, with evidence for each claim.

4. The **refutation and concession** looks at opposing viewpoints, anticipates certain objections from the audience, and concedes the validity of as much of this as possible without weakening the thesis.

5. The **summation** concludes the argument with rhetorical force, showing that this outcome or solution is best under the circumstances.

Advertising Techniques

In crafting their persuasive appeals, advertisers employ **Maslow's hierarchy of needs**. According to the psychologist Abraham Maslow's theory, most people have five basic need levels that they strive to satisfy.

1. Physiological need or life survival

2. Safety and security

3. Love and belongingness

4. Self-esteem

5. Self-actualization

Maslow theorized that human behavior and decision-making are motivated by one of the five need levels in his hierarchy. Applied to an advertiser or marketer, the ability to appeal effectively to one of these motivational drivers plays a large part in his or her potential success.

Services that are non-essential, such as custom-tailoring or massage treatments, can be marketed successfully to those in the fourth or fifth level of Maslow's hierarchy because those people are motivated by their needs for self-esteem and reaching their full potential. The same marketing campaign is unlikely to appeal to those on the first level, who are driven by the most basic needs for food and shelter.

In the same way, a single product can be marketed to different customers in different ways. A person on Maslow's second needs level might be induced to buy a luxury automobile that has important safety features and performs reliably in consumer studies. To a person on the fourth needs level, the automobile might be presented as an eye-catching purchase that will look good to peers or management.

PRODUCTION AND DISTRIBUTION OF WRITING

3.3 Production and Distribution of Writing

a. Produce clear writing by employing precise and extensive vocabulary and effective diction to control voice, style, and tone

b. Produce coherent writing by using clause-joining techniques (e.g., coordinators, subordinators, punctuation) to express logical connections between ideas

c. Identify and use clausal and phrasal modifiers to control flow, pace, and emphasis (e.g., adjective clauses, appositives, participles and verbal phrases, absolutes)

d. Identify and use devices to control focus in sentence and paragraph (e.g., active and passive voice, expletives, concrete subjects, transitional phrases)

e. Demonstrate the ability to use technology, including the Internet, to produce, publish, and update individual or shared writing products

(*California Common Core State Standards for English Language Arts, W.6–12.4–6*)

The writing teacher should understand and be able to describe how correct grammar, precise vocabulary, and appropriate diction can help students produce writing that is clear and effective. Following are some of the more important elements.

PRECISE VOCABULARY AND EFFECTIVE DICTION

The student writer should work to build a **strong vocabulary** so that he or she can choose the precisely correct word when writing. One aspect of an extensive vocabulary is recognizing the connotation of synonyms. For example, the words *mansion* and *hovel* both refer to a house, but with quite different connotations to a reader. The student writer should also recognize situations where a technical term or special language is needed to be precise.

Writers should also think about their **diction**, or voice, style, and tone in writing. A distinctive **voice** means that a writer's work sounds like no one else. After only a few sentences, the reader seems to be hearing a unique person speaking. A writer's **style** may be simple or relatively ornate and colorful, but should always be clear and accurate. **Tone** is the writer's attitude toward the reader, subject, and situation. A solemn tone would be more appropriate for an examination of automobile safety issues, while a more light-hearted tone could be used to describe the process of getting a driver's license.

Sentence Types and Clause-Joining Techniques

The student writer should understand how a variety of different sentence types can make a piece of writing more interesting and give it a sense of flow. **Types of sentences** include:

- **Simple sentence**. An independent clause containing a subject and a verb.

- **Compound sentence**. A sentence formed by joining two independent clauses using a coordinating conjunction, a semicolon, or a conjunctive adverb.

- **Complex sentence**. A sentence made up of an independent clause and one or more dependent clauses joined by subordinating conjunctions.

- **Compound-Complex Sentence**. A sentence formed from two or more independent clauses and one or more dependent clauses joined by one of a variety of conjunctions or punctuation marks.

To suggest the logical connection between ideas, the writer can use a variety of techniques to join clauses together. These **cohesive devices** include coordinating conjunctions, conjunctive adverbs, and subordinating conjunctions.

A **coordinating conjunction** (*and, but, or, nor, for, yet, so*) joins two simple sentences or independent clauses. If the clauses are closely related, they may also be joined with a semicolon.

> I took a chemistry class last summer, so I plan to take a different science class this semester.

> I took a chemistry class last summer; the teacher was excellent.

A semicolon and a **conjunctive adverb** (*indeed, moreover, consequently, however, therefore, nonetheless*) may also be used to join two independent clauses.

> I hope to have a career as a chemist someday; **consequently**, I'll be taking more chemistry classes in the future.

An independent and a dependent clause may be joined with a **subordinating conjunction** (*as, as if, before, because, although, if, since, when, whenever, unless, until, while, etc.*). The independent clause presents the main point of the sentence, while the dependent clause adds information.

> **Before** I came down with a fever, I was hoping to make the trip.

> The ice cream store stayed open **until** the last customer had been served.

The student writer should recognize how **clausal and phrasal modifiers** can be used to control the flow, pace, and emphasis of a piece of writing. A **clausal modifier** acts like an adjective or adverb in the structure of a sentence. Notice how these clauses can appear at the beginning, middle, or end of a sentence, giving the writer choices for sentence construction.

Adjective clause:

> No one could identify the man *who shouted from the opposite rooftop*.

The gift, *which sat unwrapped on the coffee table for days,* had been carefully chosen.

Adverb clause:

After the game went into extra innings, the crowd began to buzz with anticipation.

The fans knew, *once the game was over,* that they had witnessed a classic.

Phrasal modifiers can also function as adjectives or adverbs in a sentence.

Prepositional phrase as adjective:

The singer *on the brightly lit stage* acknowledged the audience's applause.

Hailstones began falling, threatening the windshield *of her new truck.*

Prepositional phrase as adverb:

Throughout the village, people awoke and peeked out their windows.

We finally found our dog Charlie sitting disconsolately *between two unfamiliar houses.*

An **appositive** is a noun or noun phrase that renames another noun nearby. It may come at the beginning or end of a sentence or be "embedded" in the middle.

An accomplished artist, Anne also prepared delicious meals for our group.

Sherman learned a great deal about the history of the area from Mr. Watkins, *the former mayor.*

I played with Muggles, *Sharon's spritely little pug,* for most of the morning.

Participles are two of the principal parts that every verb has. For example, *helped* and *jumped* are past particles and *helping* and *jumping* are present participles. They can also be used as adjectives and nouns. A present participle employed as a noun is also called a **gerund**.

Participle as an adjective:

A *sighing* wind added to the *chastened* mood of the afternoon.

Maggie's *torn* jersey, *bleeding* knees, *bruised* chin, and *crumpled* bicycle attested to the spill she had taken that morning.

Participle as a noun:

Winning requires a dedication to practice and hard work. (subject)

Our family loves *camping* in the summertime. (direct object)

Granddad gave *cooking* a whirl and proved to be a natural! (indirect object)

Before *composing* the finale, Regina listened to Duke Ellington recordings. (object of a preposition)

Another phrasal modifier is a **verbal phrase**, which is made up of a verbal (a verb that also functions as another part of speech) and all of its modifiers and objects. A verbal phrase can be a participial phrase, a gerund phrase, or an infinitive phrase, and it can function in a sentence as various parts of speech.

Washing his car in the driveway, Alex noticed a new dent in one door. (The phrase in bold is a participial phrase that functions as an adjective modifying *Alex*.)

Washing his car is the last thing Alex has to do today. (The phrase in bold is a gerund phrase that functions as a noun and the subject of the sentence.)

Alex likes **to wash his car on sunny summer afternoons**. (The phrase in bold is an infinitive phrase that functions as a direct object in the sentence.)

A less common phrasal modifier is the **absolute phrase**, which is a word group that modifies an entire sentence and consists of a noun plus at least one other word. The student writer should notice that an absolute phrase may appear at various places in a sentence.

His jacket red amidst the white snowfall, the hunter could be seen from miles away.

The hunter could be seen from miles away, *his red jacket glowing amidst the white snowfall.*

The hunter, *red jacket almost glowing in the snow,* could be seen from miles away.

Devices to Control Focus in Sentences and Paragraphs

The writer has many tools to control the focus and perspective of a written work, much as a cinematographer controls the depth of focus of a camera lens. For example, the writer can decide between active voice or passive voice in sentence construction. In the **active voice**, the subject performs the action, making the sentences more forceful and emphatic. In the **passive voice**, the object of the sentence performs the action. While passive voice is sometimes useful, student writers should mostly try to write in the active voice.

Active voice:

The **dancer thrilled** the audience with her daring leaps across the stage.

Passive voice:

The **audience was thrilled** by the dancer's leaps across the stage.

Concrete subjects are specific individuals or objects, as opposed to generalized people or things. Concrete language with things given their specific names brings a sentence or paragraph sharply into focus. *LeBron James* is more concrete than *a Cleveland Cavaliers player. A player* is even less concrete as a subject. Some subjects, such as *greatness* or *beauty,* are not concrete but abstract.

Expletives are two indefinite pronouns—*it* and *there*—that often are used as subjects in vague or weakly constructed sentences. The student writer should try to avoid using expletives in their writing.

Sentences with expletives:

It might rain tonight.

There was a cool breeze in the forest.

Rewritten to eliminate expletives:

The forecast calls for rain tonight.

A cool breeze blew through the forest.

Finally, the student writer should use **transitional words and phrases** to maintain focus and clarity in a piece of writing. The transition between ideas should be clear to the reader, as in the following examples:

Similarity or Addition

(*comparatively, coupled with, correspondingly, identically, likewise, moreover, similarly, in the same way, together with*)

In *Anna Karenina,* the landowner Levin faces a philosophical crisis, an inner debate about how best and most fruitfully to live. *In the same way,* many characters in Chekhov's stories face *similar* dilemmas about the meaning and purpose of life.

Contrast

(*conversely, instead, on the contrary, rather, yet, but, however, still, nevertheless, in contrast*)

The movie was marred from the start with script rewrites, actor defections, and production delays. *Nevertheless,* for all its seeming uncertainties, the film proved to be a box-office success.

Consequence

(*as a result, consequently, for this reason, hence, so then, subsequently, therefore, thus, thereupon, wherefore*)

Hours of rain had left the field soaked and slippery. High winds made punts and kickoffs difficult to catch. *As a result,* the championship game disappointed fans nationwide.

Example

(*chiefly, especially, for instance, particularly, in particular, including, such as, specifically*)

Alfonso's skill at cooking on his outdoor grill resulted in an array of delicious smoked meats *such as* steak, spare ribs, chicken breasts, and pork chops.

Exception

(*aside from, barring, beside, except, excluding, exclusive of, other than, outside of, save*)

Swarms of mosquitoes pestered us each evening, and the people in the neighboring cabin were rather noisy. *Aside from* those irritations, the trip to the lake pleased us all.

Generalizing

(*as a rule, usually, generally, ordinarily, for the most part*)

Heather liked to paint at all hours of the day or night, but *ordinarily* she began work at eight in the morning.

Sequence

(*at first, first of all, to begin with, in the first place, at the same time, for now, for the time being, the next step, in turn, later on, meanwhile, next, then, soon, later, while, earlier, simultaneously, afterward, in conclusion*)

At first, it was not my intention to take over as club president. *In time* I saw areas where I believed my leadership could make a difference. *Eventually* I realized that a shakeup at the top was inevitable, and I lobbied for the job.

Summarizing

(*all in all, all things considered, after all, briefly, by and large, in any case, in any event, in conclusion, on the whole, in short, in summary, in the final analysis, in the long run, on balance, to sum up, to summarize, finally*)

The grounds of the old university were maintained in a stately beauty, and the architecture of its halls and great chapel spoke of another, more serious century. Each lecturer brought intellectual fire to his or her presentation. It was, *all things considered,* the best trip I have ever taken.

CONVENTIONS OF ORAL AND WRITTEN LANGUAGE

3.4 Conventions of Oral and Written Language

a. Apply knowledge of linguistic structure to identify and use the conventions of standard English

b. Recognize, understand, and use a range of conventions in both spoken and written English, including:

- Conventions of effective sentence structure (e.g., clear pronoun reference, parallel structure, appropriate verb tense)

- Preferred usage (e.g., verb/subject agreement, pronoun agreement, idioms)

- Conventional forms of spelling

- Capitalization and punctuation

c. Adapt speech to a variety of contexts and tasks, demonstrating a command of formal English when indicated or appropriate

(*California Common Core State Standards for English Language Arts, L.6–12.1–3*)

The teacher must know and be able to apply the conventions of Standard Edited English. This includes parts of speech, sentence parts, and sentence structures.

PARTS OF SPEECH

- **Noun:** a word that names a person, place, thing, or idea. Proper nouns naming a particular person or place are capitalized, while common nouns are not.

    Common nouns: farmer, borough, basketball, democracy
    Proper nouns: Michelle Obama, Turkey, Golden Gate Bridge

- **Pronoun:** a word (*he, it, they, somebody*) used in place of a noun that identifies people, places, things, or ideas without renaming them. The noun that a pronoun replaces is its antecedent; a pronoun placed too far from its antecedent in a sentence may be vague in its reference.

- **Verb:** a word that expresses action (action verbs) or state of being (linking or helping verbs).

    Action verb: The girl *kicked* the ball.
    Linking verb: Herman *was* late for class.
    Helping verb: Edna *is* cooking lunch for us today.

- **Adjective:** a word that modifies a noun or pronoun and answers such questions as What kind? Which one? How many?

    heavy rain, the *green* hat, *fourteen* players

- **Adverb:** a word that modifies a verb, adjective, or another adverb and answers such questions as How? When? Where? How often? To what extent?

    Our lawyer argued *effectively* that the case should be dismissed.
    His fingers turned *almost* blue in the frosty air.

- **Preposition:** a word that expresses a relationship between a noun or pronoun and another word in a sentence. The noun or pronoun that usually follows a preposition is called its object. The preposition, its object, and modifiers form a prepositional phrase.

    from the store, *in* the dirt, *throughout* the play

- **Conjunction:** a word that connects words or groups of words. Conjunctions include coordinating conjunctions (*and, but, so, yet, for, nor, or*), correlative conjunctions (*either/or, not only/but also, neither/nor*), and subordinating conjunctions (*after, although, as, as if, because, before, even if, even though, how, if, lest, now that, since, unless, until, where, wherever, while*).

- **Gerund:** a present participle that always functions as a noun.

  Swimming is my favorite sport.

- **Infinitive:** a phrase made up of the word *to* and the base form of a verb (to love, to decide). It can function as an adjective, adverb, or noun.

- **Interjection:** a word or phrase that generally expresses strong emotion, such as surprise or delight.

  Incredible! Scientists have located the wrecked ship at the bottom of the sea.

- **Participle:** a verb form that usually ends in *–ed* or *–ing* and can function as an adjective but with certain characteristics of a verb.

  canned peas, *battering* winds

SENTENCE PARTS

- **Subject:** A noun or pronoun that is partnered with an action verb or being verb. The subject may also be understood as (you), as in the sentence "Take me home, please."

- **Predicate:** A verb that expresses the subject's action or state of being. The subject and predicate do not always appear next to each other or in the normal order.

  The *worker* on the tower *yelled* for assistance.
  The *worker has* often *yelled* for assistance from the tower.
  Has the *worker yelled* for assistance from the tower?

- **Direct Object:** A noun or pronoun that follows a verb and answers the question Whom? or What?

- **Indirect Object:** A noun or pronoun that follows a verb and answers the question To whom? or For what?

- **Phrase:** A group of related words that does not have a subject and predicate pair and does not express a complete thought, such as a prepositional phrase or a verbal phrase.

- **Clause:** A group of related words that contains a subject and predicate. An **independent clause** expresses a complete thought, while a **dependent clause** does not.

    Independent clause: Hatteberg hit a double
    Dependent clause: if Hatteberg hit a double

- **Conjunctions for Compounding Sentence Elements:** The coordinating conjunctions *and, but, or,* and *nor* join subjects, predicates, adjectives, adverbs, prepositional phrases, and dependent clauses within a sentence in a process called **compounding**. Subordinating conjunctions connect a dependent clause to an independent clause.

Sentence Structures

- A **declarative sentence** makes a statement and ends with a period.

    My garden extends from the porch to the back fence.

- An **interrogative sentence** asks a question and ends with a question mark.

    Why did the police stop and talk to those people?

- An **exclamatory sentence** expresses strong emotion and often ends with an exclamation point.

    We must get out of here now!

- An **imperative sentence** gives an order or makes a request.

    Hand me the tape measure. Please hold still while I measure your waist.

- A **simple sentence** is an independent clause and expresses a complete thought.

    Surfing is my favorite hobby.

- A **compound sentence** contains two or more independent clauses connected by a coordinating conjunction or a semicolon.

Surfing is my favorite hobby, but I also enjoy rock climbing.

- A **complex sentence** contains an independent clause and one or more subordinate clauses.

    While surfing is my favorite hobby, I also enjoy rock climbing.

- A **compound-complex sentence** contains two or more independent clauses and one or more subordinate clauses.

    Surfing is my favorite hobby, but I also enjoy rock climbing because fitness is important to me.

Effective Sentence Structure and Preferred Usage

The writing teacher should explain and demonstrate how proper sentence structure and preferred usage of grammatical elements makes writing easier to read and understand. Here are some points to remember.

- **Parallel structure** means that sentence elements that are alike in function should also be alike in construction. This adds to the clarity, economy, and force of a piece of writing.

    Not parallel: **Dancing** and **ability to sing** are two requirements for the lead role in this play.

    Parallel: **Dancing** and **singing** are two requirements for the lead role in this play.

    Not parallel: She likes **to dance** but not **singing**.

    Parallel: She likes **to dance** but not **to sing**.

    Not parallel: The director wondered **who the new actress was** and **about her experience in the theater**.

    Parallel: The director wondered **who the new actress was** and **what experience she'd had** in the theater.

    Not parallel: The director emphasized **collective effort**, **mutual support**, and **being responsible as a group** for the success of the production.

    Parallel: The director emphasized **collective effort**, **mutual support**, and **group responsibility** for the success of the production.

Not parallel:	The angry shopper wanted **to exchange** the item, **to obtain** a refund, or **a conversation** with the store manager.
Parallel:	The angry shopper wanted **to exchange** the item, **to obtain** a refund, or **to speak** to the store manager.

- **Clear pronoun reference** means that each pronoun in a sentence refers clearly and unmistakably to one particular noun. If necessary, the writer should rephrase the sentence to make the meaning clear.

Unclear:	While storing the goblet in the antique cabinet, Sandra broke it.
Clear:	While storing the goblet in the antique cabinet, Sandra broke the goblet.
Unclear:	If the customers don't buy all the scarves, pack them away under the counter.
Clear:	If any of the scarves are unsold, pack them away under the counter.
Unclear:	The owner told Chuck that he would be getting a raise.
Clear:	The owner congratulated Chuck on the raise he would be getting.
Unclear:	While the city coffers were full, they made poor use of it.
Clear:	While the city government had a lot of money, the council members made poor use of it.
Unclear:	I arrived late to the play, which was foolish.
Clear:	In arriving late to the play, I felt foolish.
	Or
	I arrived late to the play, which was in any case a foolish piece of work.

- **Appropriate verb tense** means that the writer indicates whether the action occurred in the past, present, or future and stays consistent with the appropriate verb tense.

Inconsistent:	Elizabeth Bishop **is** celebrated for her ability to see original details in a setting, and she **used** this skill to add color to her poems.
Consistent:	Elizabeth Bishop **is** celebrated for her ability to see original details in a setting, and she **uses** this skill to add color to her poems.

Inconsistent:	Last year, our class **completed** a project in which we **would have to interview** older relatives about past events in American history.
Consistent:	Last year, our class **completed** a project in which we **had to interview** older relatives about past events in American history.

Inconsistent:	If the weather **would** cooperate, we **can** start the game on time.
Consistent:	If the weather **would** cooperate, we **could** start the game on time.

- **Subject/verb agreement** means that a subject and verb must agree in number; that is, both must be either singular or plural.

Singular:	**Arthur has passed** every test this semester. There **is** another **test** today.
Plural:	**Arthur and Pilar have passed** every test this semester. There **are** more **tests** this week.

- **Pronoun agreement** means that a pronoun agrees in person, number, and gender with its antecedent.

Incorrect person agreement:	If a **person** hopes to succeed, **you** have to work hard.
Correct:	If a **person** hopes to succeed, **he or she** has to work hard. If **you** hope to succeed, **you** have to work hard.

Incorrect number agreement:	If **somebody** hopes to succeed, **they** have to work hard.

Correct:	If **somebody** hopes to succeed, **he or she** has to work hard.
	If **people** hope to succeed, **they** have to work hard.
Incorrect gender agreement:	If a **person** hopes to succeed, **he** has to work hard.
Correct:	If a **person** hopes to succeed, **he or she** has to work hard.
	If **people** hope to succeed, **they** have to work hard.

- **Idioms** are phrases that mean something different than the meanings of the individual words would indicate. In general, writers should use idioms sparingly in formal writing.

    Our teacher **turned a blind eye** to our dismay about the new assignment. (pretended not to see)

    Some of the applicants looked **down-at-heel**. (shabby and untidy)

    If you **bear down**, you can still get finished in time. (focus and concentrate)

CONVENTIONS OF PRONUNCIATION AND INTONATION

Given the inconsistency between the sound and spelling of many English words, a dictionary is a helpful guide to how words should be pronounced. To give a simple example, the words *rover, mover,* and *lover* would seem to be rhymes but are actually all pronounced differently.

In the same way, the words *fees, freeze, seize, please, sleaze, cheese,* and *keys* have various spellings for the /eez/ sound but are actually rhyming words. There are also words that have British pronunciations that differ from the American versions, such as *garage* (GAIR ahzh), *laboratory* (luh BOR uh tree), and *fertile* (FUR tile).

Intonation is the stress placed on different words in a sentence depending on its meaning. A speaker's voice will rise and fall in patterns that are familiar to a native speaker of the language. For example, the poet Robert Frost believed that a listener could make out the gist of an argument from behind a closed door just by hearing the stresses and sentence sounds of the dialogue.

CONVENTIONAL FORMS OF SPELLING

As detailed in Chapter 3, the difficulty of spelling many English words comes from the changes the language has undergone from its Anglo-Saxon origins to modern English. These include the huge number of words imported from other languages. The student writer should strive to spell accurately, using a dictionary when necessary and keeping a list of troublesome words.

Technological aids such as spell-check programs can also help, although these may also introduce new errors. Students should develop etymological (word origin), phonological (sound), visual (sight), and morphemic (meaning of word parts) skills to analyze spelling, and use spelling rules such as "*i* before *e* except after *c* or when sounded as *ay* as in *neighbor* or *weigh*." They should also be aware of spelling variants between American and British English.

Capitalization and Punctuation

A successful piece of writing avoids errors in **capitalization and punctuation**. Words that should be capitalized include:

- the first word in a sentence

- the first word of a direct quote

- proper nouns

- proper adjectives (Swedish ambassador)

- titles (Mrs., Dr., Senator)

- peoples and nationalities

- the major words in titles of books, plays, poems, etc.

- names of organizations, schools, government agencies

- heavenly bodies

- nations, states, cities

Errors in punctuation crop up most frequently in comma use. Commas should be used to:

- separate three or more items in a series

    He got out a pan, filled it with water, and placed it on the stove. (The comma before *and* is optional, although using it can avoid misreadings.)

- connect two independent clauses

    She cooked the spaghetti, and I prepared the sauce.

- set off introductory elements

    Gazing at the clouds, Roberto predicted that it would soon rain.
    Demario, your report is excellent!

- set off parenthetical elements

    Ranger, his German Shepherd, patrolled the backyard.

- separate coordinate adjectives

    A short, shifty, nervous young man walked into our store.

- set off quoted material

    It was Shakespeare who wrote, "The quality of mercy is not strained."

- avoid possible confusion or misreading

    Inside, the house was almost ready for the coming celebration.

RESEARCH TO BUILD AND PRESENT KNOWLEDGE

3.5 Research to Build and Present Knowledge

a. Demonstrate knowledge of strategies for developing and applying research questions

b. Demonstrate knowledge of methods of inquiry and investigation

c. Gather relevant information from multiple authoritative print and digital sources, using advanced searches effectively; assess the strengths and limitations of each source in terms of the task, purpose, and knowledge; and critically evaluate the quality of the sources

d. Interpret and apply findings

e. Integrate information into a written text selectively to maintain the flow of ideas, avoiding plagiarism and overreliance on any one source and following professional conventions and ethical standards of citation and attribution, including footnotes and endnotes

(*California Common Core State Standards for English Language Arts, L.6–12.7–8*)

Note: *Content from SMR 3.5 Research to Build and Present Knowledge is tested in ten multiple-choice questions in Subtest I. This content is not tested in the writing prompts in Subtest III.*

Students must write many research papers during high school. These projects provide practice in such skills as focusing a topic, using and citing multiple sources for research, and analyzing and organizing research materials. The following sections describe the basic steps of the research process.

Develop and Apply Research Questions

Once a student writer has chosen a topic, he or she must narrow it or bring it into focus. The best way to do this is to state the topic idea as a **research question**. For example, the topic "water" could be narrowed to the question "What effects will government programs regarding water use have on the future of agriculture in southern California?" This question provides "restrictors" that limit the topic and provide ideas for research, such as "government programs regarding water use," "the future of agriculture," and "southern California." Further research will allow the student to rewrite the research question as a **thesis statement** that makes an assertion or recommendation: "Government programs regarding water use are vital to the future of agriculture in southern California."

Demonstrate Methods of Inquiry and Investigation

The student writer should be urged to develop skills of **inquiry and investigation** by finding topics of interest, posing questions about the topic, researching the answers, and then following through with fact-supported conclusions and ideas for further research.

The teacher can aid this process by asking questions that challenge lazy assumptions and spur the student to test the validity of his or her conclusions.

Identify and Use Multiple Resources

Once the student has a research question or thesis statement, he or she should look for information and supporting details in various sources, including online databases, encyclopedias and dictionaries, library books and journals, and bibliographies.

Some of the best search engines for students include:

- Google Scholar, for finding papers, abstracts, citations, and scholarly literature

- iSEEK, for editor-reviewed search results from universities, government sites, and other noncommercial sources

- DMOZ, or the Open Directory Project, for searchable access to millions of links chosen by expert volunteers from many fields

- OJOSE, or the Online JOurnal Search Engine, for finding and downloading scientific publications from more than 60 different databases

- Scirus, for scientific journal articles, scientists' web pages, and institutional sources of information

- Dogpile, Whonu, and MetaCrawler, for searching other search engines to obtain a comprehensive results list

A helpful source for periodicals and journal articles is *The Readers' Guide to Periodical Literature,* which is available in most libraries. Ideas for further research in books and articles can also be found in the bibliography at the back of a book. Audiovisual materials such as videos, DVDs, and audio recordings are also valuable sources of information.

The student should also be aware of differences between **primary and secondary sources**. For example, in researching the Battle of Appomattox Court House, the memoirs of Ulysses S. Grant would be a primary source (written by an observer or participant), while a book such as *Lee's Last Retreat: The Flight to Appomattox* would be a secondary source, written by a later historian.

The student must also **evaluate the quality and usefulness** of sources. Items to consider include:

- Who is the author? What are his or her credentials, qualifications, or other publications?

- What is the author's perspective on the topic? Is it narrow or general? Does it suit the student writer's needs for the research question?

- What year was the source published? Is the material up to date? Is there an updated revision available?

- Is the point of view objective? Does the author have an ulterior motive or a political axe to grind? Can the facts and details be trusted?

- Who is the intended audience for the source? Is the material simplified for a younger audience? Is it mainly for an academic reader?

- Who published the source? Is this organization biased in some way?

Interpret and Apply Findings

Once the student writer has found and reviewed a number of sources, he or she must interpret the information and apply it to the writing project. Source materials may convince the writer to change the research question or thesis statement and refocus the project.

Avoid Plagiarism

Plagiarism is the use of another writer's ideas and language without authorization and the presentation of them as one's own work. To avoid plagiarism in a research paper, the student writer must cite each source of information using footnotes, endnotes, or references in parentheses.

Material quoted verbatim from another writer should also be presented in quotation marks along with the writer's name and professional information. The student writer should be aware that Internet sources have made it much easier for teachers or graders to catch students who are guilty of plagiarism. There are even detection services available online such as MyDropBox.com and Turnitin.

Use Professional Conventions of Citation and Attribution

The student writer should carefully cite each source of information used in a research paper. The three most common styles for citation are the Modern Language Association (MLA), the American Psychological Association (APA), and the *Chicago Manual of Style*. Below are some examples based on the MLA documentation style for research papers.

Book

Gordon, Charlotte. *Romantic Outlaws: The Extraordinary Lives of Mary Wollstonecraft and Her Daughter Mary Shelley.* New York: Random House, 2015. Print.

Book with more than one author

Campbell, Richard, Christopher R. Martin, and Bettina Fabos. *Media and Culture: An Introduction to Mass Communication.* Bedford/St. Martin's, 2014. Print.

Article in a book

Ahmedi, Fauzia Erfan. "Welcoming Courtyards: Hospitality, Spirituality, and Gender." *Feminism and Hospitality: Gender in the Host/Guest Relationship.* Ed. Maurice Hamington. Lanham: Lexington Books, 2010. 109–24. Print.

Article in a journal

Laing, Jennifer, and Warwick Frost. "How Green Was My Festival: Exploring Challenges and Opportunities Associated with Staging Green Events." *International Journal of Hospitality Management* 29.2 (2010): 261–7. Print.

Article in a magazine

Rakoff, Jed S. "Why Innocent People Plead Guilty." *New York Review of Books,* 20 Nov. 2014: 16-18. Print.

Article in a newspaper

Binkley, Christina. "Fashion's Secret Blockbusters." *Wall Street Journal*, 28 May 2015, D1. Print.

Article in a newspaper online

Pollack, Andrew. "Stem Cell Research Papers Are Retracted." *New York Times,* 2 July, 2014. www.nytimes.com.

Encyclopedia entry

Mercuri, Becky. "Cookies." *The Oxford Encyclopedia of Food and Drink in America*. Ed. Andrew F. Smith. Vol. 1. 2004. Print.

Film or video

Magic in the Moonlight. Dir. Woody Allen. 2014. DVD. Sony Pictures Home Entertainment, 2014.

CD-ROM

"Marriage." *Encyclopedia Judaica*. CD-ROM. Vers. 1.0. Jerusalem: Judaica Multimedia, 1997.

Sound recording

Miranda Lambert. *Platinum*. RCA, 2014. CD.

Effective Presentation Methods

The student writer should be encouraged to consider how best to present a research paper, possibly including the use of multi-media formats. A PowerPoint presentation, for example, helps the student learn to condense information into main ideas and supporting details using a variety of charts, bulleted lists of facts, and graphic organizers. Such a presentation can be "self-playing," meaning that the slides and special effects advance automatically at a predetermined rate with no manual operation, or manually controlled by the speaker with mouse clicks.

The second option allows the presenter to increase discussion time and take questions during the presentation if desired. Such a presentation might even include audiovisual elements such as video clips and interactive maps. After making a class presentation, student writers can then submit the final paper in a "text only" format for the teacher to review.

Communications: Speech, Media, and Creative Performance

5

On the CSET: English Subtest IV, you will have 1 hour and 30 minutes to respond to four short-answer questions in three main areas of Communications:

- **Non-Written Communication** will test your ability to identify features of oral performance in a variety of forms, from extemporaneous speaking to prepared debate. You should also demonstrate knowledge of various performance skills related to oral communication, such as diction, enunciation, and gestures, and be able to express principles of the speaker/audience interrelationship. You must be able to evaluate a speaker's point of view, reasoning, and use of evidence and rhetoric. You must be able to identify and use collaborative communication skills in various discussion formats and in a variety of roles. Your ability to present information, findings, and supporting evidence to convey a distinct perspective and logical argument will also be tested. You must also demonstrate knowledge of skills needed for planning and delivering a reflective narrative and an argument that supports a precise claim.

- **Media Analysis and Applications** will require you to analyze the impact on society of a variety of media forms, from television and film to the Internet. You must be able recognize and evaluate media strategies to inform, persuade, entertain, and transmit culture. You should be able to analyze persuasive speech in media, including patterns of organization and use of persuasive language. You must identify the aesthetic effects of a media presentation. You must be able to integrate multiple sources of information in various media and formats in order to make informed decisions and solve problems. You must also know how to make strategic use of digital media—such as videos and Microsoft PowerPoint—in presentations.

- **Dramatic Performance** will require you to describe and use a range of rehearsal strategies, from teambuilding to vocal exercises, to effectively mount a dramatic production. You must know how to employ basic elements of character analysis and acting approaches to reveal character and relationships. You should be able to analyze dramatic works and use textual evidence to make choices about play production. You must know and be able to apply the fundamentals of stage directing and show facility in a variety of oral performance traditions, including storytelling and recitation.

PREPARING FOR CSET: ENGLISH SUBTEST IV

On CSET: English Subtest IV, you will answer four short-response questions covering the three major sections in this chapter. You will have a one-page lined response sheet for your answer to each question. You should read and respond to each short-answer question in about 15 minutes. Subtest IV does not include any multiple-choice questions.

For each constructed-response question in Subtest IV, you should write a response of about 75–125 words, although you may write longer responses if you prefer. Each response will be assessed according to the subject-matter knowledge and skills they demonstrate, not writing ability. You should, however, write clearly enough to allow for a valid judgment of your knowledge and skills regarding the subject matter. You should write for an audience of educators in the field.

The short-response questions in Subtest IV require teacher candidates to demonstrate the breadth of knowledge needed to integrate journalism, technological media, speech, and dramatic performance into the language arts curriculum, while also showing sensitivity to cultural approaches to communication.

One short-response question might address the challenges of public speaking. It might cover the skills necessary for effective oral communication or ways to handle problems in speaker-audience interactions. Another question might deal with the issue of credibility and reliability in the media or the factors that make for effective advertising. Another question might present a draft of a reflective narrative and ask for ways it could be improved for more effective oral presentation.

A new emphasis in the CSET: English Subtest IV is on the analysis of dramatic works in staging student productions. One short-response question might require you to analyze an excerpt from a play and use textual evidence to support decisions about play production values, such as blocking, lighting, and direction of actors. Another type of question might address rehearsal strategies for different productions, including a fast-paced farce, a musical, and a dialogue-driven comedy.

Your responses will be assessed based on the following:

- **Purpose:** How well your response focuses on the task set by the prompt in relation to relevant CSET: English subject matter requirements.

- **Subject Matter Knowledge:** How well you apply accurate knowledge about CSET: English subject matter in your response.

- **Support:** How well and how appropriately you use evidence from relevant CSET: English subject matter requirements to support your response.

You will not use any reference materials in the testing session. All the necessary information will be included with the writing prompts. Read each prompt carefully and make sure you understand your task before you begin to write. Think about how to organize your responses to address each prompt completely. Check your work and make any changes needed to improve your responses.

As with the information in Chapters 2, 3, and 4, the following descriptions are meant to provide a general idea of what you are expected to know for the CSET: English Subtest IV. For further research, you should consult Curriculum Frameworks and Instructional Materials from the California Department of Education (2014) at *http://www.cde.ca.gov/ci/cr/cf/allfwks.asp*. You might also consult the following sources:

- Communication

The Art of Public Speaking by Stephen Lucas (2005)

The Debater's Guide, Fourth Edition by Jon M. Ericson, James J. Murphy, and Raymond Bud Zeuschner (2011)

Public Speaking for College and Career by Hamilton Gregory (2004)

Public Speaking: Strategies for Success by David Zarefsky (2010)

- Media Analysis

Digital and Media Literacy: Connecting Culture and Classroom by Renee Hobbs (2011)

How Fantasy Becomes Reality: Seeing Through Media Influence by Karen E. Dill (2009)

Media and Culture: An Introduction to Mass Communication by Richard Campbell, Christopher R. Martin, and Bettina Fabos (2011)

The Teacher's Guide to Media Literacy: Critical Thinking in a Multimedia World by Cyndy L. Scheibe and Faith Rogow (2012)

- Dramatic Performance

The Drama Teacher's Survival Guide: A Complete Toolkit for Theatre Arts by Margaret Johnson (2007)

The Stage and the School by Harry H. Schanker and Katharine Anne Ommanney (2005)

Teaching Drama in Primary and Secondary Schools: An Integrated Approach by Michael Fleming (2001)

Theatre in the Secondary School Classroom: Methods and Strategies for the Beginning Teacher by Jim Patterson, Donna McKenna-Crook, and Melissa Swick (2006)

NON-WRITTEN COMMUNICATION

4.1 Non-Written Communication

a. Identify features of, and deliver oral performance in, a variety of forms (e.g., impromptu, extemporaneous, persuasive, expository, interpretive, debate)

b. Demonstrate knowledge of performance skills (e.g., diction, clear enunciation, vocal rate, range, pitch, and volume; gestures and posture; appropriate eye contact; response to audience)

c. Articulate principles of speaker/audience interrelationship (e.g., interpersonal communication, group dynamics, public address)

d. Evaluate a speaker's point of view, reasoning and use of evidence and rhetoric, assessing the stance, premises, links among ideas, word choice, points of emphasis, and tone

e. Identify and demonstrate collaborative communication skills in discussions (e.g., one on one, in groups, teacher-led) and in a variety of roles (e.g., listening supportively, facilitating, synthesizing, stimulating higher-level critical thinking through inquiry)

f. Present information, findings, and supporting evidence (e.g., reflective, historical investigation, response to literature presentations), conveying a clear and distinct perspective and a logical argument, such that listeners can follow the line of reasoning, alternative or opposing perspectives are addressed, and the organization, development, substance, and style are appropriate to purpose, audience, and a range of formal and informal tasks

g. Demonstrate knowledge of skills needed for planning and delivering a reflective narrative that explores the significance of a personal experience, event, or concern; uses sensory language to convey a vivid picture; includes appropriate narrative techniques (e.g., dialogue, pacing, description); and draws comparisons between the specific incident and broader themes

h. Demonstrate knowledge of skills needed for planning and presenting an argument that supports a precise claim; provides a logical sequence for claims, counter-claims, and evidence; uses rhetorical devices to support assertions (e.g., analogy, appeal to logic through reasoning, appeal to emotion or ethical belief); uses varied syntax to link major sections of the presentation to create cohesion and clarity; and provides a concluding statement that supports the argument presented

(California Common Core State Standards for English Language Arts, SL.6–12.1, SL6–12.3–5)

FEATURES AND FORMS OF ORAL COMMUNICATION

As with written communication, the purpose of oral communication or speech is to provide a message to an audience or receiver. The effectiveness of oral communication depends on both the skill of the speaker and the listening ability of the audience (whether one person or a group). The major forms of speech include the following:

- **Impromptu speech** is delivered on the spur of the moment with no preparation beforehand. This form of speech or casual remarks is less structured and less supported by facts and evidence than other forms in order to allow for spontaneity. Although impromptu speech is spontaneous, the ideas presented must still be supported with statements that demonstrate pertinence, variety, and detail.

- **Extemporaneous speech** is a short, informal speech on a provided topic that is made without extensive time for preparation. This form of speech is delivered without benefit of text or notes and is improvised rather than composed.

- **Persuasive speech** is a more tightly focused form designed to persuade the audience to believe something, agree with some viewpoint, or take some action. This form of speech can be organized in different ways, including cause-effect, problem-solution, comparison-contrast, assertion-reasons, and motivated sequence.

  The last example, also known as **Monroe's Motivated Sequence**, is frequently used to organize persuasive speeches. It includes the following steps:

  1. Attention (getting the audience's attention)

  2. Need (describing the problem and showing the need for a solution)

  3. Satisfaction (presenting a solution that satisfies the need)

  4. Visualization (visualizing the result of the solution)

  5. Action (requesting the audience to approve or take action)

- **Expository speech** is intended to be informative and does not express the speaker's personal opinion. This form of speech presents information that is accepted as factual.

- **Interpretative speech** is intended to bring to life a text or piece of literature through the creative use of voice, gesture, and facial expression. This form of speech may include a Shakespearean soliloquy, a Brownian dramatic monologue, a brief scene from a play for one or two speakers, or a humorous story such as a tall tale.

- **Debate** is a structured program or contest of formal arguments that take opposing points of view. This form of speech contains opinions that are supported by facts and examples.

Any debate begins with a **proposition**, such as "Be it resolved: Learning a foreign language should be required for all high school students." The **proposition side** in the debate advocates adopting the resolution or argues in favor of it, while the **opposition side** tries to refute the resolution. Usually there is a judge whose task is to decide the winner, although some debate formats allow the audience to participate in this decision.

The oldest and probably most popular debate format in American high schools is the **team policy debate**. In this version, the proposition side is called the **Affirmative or Aff** and the opposition side is called the **Negative or Neg**. Each team has two debaters for a total of four participants (not counting the judge or audience).

A team policy debate includes eight speeches in all. The first four, which are each limited to eight minutes, are called constructive speeches, because the teams use them to lay out the main points of their best arguments. The last four speeches, which are limited to four minutes apiece, are called rebuttals, because the teams use them to extend, apply, and challenge the arguments that have already been made. There may also be a three-minute cross-examination period following the round of constructive speeches.

Team policy debate focuses on the ability to gather evidence and organize a response rather than the ability to persuade. **The Lincoln-Douglas debate** format places more emphasis on persuasive speaking, usually in a discussion of competing ethical values or actions. This format is based on the famous debates between Illinois senatorial candidates Abraham Lincoln and Stephen A. Douglas in the 1850s. It is a one-on-one debate consisting of five speeches and two cross-examination periods. While the Affirmative speaker has one more opportunity to speak than the Negative speaker, both have the same total speaking time.

INDIVIDUAL PERFORMANCE SKILLS IN ORAL COMMUNICATION

Students in English-Language Arts classes should practice oral communication in a variety of settings and situations, including one-on-one conversations, group discussions, and public speaking. In all these types of speech, the student should strive to choose words carefully, speak clearly and confidently, avoid long-windedness or wordiness, present ideas in a logical order, listen closely to what other speakers have to say, and use effective gestures and body language to emphasize meaning. In addition, there are specific performance skills that can make a student a more effective speaker and listener.

- **Diction** is the accent, inflection, intonation, and speech-sound quality employed by a speaker. A successful speaker has an accent and intonation that is easily heard and understood by the audience. News anchors, sports announcers, and actors often speak in a general accent that the audience recognizes and understands. The speaker may also vary his or her intonation or sentence sounds.

  For example, some sentences should end in a rising intonation, like a question, but not all sentences should end this way. Proper diction also includes the ability to "hit" or emphasize important words and phrases to communicate important ideas. A speaker with good diction also avoids "vocal pauses" such as *um* or *er*, or repeated words that become verbal tics such as *like* or *you know*.

- **Enunciation** is the ability to speak clearly and articulate each speech sound without stumbling or saying the wrong words. Actors sometimes practice enunciation with "tongue twisters" (such as "rubber baby buggy bumpers") or lines with difficult combinations of sounds, such as this passage from Gilbert and Sullivan's *The Pirates of Penzance*:

  > I am the very pattern of a modern Major-General,
  > I've information vegetable, animal, and mineral;
  > I know the Kings of England, and I quote the fights historical
  > From Marathon to Waterloo, in order categorical;
  > I'm very well acquainted too with matters mathematical,
  > I understand equations, both the simple and quadratical;
  > About binomial theorem I'm teeming with a lot o' news,
  > With many cheerful facts about the square of the hypotenuse.
  > I'm very good at integral and differential calculus,
  > I know the scientific names of beings animalcules,
  > In short, in matters vegetable, animal, and mineral,
  > I am the very model of a modern Major-General.

- **Volume** is the loudness or softness of speech sounds. While a public speaker should try to speak loudly enough to be heard at all times, he or she should also vary the volume to emphasize certain points and passages and occasionally jolt the listeners back to attention. Volume is also related to the resonance of a voice, meaning that speakers should try to maintain as full and rich a sound as their voices can achieve.

- **Rate** or pace is the speed at which a speaker delivers words. Often, students must be reminded to slow down when speaking to a large group so as not to sound nervous or flustered. Speaking rate is often related to the comfort level of the speaker and the listener. For example, a person may speak very rapidly to friends and still expect to be understood.

- **Pitch** is like the high and low notes of music. A speaker that is able to vary his or her pitch has a greater **range** of speech sounds, and tends to have a more pleasant and interesting speaking voice, while one who is unable to do this may speak in a boring monotone. One aid to better volume, rate, and pitch is **proper breathing**. A nervous speaker may take shallow breaths that lead to a softer voice and a narrower range of speech sounds. A speaker should try to take deep breaths from the diaphragm, which tends to have a calming effect and provides for better volume and range.

- **Body language and gestures** can be used to emphasize main points or even to add humor. For example, a woman presenting a sentence she doesn't agree with might pause, look at the audience, and raise her eyebrows in disbelief. A professor describing a situation "that would make you tear your hair out" might casually run his fingers over his own sparsely covered scalp. Such movements should be used sparingly, however, and should not be stilted or artificial. Otherwise, the speaker should stand straight and still, without unnecessary or distracting fidgets.

- **Eye contact** can be used to maintain a connection with the members of the audience and also to gauge audience reaction during a speech. The speaker should make eye contact with various listeners, moving his or her gaze smoothly around the room or auditorium. If a speech is being read, the speaker should remember to look up occasionally from the written text and establish eye contact.

- **Response to the audience** involves the speaker being aware of nonverbal signals that indicate something the audience might want or need. If some audience members are leaning forward or cupping their ears, the speaker should increase the volume of his or her voice. If some listeners look quizzical about a certain point, the speaker might repeat it or restate it in clearer language.

The speaker should also be ready to answer questions or discuss the topic of the speech after it is finished. A speaker can practice responding to the audience in rehearsals or run-throughs. Students should try not to get defensive about any criticism, and should listen carefully and even take notes about suggestions for improvement in the speech.

PRINCIPLES OF SPEAKER/AUDIENCE INTERRELATIONSHIP

A successful interrelationship between speaker and audience, whether personal or in a group, depends on **active listening skills**. In the English-Language Arts classroom, the teacher should frequently remind students to listen closely. This helps avoid misunderstandings and allows students to participate in discussions and respond more effectively in class. Listeners should always be focused on the speaker's topic, the main ideas presented, and how those ideas fit together.

In interpersonal communication, such as an interview or a conversation, the listener can ask more pertinent questions if he or she is paying close attention to the other speaker. In group dynamics, such as class discussions, good listening skills involve knowing when to listen and when to speak, how to stay on topic and add to the discussion, and how to question or disagree with a speaker without being disrespectful or rude.

In a group forum or classroom lecture, the listener might take notes in order to remember the main ideas and important details. To elicit more creative responses from listeners, the teacher should ask open-ended questions about the topic. Instead of asking, "Do you agree with the speaker's point of view?" the teacher might ask, "What problems do you foresee with the solution that the speaker recommends?"

In dealing with an audience, a speaker should be prepared for various types of response. Often, an audience response can be used to the speaker's advantage, as in these scenarios:

- A hostile member of the audience begins heckling during the speech. As the speaker, you should remain calm and reasonable. At first, you might acknowledge the heckling with a slight pause and then continue. If the heckling goes on, you should respond calmly—for example, you might tell the heckler that questions or comments will be addressed after the speech. You might use humor to defuse the situation, or appeal to fairness and good manners. Above all, remain polite and set the tone. If the heckler continues to be rude and unreasonable, the audience's sympathy and respect will probably go to you, the speaker. If the heckler's interruptions continue, you may ask to have the person removed from the hall as a last resort.

- During a presentation, you notice from the audience members' body language and comments that they already know a great deal about the topic. A possible response is to change course and allow the audience to determine where the presentation goes. You might introduce facts and details that you hadn't planned to include because they seemed to be too "insider" oriented. You might simply take questions sooner and allow for a group discussion.

- The audience appears skeptical about what you are saying and are sitting with folded arms and blank expressions. If you are speaking on a controversial issue, acknowledge the audience's concerns. It's not enough simply to say, "I understand how you're feeling." Audience members will think to themselves, "No, you don't! How could you?" Instead, be specific in addressing the causes of their unease. This is like "naming the elephant in the room," or acknowledging at the start what everyone is thinking. Demonstrate that you understand why the issue is difficult or emotional and find areas of common ground from which to begin. For example, in a speech in support of building a new highway bridge in an old suburb, point out that change can be difficult at first but that it often brings new convenience and other benefits that outweigh the temporary disruption.

MEDIA ANALYSIS AND APPLICATIONS

4.2 Media Analysis and Applications

a. Analyze the impact on society of a variety of media forms (e.g., television, advertising, radio, Internet, film)

b. Recognize and evaluate strategies used by media to inform, persuade, entertain, and transmit culture, including rhetorical techniques such as logical fallacies, appeals to emotion, and analogies

c. Analyze persuasive speech in media and understand the patterns of organization and the use of persuasive language, reasoning, and proof

d. Identify aesthetic effects of a media presentation

e. Integrate multiple sources of information presented in diverse media and formats (e.g., visually, quantitatively, orally) in order to make informed decisions and solve problems, evaluating the credibility and accuracy of each source and noting any discrepancies among the data

f. Demonstrate knowledge of how to make strategic use of digital media (e.g., textual, graphical, audio, visual, and interactive elements) in presentations to enhance understanding of findings, reasoning, and evidence and to add interest

(Visual and Performing Arts Content Standards for California Public Schools, Theatre, Grades 6–12, 5.0: Connections, Relationships, Applications; California Common Core State Standards for English Language Arts, SL.6–12.2, SL6–12.5)

Media is the overall term for the various kinds of entertainment and information channels that have become such an important part of the modern world. Media—or mass media, as it is often called—includes visual, audio, and print mediums, including television, film, radio, books, newspapers, magazines, newsletters, billboards, DVDs, CDs, video games, Internet websites, and social media. Each medium plays a different role in communicating, informing, and persuading its target audience.

A person encounters media when he or she sees a television screen, hears a radio or music playing in a department store, sees a sign pulled by a small airplane, sends an email by smart phone, or looks up a word on a computer. An English-Language Arts teacher must be able to analyze and recognize various characteristics of media and how they impact consumers.

MEDIA FORMS AND THEIR IMPACT ON SOCIETY

In today's world, the explosion of new forms of media means that people get more information than ever before from sources other than traditional printed texts. As a result, students must develop **media literacy**, which will enable them to use and interact with a variety of media forms.

Print

In the mid-1400s, Johannes Gutenberg revolutionized the printing of written materials with his invention of a printing press with movable type. This hand press enabled printers to produce books and pamphlets quickly and inexpensively, and made printed materials widely available for the first time. In 1605, the first weekly newspaper appeared in Antwerp, with the first English language daily paper, *The Daily Courant,* starting a hundred years later in Amsterdam.

The 1800s brought further innovations in printing, including the invention of a type-composing machine in 1841; the advent of a cylinder press that could print 8,000 sheets an hour; and a process for mass-producing paper from wood pulp. These milestones brought about a new age of literacy in the West. Books, journals, newspapers, magazines, pamphlets, posters, and handbills poured forth from the presses, spreading information and opinions to all levels of society.

Today, faced with competition from online sources of news and entertainment, newspapers and magazines are struggling to survive. Some have set up pay sites on the internet, but many offer their material for free and hope to profit from online advertising. While printed sources still survive, many publications are moving towards digital presentation on personal computers, smartphones, and tablets.

Radio

Originally called "the wireless telegraph," radio was invented by a Serbian named Nikola Tesla, who came up with the theoretical model, and Guglielmo Marconi, an Italian who first transmitted coded signals in 1896. Eight years later in Massachusetts, a General Electric Company engineer named Ernst Alexanderson built a two-kilowatt, 100,000-cycle radio set that transmitted a violin performance on Christmas Eve, 1906—the initial American radio broadcast.

By the 1920s, radio had become the first electronic-based mass medium and a growing source for news and entertainment. President Franklin D. Roosevelt delivered radio speeches he called "fireside chats" to explain new government programs and reassure the nation during hard economic times and the onset of World War II. Radio also influenced musical styles and tastes, broadcasting big band jazz shows in the 1930s and 1940s and introducing rock and roll to car radios in the 1950s and to new portable transistor sets in the 1960s.

Today, radio remains a popular source for music and information. Political "talk radio" continues to attract large audiences. Satellite radio services such as Sirius XM broadcast from satellites primarily to cars. These services feature hundreds of channels of music in many genres, news, sports, and talk.

Film

Commercial motion pictures, or movies, began in 1889 when Thomas Edison and W. K. Dickson developed the Kinetoscope, a device in which celluloid film was moved past a light. By 1894, coin-operated Kinetoscopes, dubbed "peepshows," appeared in New York City. A year later in Paris, the Lumière brothers patented a combination movie camera and projector that could project large movie images for viewing by many people at once. The first decade of the twentieth century saw many more innovations, including the production of films that told a story, such as *The Great Train Robbery*; the introduction of nickelodeons, or early movie theaters; and the beginnings of animated cartoons.

Soon, the American movie business, with its studios and stables of popular actors, had established itself in Hollywood, California, where mild weather and abundant sunshine made outdoor filming possible year round. Movie stars such as Mary Pickford, Douglas Fairbanks, and Charlie Chaplin became worldwide celebrities, and fan magazines sprang up to capitalize on their popularity.

In 1927, silent movies gave way to "talkies," or movies with synchronized sound. The "silver screen" (so called because early movies were filmed in black and white) affected fashion, manners, and slang across the nation. When, in a 1930s film, Clark Gable removed his shirt onscreen, revealing his bare chest, the sales of men's undershirts plummeted. Newsreels showed moviegoers the events and personalities they knew from newspapers. During World War II, Hollywood produced dozens of films depicting the American war effort against the Axis powers.

Movies also reflected and sometimes led changes in community standards about propriety and decency. As early as 1909, the New York Board of Motion Picture Censorship persuaded most major studios to submit their films for board approval. In 1930 a group comprised of movie producers and distributors passed The Motion Picture Production Code, also called "The Hays Code" for Will H. Hays, the group's president.

A few years later, Catholic bishops established their own Legion of Decency to evaluate the contents of movies and advise congregations about the moral content of certain films. The Production Code forbade profanity, nudity, or the depiction of sexual situations or drug use, and even suggestive jokes could be grounds for censorship. It was not until societal standards began to change in the 1960s that the Production Code was replaced by a new rating system (currently: G, PG, PG-13, R, or NC-17) that served as a cautionary warning to parents about content.

American society's struggle with racial issues also found its counterpart on the screen. Silent films and early talkies featured African Americans in subservient roles or strictly as musical entertainers, as in short films featuring Louis Armstrong or Duke Ellington. Occasionally "race films" with all-black casts broke through to a larger audience.

As society changed with passage of the Civil Rights Act of 1964, movies increasingly began to feature African Americans in starring roles and larger productions. Movies such as *Lilies of the Valley, The Color Purple, Glory, 12 Years a Slave, 42,* and *Selma* have brought black history and black experience to mainstream audiences in America. Similarly Native Americans went from stereotypical roles in westerns to more nuanced portrayals in films such as *Dances with Wolves* and *Smoke Signals.*

Technology continues to bring many changes to the ways people watch movies and to the images they see on the screen. With the advent of videocassettes and later DVDs, movies could be watched at home and individual scenes studied in detail. Improvements in filmmaking technology, from cameras and camera movement to sound recording to editing, have provided filmmakers with a wide array of new options.

Computer-generated imagery (CGI) has revolutionized movie effects with realistic digital images. This in turn has fostered an explosion of films featuring digital effects, many of them based on comic books and fantasy novels, such as *X-Men, Iron Man, The Dark Knight, The Avengers,* and *The Lord of the Rings* trilogy. The growth of worldwide markets for films and DVDs has also changed the movie business. Hollywood studios now earn almost 70 percent of their revenues from international markets.

Film: Formal and Technical Considerations

In analyzing the aesthetic effect of a film (or television drama), the student should be familiar with some of the technical aspects of film production.

1. **The Camera Shot**

   - long shot or establishing shot

   - close-up

   - medium shot

   - low angle or high angle

   - reaction shot

- zoom (fast/slow/in/out)

- freeze frame

- slow motion

- soft focus, sharp focus, deep focus

- subjective shot

- point-of-view shot

- special effects

2. **Camera Movement**

   - stationary camera

   - fixed axis camera: pan or tilt

   - dolly, tracking, trucking shots

   - crane shots

   - hand-held camera or steady-cam

3. **Lighting**

   - back-lighting, front-lighting, highlighting

   - natural vs. artificial sources of lighting

   - black/white contrast or chiaroscuro

   - harsh/soft, cold/warm lighting

   - high-key, low-key lighting

4. **Composition**

   - position of characters in frame (foreground/background, center/off-center, etc.)

   - view of character (unobstructed, hidden, profile, silhouette, etc.)

   - décor and setting as mood setting or commentary on character or situation

   - balanced/unbalanced

- arrangement of shapes

- arrangement of colors

5. **Editing**

  - pace or tempo

  - rhythm

  - disjointed/continuous

  - dissolve

  - fade-in or fade-out

  - cross-cut

  - jump cut

  - flashback or flash-forward

6. **Sound**

  - dialogue

  - music

  - sound effects

  - off-screen and on-screen sounds

  - use of silence

7. *Mise en scène* **(a French term for "putting the scene together")**

  - setting and props (architecture and interior design)

  - costumes, hairstyles, and make-up

  - body language and facial expressions of the actors

  - overall use of color and design

Television

The most ubiquitous of modern electronic media is television. Early experiments with the cathode ray tube led to Philo Taylor Farnsworth's working model of electronic television in 1927. This is the basis for all modern televisions, or TVs. Early television systems were black and white, with color sets becoming widespread only in the late 1960s. The NTSC standard mandated by the Federal Communications Commission (FCC) called for 525 lines of vertical resolution, played back at 30 frames per second with the audio carried by frequency modulation.

Today's High Definition television standard increased the number of lines of resolution to 1,080, bringing a much sharper resolution. The television technology that most affected consumers, however, might be the videocassette recorder, or VCR, which allowed viewers to record programs for later playback.

By 1988, more than sixty percent of American homes had VCRs. Videos of feature films exploded in popularity, and were then replaced by digitally recorded movies or DVDs of even higher quality. Now Blu-ray technology and flat-screen plasma and LCD televisions allow viewers to watch movies at home in circumstances that mimic a theater's picture and sound quality.

Television began strictly as a broadcast medium, with three major national networks providing programming and local broadcast licenses tightly controlled by the FCC. Cable networks, known as "pay TV," which had been around since the 1950s, came into their own in the 1980s with Ted Turner's superstation WTBS in Atlanta, Georgia, one of the early leaders.

Cable systems and digital satellite dishes enabled viewers to choose from dozens and then hundreds of channels. Specialized networks for news, sports, home improvement, cooking, and even cartoons sprang up and fragmented the national audience. Today only huge events like the Super Bowl continue to garner large national audiences to rival those of broadcast television's dominance in the 1960s and 1970s.

Like radio, early television broadcasts focused on scripted dramas, light comedies, and musical variety programs. *I Love Lucy,* a comedy featuring Lucille Ball and Desi Arnaz, became a staple of Americans' viewing habits.

Talk shows such as *The Tonight Show with Johnny Carson* featured a mix of guests including movie stars, musicians, and people in the news. Events such as the first American television appearance of the English pop group the Beatles on the *Ed Sullivan Show* drew more than 73 million viewers on a Sunday night.

The mass audience that television produced gave it an oversized influence on styles, opinions, tastes, and fads. When President John F. Kennedy was assassinated in November 1963, shocked and grieving Americans remained glued to their television sets for days. In 1969, Neil Armstrong's first steps on the moon also riveted viewers. News anchors such as Edward R. Murrow and Walter Cronkite gained the trust of viewers, to the extent that they could sometimes affect the course of events.

In 1968, Cronkite ended his news program with a statement that the United States military was "mired in stalemate" in Vietnam and that America's leaders should negotiate to end the war. President Lyndon B. Johnson is supposed to have said, "If I've lost Cronkite I've lost Middle America," and indeed Johnson soon announced he would not be running for re-election. A 1949 FCC ruling called the Fairness Doctrine made broadcasters responsible for seeking out and presenting all sides of a controversial issue. This tended to blunt any tendency toward political advocacy on TV. Once the doctrine was repealed in 1987, broadcasters could openly express political opinions. Today, cable news programs often have liberal or conservative political slants—a situation that, according to some critics, has further polarized the nation politically.

Television also addressed controversial topics in other ways. Shows such as *All in the Family* and *M*A*S*H* managed to combine broad comedy with an examination of social issues. The Public Broadcasting Service helped educate children as well as entertain them with its *Sesame Street* program.

The 1977 miniseries *Roots* won an enormous audience for its tale of how Africans were captured and brought to America as slaves. *The Day After,* a 1983 made-for-TV movie, drew high ratings and sparked a national conversation about nuclear weapons with its story of a thermonuclear war between the United States and the Soviet Union.

More recently, cable networks and online streaming services have created their own series with great success. HBO's series *The Sopranos,* which debuted in 1999, told the story of a New Jersey mobster who balances family problems with Mafia intrigues. *The Sopranos* ushered in a wave of gritty television productions such as *The Wire, Breaking Bad,* and *Boardwalk Empire.* Cable also presented racier fare, such as HBO's *Sex and the City* and Showtime's *Californication,* both of which avoided the censorship restrictions of network TV. Series such as *Mad Men,* about advertising executives in 1960s Manhattan, examined changes in societal mores.

Streaming services such as Netflix began to release entire seasons of a series at once, encouraging viewers to "binge watch" episodes over a short period of time. Overall, the advent of cable, home video, streaming services, and other entertainment options has served to fragment the national audience for television and reduced its ability to impact society as in the days of *The Ed Sullivan Show* and *I Love Lucy*.

Advertising

While advertising encompasses print, radio, billboards, and direct mail, its greatest effect on Americans has come through television commercials. Early advertisers on television would sponsor entire programs and lend their company's name to the production. Many companies hired celebrity spokespersons for their ads, while others developed their own recognizable representatives, human and nonhuman, such as Mr. Clean, Flo, the Jolly Green Giant, Ronald McDonald, and Charlie the Tuna.

Advertising "jingles," or songs, sometimes became commercial hits, as with Coca-Cola's 1971 "I'd Like to Teach the World to Sing," which sold more than a million copies. TV ads can also influence politics. Negative political advertising began with Lyndon Johnson's "daisy" commercial, in which a mushroom cloud erupting behind a little girl suggested that opposing candidate Barry Goldwater would not hesitate to use nuclear weapons. In a 1984 presidential debate, candidate Walter Mondale quoted the line "Where's the beef?" from a fast-food commercial to indicate that President Ronald Reagan's policies lacked substance.

Critics often have urged the government to curb advertising of harmful products. In 1971, Congress banned cigarette advertising on radio and TV, resulting in a loss of more than $220 million in revenue. A year later, the National Association of Broadcasters and the major networks reduced commercial time in children's weekend shows from 16 minutes an hour to 12 minutes an hour. They also banned "tie-ins," or the mention of products in a program context or the use of program hosts or cartoon characters as commercial pitchmen. Critics also pointed to the allegedly harmful effect of ads for sugary cereals, cookies, candy, and soft drinks during children's programming.

By the 1990s, advertisers sought new ways to reach viewers. One solution was the infomercial, a 30-minute or hour-long program devoted to marketing and selling a product or service and often featuring a celebrity host. While television remains the most important medium for advertisers, some worry about the advent of digital video recorders (DVRs), which allow viewers to edit out or skip commercials when watching a program.

Live events such as the NFL's Super Bowl command the highest prices for commercials, since they offer advertisers the increasingly rare opportunity of reaching an audience in real time.

The Internet

Begun by visionary thinkers in the early 1960s who saw the potential value of linking computers to share information in scientific and military fields, the Internet has grown today into the main conduit of information in the world. The Internet was brought online in 1969, and connected four major computers at western universities. It was designed to provide a communications network that would remain in operation even if some of the major sites were down. This was achieved with routers, which directed traffic around the network using alternate routes.

Early in the Internet's development, users included only computer experts, scientists, and engineers employing a very complex system or "language." More practical applications soon arose, as when libraries began to automate and network their catalogs using the Internet. By the mid-1980s, standardized commands allowed nontechnical people to use features of the Internet such as email and file transfer protocol (FTP), although it was still not easy. In 1989, a system for embedding links in text to link to other text became the basis for the World Wide Web. In 1993 the first graphical browser allowed nontechnical users to navigate between sites with ease. By 1998 Microsoft's Internet Explorer became the dominant Internet browser.

At first, businesses struggled to find ways to use the internet for commerce. In the late 1990s, the "dot.com boom" collapsed as technology companies faced the difficulties of making profits from websites. Since then, savvy entrepreneurs like Amazon have found success in selling books, CDs, and other products online by relying on quick service and razor-thin profit margins. Other sites such as eBay helped customers set up online auctions for a variety of items. As people became more confident in security on the Internet, they increasingly turned to websites for shopping. In the last few years, the rapid growth of wireless technology and mobile devices has enabled people to use the Internet to obtain information or communicate no matter where they are. In addition, social networking sites appear to hold great potential for sales and marketing.

Social Media

Social media are Internet sites where people can interact freely, sharing and discussing information about each other and the world using a mix of words, images, videos, and audio. The forms of social media include:

- **Blogs.** Short for the portmanteau word *weblog,* the blog began about 1997 as a way for writers to share their words online. While a blog is basically a personal website, it can function as a diary, a daily pulpit, a political soapbox, an outlet for breaking news, or a collection of links to other websites and blogs. Some student writers may already be **blogging**—that is, writing a blog on a regular basis. Newer material, called posts, appears at the top of the blog, so that readers can check in to see fresh content. Bloggers often receive feedback in the form of emails or posted comments at the end of stories.

- **Forums and message boards.** These are online discussion websites where a host and visitors can hold conversations in the form of posted messages. The messages remain to be viewed at any future time, so that users can join the conversation even if they weren't online when it started. In 1978, two Chicago computer hobbyists invented the message board or bulletin board system to keep friends informed about meetings and news and to share information with posts. Today, there are online forums on almost any topic, from fashion to literature.

- **Social networks and social gaming.** A social network is a website that functions as an online community of Internet users. The users may share common interests, such as hobbies, politics, or religion, or they may seek mutual friends. Once a person is granted access to a social networking website, he or she can begin reading the profiles of other members and possibly even sharing information with them. The most popular social networking sites include Facebook, Twitter, LinkedIn, Pinterest, Instagram, and YouTube. Some sites are also devoted to social gaming, in which users interact to play games, from Scrabble-like word games to complicated sword-and-sorcery role-playing games such as *World of Warcraft.*

- **Wikis.** A wiki is a piece of server software that enables users to create and edit Web page content using an Internet browser. These "open editing" sites support hyperlinks, or links to other websites or blogs, and are simple enough to be used by writers with little or no technical expertise. The most popular wiki is probably Wikipedia, an online encyclopedia that launched in 2001 and is collaboratively created and edited by more than 100,000 volunteers.

While on the topic of social media, the English-Language Arts teacher should remind students about the drawbacks and dangers of social networking. Once words or images are posted online, hundreds or even thousands of people may see them. A rash post or up-loaded video can be embarrassing, so thought must be given to each piece of information that is shared. Also, there are online predators and scam artists who should be avoided at all costs. The best advice is to proceed with caution online, just as a person would in a crowded real-life setting.

Recognizing Media Strategies

A media-literate student must acquire critical thinking skills to analyze and critique **media messages** for bias, authoritativeness, and hidden motives of persuasion, enabling the student to see how various media affect individuals and society. To help students develop these skills, the English–Language Arts teacher should emphasize the role that the mass media play in a democracy and the constraints under which they operate due to sponsorship from advertisers, production costs, and the pressure of community standards. Students should be critical consumers of media messages, with an eye to the specific purpose for each kind of message.

The mass media generally has four purposes:

- inform

- persuade

- entertain

- transmit culture

Often two or more of these purposes are combined in a media production, such as a political talk show that recounts the day's events and features panel discussions of the issues involved with entertaining personalities. This merging of the media's purposes is sometimes referred to as "infotainment."

According to the National Communication Association, media-literate students should recognize and apply the following ideas in their daily lives:

- Media does not reflect the world, but instead is a construction of the world through the use of media effects.

- Media portrays a constructed reality instead of an actual reality.

- Media messages are interpreted individually; no two people will interpret a given message the same way.

- Media messages are commercially produced. Sponsors and underwriters usually promote their own agendas.

- Media images often portray ideological and value-laden messages.

- Media messages have powerful social and political impact.

- The form and content of media messages are closely related. Even though various media cover the same stories or events, interpretations of these events are often directly related to the media form.

In general, a student should learn to ask the following **media-analysis questions** in considering any media message, whether it is a news report, debate, editorial, or dramatic presentation.

- What kind of message is being presented?

- Who created it?

- Who is the intended audience?

- How are the words, images, and sounds employed to influence audience response?

- What examples, if any, of bias or stereotypes are included?

- How does this message compare to your own experience of the world?

- Is another side of the argument or other important details left out of the message?

To give students practice in analyzing and critiquing media messages, the teacher can provide a variety of lessons about identifying point of view and bias, interpreting data, distinguishing between fact and fiction, analyzing the authority of sources, and other skills.

For example, students might be asked to describe how they would evaluate the reliability and credibility of a particular news story in the media. Students should respond that reliable and credible news reporting is marked by accuracy, objectivity, balance, and thoroughness. They should also consider whether the reporter speculates or shows bias in some way, whether the reporter's sources are valid and independent or unreliable and partisan, and whether the news organization itself is reliable. Another good exercise is to compare two or more news stories on the same topic to decide which is most accurate and complete.

Other useful class exercises in critiquing media include:

- Examine the aesthetic and emotional effect of a scene in a movie or television show using the technical knowledge of sound, camera angles, camera motion, lighting, editing, and color usage.

- Evaluate a television advertisement by analyzing its language and sound, its intended audience demographic, and its usage of loaded terms or persuasive devices.

- Work in small groups to construct a newscast from current events, drawing upon knowledge of audience, sponsor, sequence, slant, style, and scope.

Effective and Creative Media Presentation

As students gain experience in analyzing media strategies, they can identify aesthetic effects that will improve their own multimedia presentations. Desktop publishing software allows users to present a written report in a sophisticated page layout with multiple columns and with images such as photos, artwork, charts and graphs, and typographical effects. Most word-processing programs also have these capabilities. Using these software aids, students can experiment with page layouts, fonts, graphics, and other elements. Students may also employ video, animation, music, and slideshow presentations to add interest. At the end of a student presentation, the teacher should hold a class discussion about its aesthetic elements, how effective it was overall, and how it could be improved.

Dramatic Performance

A secondary-level English–Language Arts teacher must be able to organize and mount dramatic productions effectively. In the course of rehearsing and performing plays, the students should:

- Develop interpersonal and problem-solving skills through group interaction and collaboration.

- Understand and apply the creative process to the fundamental skills of acting and directing.

- Understand and apply the creative process to skills of design and technical production.

- Analyze and assess the characteristics and meanings of traditional and modern forms of drama.

Rehearsal Strategies

In preparing to stage a play, the teacher should use **teambuilding exercises** to develop strong teamwork skills among the students. Actors and backstage workers must be able to trust each other in order to create a successful performance. No matter how well rehearsed the actors are, unexpected elements will crop up during a performance, calling for instantaneous adjustment of the part of the whole company. Some simple teambuilding exercises include:

- **Ice breaker.** Pass a box of tissues around and have each participant take as many sheets as he or she chooses. Then have each person tell the group one personal detail for each sheet taken.

- **Trust builder.** Pair up students and blindfold one member of each pair. Have the sighted students lead the blindfolded students around the room or the stage for several minutes and then switch roles.

- **Team juggling.** Have students work as a team to juggle several objects, adding more balls or objects until team members begin dropping them. Challenge the students to figure out how to juggle more balls or objects.

The teacher must also deal with **scheduling** and **organizing resources**. It helps to list the resources available to the production. The teacher may need to check with school administrators and other teachers about the budget, equipment, and availability of school facilities. The teacher can then set priorities about choice of play, auditions, rehearsals, and performance.

- **Selecting a play.** The play should be age appropriate for high school students and approved by school administrators. Also, the stage should have the necessary technical capabilities for the production.

- **Holding auditions.** Allow students to try out for the various roles in the play. Often, teachers will steer leading roles to older students who are capable of performing the parts, but this is optional.

- **Organizing a stage crew.** The production will require crew members capable of handling sound, lighting, props, costumes, and other technical details. Students who act in one production may take stage crew positions in another.

- **Rehearsing.** The teacher should oversee all the details of preparing the production, from holding rehearsals with the actors to arranging for stage crew members to practice their duties. The teacher must also monitor the students whose job is to acquire props, build sets, and create costumes. For a musical play, the teacher should insist that musicians join several rehearsals as well.

Approaches to Acting

The actor should try to portray a character in ways that fit the overall intentions of the play's author and the director. Each actor should read the entire play carefully—several times, if possible—and try to understand the character he or she is playing. The actor should highlight his or her lines in the play and begin memorizing them.

Each student actor should strive to become the character by thinking about that character's background, motivation, and emotional makeup. The actor should consider what gestures, movements, and speech inflections best express the character's personality. If the actor has done the background work and feels comfortable in the role, his or her performance will be more believable to the audience.

To help the actors develop their roles, the teacher can have them do **improvisations** in which they speak or interact with each other spontaneously in character. Actors can also practice speaking precisely, or correct elocution; projecting his or her voice so the audience can hear each line, speaking with an accent or different intonations, and performing various kinds of movements that suggest character traits. Storytelling, reciting poetry, and performing dramatic monologues also help improve diction and oral performance skills.

When rehearsing a scene with others, the actor should consider the following:

- **Relationship:** How does the character feel about the other person or people in the scene? Does the character feel love or hatred? Does the character feel pity or remorse?

- **Conflict:** The basis of every plot is conflict, so the actor must focus on the conflict in every scene. One character wants something, the other character wants the opposite—and only one can be successful.

- **Motivation:** Why is the character acting this way? What background details account for his or her actions? Deciding on motivation will help the actor develop a performance that is consistent from start to finish.

- **Setting:** Where is the character during each scene and how does the setting affect his or her reactions or emotions? Whose property is it and what other people are around? Does the character feel safe or threatened?

Stage Crew and Principles of Theatrical Design

The **stage crew** performs the various duties necessary for a successful performance. These duties involve the principles of theatrical design.

- The **set designer** creates the background, scenery, and décor for the production.

- The **costume designer** researches, designs, and makes the costumes for the characters.

- The **lighting designer** controls the lighting of the set and the actors. This involves manipulating the key light, or main light; the fill light, or the light that softens harsh shadows created by the key light; and the back light, which is used to visually separate the actors downstage from the background.

- The **sound engineer** prepares and performs or directs sound effects, offstage voices, and incidental music.

- The **props person** researches, locates, and distributes the various "props," or stage properties, necessary for the production.

- The **stage manager** takes charge of stage instructions, oversees the stage crew, and handles the details of rehearsal.

Fundamentals of Stage Directing

Typically the English–Language Arts teacher serves as the director of a school production. Besides the tasks outlined above in Rehearsal Strategies, the director should apply the following skills.

Conceptualization involves determining the class's approach to the play and what the play should say to the audience. For example, a production of Shakespeare's *As You Like It* might be performed in Edwardian dress and emphasize the comic differences between the aristocratic characters of the court and the working class or rustic characters in the Arden forest. On the other hand, a production of Arthur Miller's *The Crucible* might be based on class research about the anticommunism controversies of the 1950s and how Miller compares these conflicts to the paranoid "witch hunt" of his play.

Blocking means planning and executing the patterns of onstage movement in a play. In theatrical parlance, the areas of the stage are as follows:

Upstage Right	Upstage Center	Upstage Left
Right Center	Center Stage	Left Center
Downstage Right	Downstage Center	Downstage Left

In this arrangement, "upstage" refers to the back of the stage, "downstage" refers to the section closest to the audience, and "left" and "right" refer to the actors' left and right as they face the audience.

Successful blocking grabs the audience's attention, unfolds the events with increasing urgency, and focuses the audience's attention on individual actors or small groups when necessary. Directors learn to arrange actors in triangular relationships to build tension, or to move actors in diagonal lines (upstage left to downstage right) to create more interesting movement.

Blocking can also paint group pictures with the ensemble to suggest harmony or discord, or focus the audience's attention on a certain actor. For example, if a director of a realistic play wants to focus audience attention on a single actor without using special lighting, he or she might have the actor make a sudden movement, such as standing or sitting, or make a sound, such as a loud sigh or the thud of a chair on the stage.

Since the eyes of an observer tend to move from left to right, the director might have Hamlet declaim "To be or not to be" in a halting gait toward the downstage left corner. In general, the director should choose eight to ten "framing moments" that the audience should remember from the play and work out methods to emphasize these moments with appropriate stage movement (or absence of movement).

Tempo is the pace of a play's movement and dialogue. A director should strive to maintain a brisk pace that moves the action along without confusing the audience. Every plot requires changes of tempo to create focus on dramatic high points. In addition, some types of theater, such as farce or absurdist comedy, call for more rapid and even frenzied movement to be successful.

The cast of a farce might be having trouble enunciating the lines clearly while moving briskly around the stage. There are several possible solutions a director can try in rehearsal. The actors might stand absolutely still and practice rattling off their lines very quickly and with exaggerated clarity but no effort to be expressive. This helps them deliver the dialogue without thinking so that when they resume their stage movements the lines pour out effortlessly. It might also bring out the absurdity of the words and encourage more imaginative line readings.

Another method is to rehearse the stage movements repeatedly at even greater speed but without the dialogue. This tends to reinforce muscle memory, and enables the actors to feel at ease when performing the stage business at a slightly slower speed.

Dramatic arc is the overall movement of the play from introduction and rising action to falling action and conclusion. A successful performance finds the appropriate rhythm of the play and follows it through the main stages of dramatic arc.

1. **Exposition/Introduction**—Introduces the main characters and sets the scene.

2. **Inciting Incident**—Presents the moment when a problem or conflict arises, which will drive the rest of the story.

3. **Rising Action**—The intensity of events increases as the conflict grows.

4. **Climax**—The turning point occurs in which the situation changes for better or worse.

5. **Falling Action**—Suspense is prolonged as difficulties are confronted and questions are answered. The conflict often is overcome in this stage.

6. **Resolution/Denouement**—The remaining issues are settled. A sense of normalcy or peace is reinstated. Characters are reconciled and actions are validated. Sometimes future possibilities are presented.

PRACTICE TEST 1

CSET: English Subtest I

Also available at the REA Study Center (*www.rea.com/studycenter*)

This practice test is also available online at the REA Study Center. The CSET: English test is only offered as a computer-based exam; therefore, we recommend that you take the online version of the practice test to receive these added benefits:

- **Timed testing conditions** – helps you gauge how much time you can spend on each question

- **Automatic scoring** – find out how you did on the test, instantly

- **On-screen detailed explanations of answers** – gives you the correct answer and explains why the other answer choices are wrong

- **Diagnostic score reports** – pinpoint where you're strongest and where you need to focus your study

Practice Test 1, Subtest I
Answer Sheet

1. Ⓐ Ⓑ Ⓒ Ⓓ
2. Ⓐ Ⓑ Ⓒ Ⓓ
3. Ⓐ Ⓑ Ⓒ Ⓓ
4. Ⓐ Ⓑ Ⓒ Ⓓ
5. Ⓐ Ⓑ Ⓒ Ⓓ
6. Ⓐ Ⓑ Ⓒ Ⓓ
7. Ⓐ Ⓑ Ⓒ Ⓓ
8. Ⓐ Ⓑ Ⓒ Ⓓ
9. Ⓐ Ⓑ Ⓒ Ⓓ
10. Ⓐ Ⓑ Ⓒ Ⓓ
11. Ⓐ Ⓑ Ⓒ Ⓓ
12. Ⓐ Ⓑ Ⓒ Ⓓ
13. Ⓐ Ⓑ Ⓒ Ⓓ
14. Ⓐ Ⓑ Ⓒ Ⓓ
15. Ⓐ Ⓑ Ⓒ Ⓓ
16. Ⓐ Ⓑ Ⓒ Ⓓ
17. Ⓐ Ⓑ Ⓒ Ⓓ
18. Ⓐ Ⓑ Ⓒ Ⓓ
19. Ⓐ Ⓑ Ⓒ Ⓓ
20. Ⓐ Ⓑ Ⓒ Ⓓ
21. Ⓐ Ⓑ Ⓒ Ⓓ
22. Ⓐ Ⓑ Ⓒ Ⓓ
23. Ⓐ Ⓑ Ⓒ Ⓓ
24. Ⓐ Ⓑ Ⓒ Ⓓ
25. Ⓐ Ⓑ Ⓒ Ⓓ

26. Ⓐ Ⓑ Ⓒ Ⓓ
27. Ⓐ Ⓑ Ⓒ Ⓓ
28. Ⓐ Ⓑ Ⓒ Ⓓ
29. Ⓐ Ⓑ Ⓒ Ⓓ
30. Ⓐ Ⓑ Ⓒ Ⓓ
31. Ⓐ Ⓑ Ⓒ Ⓓ
32. Ⓐ Ⓑ Ⓒ Ⓓ
33. Ⓐ Ⓑ Ⓒ Ⓓ
34. Ⓐ Ⓑ Ⓒ Ⓓ
35. Ⓐ Ⓑ Ⓒ Ⓓ
36. Ⓐ Ⓑ Ⓒ Ⓓ
37. Ⓐ Ⓑ Ⓒ Ⓓ
38. Ⓐ Ⓑ Ⓒ Ⓓ
39. Ⓐ Ⓑ Ⓒ Ⓓ
40. Ⓐ Ⓑ Ⓒ Ⓓ
41. Ⓐ Ⓑ Ⓒ Ⓓ
42. Ⓐ Ⓑ Ⓒ Ⓓ
43. Ⓐ Ⓑ Ⓒ Ⓓ
44. Ⓐ Ⓑ Ⓒ Ⓓ
45. Ⓐ Ⓑ Ⓒ Ⓓ
46. Ⓐ Ⓑ Ⓒ Ⓓ
47. Ⓐ Ⓑ Ⓒ Ⓓ
48. Ⓐ Ⓑ Ⓒ Ⓓ
49. Ⓐ Ⓑ Ⓒ Ⓓ
50. Ⓐ Ⓑ Ⓒ Ⓓ

Practice Test 1, Subtest I
Reading Literature and Informational Texts; Composition and Rhetoric

1. **Read the passage below. Then answer the question that follows.**

> Master Crow was perched on a tree,
> Holding a cheese in his beak.
> Master Fox, drawn by the odor,
> Responded with something like this:
> "Well hello, Mister Crow!
> How handsome you are! How fine you look to me!
> Really, if your voice
> Is a match for your feathers
> You're the phoenix of all the creatures of the woods."
> At these words, the Crow was overjoyed
> And to show off his beautiful voice
> He opened his beak wide, and let the cheese fall.
> The Fox snatched it, and said, "My good fellow,
> Learn that each and every flatterer
> Lives at the expense of the one who listens to him.
> This lesson is worth a cheese, without doubt."
> The Crow, ashamed and embarrassed,
> Swore, but a bit too late, not to be fooled again.

This passage is most characteristic of which of the following literary forms often associated with the oral tradition?

A. legend

B. fairy tale

C. trickster tale

D. fable

2. Literary works such as Aldous Huxley's *Brave New World,* Yevgeny Zamyatin's *We,* and George Orwell's *1984* are examples of which of the following novelistic forms?

A. *bildungsroman* or "novel of formation"

B. dystopian novel

C. *nouveau roman* or "new novel"

D. postmodern novel

3. **Read the passage below from *Troilus and Cressida*, a play by William Shakespeare.**

> Oh, when degree is shak'd,
> Which is the ladder to all high designs,
> The enterprise is sick. How could communities,
> Degrees in schools and brotherhoods in cities,
> Peaceful commerce from dividable shores,
> The primogenitive and due of birth,
> Prerogative of age, crowns scepters laurels,
> But by degree stand in authentic place?
> Take but degree away, untune that string,
> And hark what discord follows.

primogenitive: having to do with the exclusive right of inheritance belonging to the eldest son

prerogative: an exclusive power, right, or privilege

This passage reflects the Elizabethan world view in its assertion that

A. "degree," or a hierarchy of authority and power, are necessary to a smoothly functioning society.

B. democracy and fundamental equality among citizens are the bedrock values of a strong nation-state.

C. "discord" or political chaos is the result of too much power being concentrated in the hands of a few ("crowns scepters laurels").

D. the destiny of mankind is linked to the movement of the stars, and everyone is subject to a capricious fate.

4. A recurring feature of literature written for young adults is

A. an emphasis on the history of a place or group of people.

B. a focus on the thoughts and reactions of an individual character in a situation that takes place over a relatively short period.

C. a thoughtful consideration of a social problem and how it affects a variety of characters.

D. a satirical presentation of the motivations and actions of a wide range of characters over a long period of time.

5. **Read the passage below, then answer the question that follows.**

> *In 1744 the Virginia Legislature invited the Six Nations to send six youths to the College of William and Mary in Williamsburg. This reply is by Canassatego, an Iroquois.*
>
> We know you highly esteem the kind of Learning taught in these Colleges, and the maintenance of our young Men, while with you, would be very expensive to you. We are convinced, therefore, that you mean to do us Good by your Proposal; and we thank you heartily. But you who are so wise must know that different Nations have different Conceptions of things; and you will not therefore take it amiss, if our ideas of this kind of Education happens not to be the same with yours. We have had some experience of it. Several of our young People were formerly brought up in the Colleges of the Northern Provinces; they were instructed in all your Sciences; but, when they came back to us, they were bad Runners, ignorant of every means of living in the Woods, unable to bear either Cold or Hunger, knew neither how to build a Cabin, take a deer, or kill an enemy, spoke our language imperfectly, were therefore neither fit for hunters, Warriors, nor Counsellors; they were totally good for nothing. We are however not the less obliged for your kind Offer, tho' we decline accepting it; and to show our grateful Sense of it, if the Gentlemen of Virginia shall send us a Dozen of their Sons, we will take great care of their Education, instruct them in all we know, and make Men of them.

This passage is typical of a Native American writer in that it addresses

A. the importance of educating young Native Americans in the ways of Europeans.

B. the need to retain cultural and social differences among different groups of Native Americans.

C. the dangers of surrendering to European forms of education and losing touch with traditional Native American cultural values.

D. the spiritual emptiness that results from trying to live in two cultures at once.

6. What was a main function of the chorus in ancient Greek theater?

A. to perform the leading parts in a drama

B. to provide a means of solving a character's problem by divine intervention

C. to surround the stage and ceremoniously follow the action in silence

D. to provide background information to help the audience follow the play

7. Literary works by British poets of the Romantic period such as John Keats, Percy Bysshe Shelley, and William Wordsworth tend to share which of the following characteristics?

    A. an emphasis on satire and a habit of philosophizing about man's place in the world using witty, aphoristic verse

    B. a reliance on nature for inspiration and a habit of closely examining human feelings and emotions

    C. an ironic view of the modern world and a habit of presenting the absurdity of the human condition

    D. a conservative view of British traditions and a habit of ruminating about the beauties of country life and nature

8. **Read the excerpt from the poem "When I Was Growing Up" by Nellie Wong. Then answer the question that follows.**

    I know now that once I longed to be white.
    How? you ask.
    Let me tell you the ways.

    > when I was growing up, people told me
    > I was dark and I believed my own darkness
    > in the mirror, in my soul, my own narrow vision

    > > when I was growing up, my sisters with fair skin got praised
    > > for their beauty, and in the dark
    > > I fell further, crushed between high walls

    > when I was growing up, I read magazines
    > and saw movies, blonde movie stars, white skin,
    > sensuous lips and to be elevated, to become
    > a woman, a desirable woman, I began to wear
    > imaginary pale skin

    In this poem, Wong is dramatizing what elements of immigrant experience in the modern U.S.?

    A. the struggle with feelings of inferiority or exclusion

    B. the prevalence of racism in the society at large

    C. the difficulties of growing up as a female in a male-dominated culture

    D. the need to compete constantly in order to assert one's place in society

9. **Read the excerpt below from *The Art Spirit* by Robert Henri. Then answer the question that follows.**

> One of the great difficulties of an art student is to decide between his own natural impressions and what he thinks should be his impressions. When the majority of students and the majority of so-called arrived artists go out into landscape, saying they intend to look for a "motive," they too often mean, unconsciously enough, that it is their intention to look until they have found an arrangement in the landscape most like some one of the pictures they have seen and liked in the galleries. A hundred times, perhaps, they have walked by their own subject, felt it, enjoyed it, but having no estimate of their own personal sensations, lacking faith in themselves, pass on until they come to this established taste of another. And here they would be ashamed if they did not appreciate, for this is an approved taste, and they try to adopt it because it is what they think they should like whether they really do so or not.

In this excerpt, the author infers that an art student should

   A.   experiment with many different styles.

   B.   study works of art in galleries.

   C.   condemn the taste of others.

   D.   strive for originality.

10. **Read the passage below from *The Great Gatsby*, a novel by F. Scott Fitzgerald. Then answer the question that follows.**

> *In the novel, the narrator Nick Carraway is alone at night on the beach at Long Island, thinking about his friend Jay Gatsby, whose love for Nick's cousin Daisy has taken a tragic turn.*
>
> And as I sat there brooding on the old, unknown world, I thought of Gatsby's wonder when he first picked out the green light at the end of Daisy's dock. He had come a long way to this blue lawn, and his dream must have seemed so close that he could hardly fail to grasp it. He did not know that it was already behind him, somewhere back in that vast obscurity beyond the city, where the dark fields of the republic rolled on under the night.
>
> Gatsby believed in the green light, the orgiastic future that year by year recedes before us. It eluded us then, but that's no matter—tomorrow we will run faster, stretch out our arms farther. . . . And one fine morning —

Which of the following best describes the use of a literary device in this passage?

A. The first-person point of view registers the narrator's naïve view of people who believe their dreams can come true.

B. Imagery and descriptive details stress the difference between the obscurity of the setting and the clarity of Gatsby's dreams.

C. The green light is used as a symbol to represent Gatsby's dream of a future happiness that was always eluding him.

D. A flashback to the first time Gatsby saw the green light on Daisy's dock emphasizes that dreams are more important than reality.

11. Which poetic form is generally written in blank verse, elucidates the thoughts and emotions of a character in a particular situation, and was particularly important to the work of such nineteenth-century poets as Robert Browning and Alfred, Lord Tennyson?

A. ballad

B. sonnet

C. dramatic monologue

D. epithalamium

12. **Read "The Pike," a poem by Amy Lowell. Then answer the question that follows.**

> In the brown water,
> Thick and silver-sheened in the sunshine,
> Liquid and cool in the shade of the reeds,
> A pike dozed.
> Lost among the shadows of stems
> He lay unnoticed.
> Suddenly he flicked his tail,
> And a green-and-copper brightness
> Ran under the water.
>
> Out from under the reeds
> Came the olive-green light,
> And orange flashed up
> Through the sun-thickened water.
> So the fish passed across the pool,
> Green and copper,
> A darkness and a gleam,
> And the blurred reflections of the willows on the opposite bank
> Received it.

The style and subject matter of this poem are most characteristic of poetry from which of the following literary movements?

A. Imagist

B. New Formalist

C. Parnassian

D. Symbolist

13. The allegorical play *Everyman* is probably the best-known example of what kind of drama?

A. Theatre of the Absurd

B. medieval morality play

C. restoration comedy

D. Jacobean revenge play

14. **Read the excerpt from Alexander Pope's Essay on Man. Then answer the question that follows.**

> Know then thyself, presume not God to scan;
> The proper study of Mankind is Man.
> Placed on this isthmus of a middle state,
> A being darkly wise, and rudely great:
> With too much knowledge for the Skeptic side,
> With too much weakness for the Stoic's pride,
> He hangs between; in doubt to act, or rest;
> In doubt to deem himself a God, or Beast;
> In doubt his Mind or Body to prefer;
> Born but to die, and reasoning but to err;
> Alike in ignorance, his reason such,
> Whether he thinks too little, or too much:
> Chaos of Thought and Passion, all confused;
> Still by himself abused, or disabused;
> Created half to rise, and half to fall;
> Great lord of all things, yet a prey to all;
> Sole judge of Truth, in endless Error hurled:
> The glory, jest, and riddle of the world!

In what way does this excerpt represent the literary approach of neoclassical writers?

A. It is concerned mainly with the author's own thoughts and feelings about the world and expresses these thoughts in heavily emotional language.

B. It focuses on the absurdity of man's place in a godless universe and the impossibility of achieving peace and understanding.

C. It generalizes about the condition of mankind in witty, aphoristic verse.

D. It expresses ideas in an impressionistic, indirect style that alludes to literature of the past and makes great demands upon the reader.

15. **Read the passage from** *Sweet Summer: Growing Up with and without My Dad* **by Bebe Moore Campbell. Then answer the question that follows.**

> From Ruby's I could have walked to Grandma's blindfolded, the land around me was so familiar. I could have followed the smell of the country night air so weighted with watermelons, roses and the potent stench from the hog pens. We crossed the bridge running over the canal that bordered South Mills. A sign announced that we had entered Pasquotank County. On either side of us, spread out like an open fan, were fields of corn, soybeans, peanuts and melons. White and brick frame houses broke up the landscape. Some belonged to white folks, some to colored. We reached Morgan's Corner and my stomach started quivering. It was where I bought my Baby Ruths and comic books! As my father's car slowed, my eyes scanned the fields of corn and soybeans for the opening to Grandma's. There it was!

Which of the following best describes the mood of the passage?

A. The speaker's initial expectations of happiness are spoiled by reminders of a segregated past.

B. The speaker's familiarity with the landscape and surroundings fills her with a sense of excitement.

C. The speaker's memories of the familiar sights she sees reinforce her bitter awareness of the limitations of rural life.

D. The speaker's sudden recognition of how beautiful the land is triggers her remorse for all that she has lost by moving away.

16. **Read the passage below from "A Cow's Ruminations." Then answer the question that follows.**

    The narrator of the poem is a cow in a field.

    I know them mostly as flashes, expressions of speed,
    Flicking past in metal shells, heedless of my breed.
    My own focus (as always, such is my lot)
    Is finding in this vast field one large spot
    Of delicious shade. To them such slow pursuits
    As shade and breeze and tender shoots
    Pale before restlessness, and so they miss
    The calming satisfactions of all this.

    This passage most clearly illustrates which of the following poetic devices?

    A.   use of conventions associated with the pastoral genre to satirize the modern world of highways and automobiles

    B.   use of analogy to portray the similarities between cattle and people

    C.   use of onomatopoeia to recreate the sounds of the wind and rushing cars

    D.   use of personification to suggest that animals have a stronger connection to nature than human beings

17. **Read the following passage analyzing the novel *London Fields* by British author Martin Amis. Then answer the question that follows.**

    The protagonist of *London Fields* sees television as the best part of reality—a perfect world comprised of all the glamour, fantasy, wealth, and security anyone could desire. Experiential reality itself is presented as harsh, confusing, fragmented, and frustrating. As a result, the protagonist chooses television as his "exemplary reality, all beautifully and gracefully interconnected, where nothing hurt much and nobody got old."

    Which of the following best describes Amis's approach to fiction as discussed in this passage?

    A.   postmodernist

    B.   modernist

    C.   Symbolist

    D.   realist

18. **Read the excerpt below from *The Art of Love*, a work by the Roman poet Ovid. Then answer the question that follows.**

> Who hopes to keep his loved one on the hooks
> Must make her think he's ravished by her looks.
> If she's in silk, her taste in silks admire,
> In Tyrian colors, praise the gowns of Tyre.
> In gold, herself's more precious far than gold,
> If tweed's her choice, her choice of tweed uphold.
> In negligee, cry how she burns and thrills —
> But add in anxious tones, "Beware of chills."

Which of the following themes characteristic of the works of Ovid is best exemplified in this passage?

A.   the emotional torment of romantic love

B.   the falsity of the upper classes in Roman society

C.   the need for clever stratagems to achieve romantic success

D.   the overindulgence of the wealthy in sensual pleasures

19. **Read the following passage. Then answer the question that follows.**

> … I was soon reduced so low that it was necessary to keep me almost always on deck and from my extreme youth I was not put in fetters. In this situation I expected every hour to share the fate of my companions, some of whom were almost daily brought upon the deck at the point of death, which I began to hope would soon put an end to my miseries. Often did I think many of the inhabitants of the deep much more happy than myself. I envied them the freedom they enjoyed, and as often wished I could change my condition for theirs. Every circumstance I met with, served only to render my state more painful and heightened my apprehensions and my opinion of the cruelty [of the crew].

This passage is an example of what kind of traditional American literary form?

A.   immigrant's journal

B.   slave narrative

C.   exposé of child labor

D.   political pamphlet

20. **Read the poem "1914" by Wilfred Owen. Then answer the question that follows.**

> War broke: and now the Winter of the world
> With perishing great darkness closes in.
> The foul tornado, centred at Berlin,
> Is over all the width of Europe whirled,
> Rending the sails of progress. Rent or furled
> Are all Art's ensigns. Verse wails. Now begin
> Famines of thought and feeling. Love's wine's thin.
> The grain of human Autumn rots, down-hurled.
>
> For after Spring had bloomed in early Greece,
> And Summer blazed her glory out with Rome,
> An Autumn softly fell, a harvest home,
> A slow grand age, and rich with all increase.
> But now, for us, wild Winter, and the need
> Of sowings for new Spring, and blood for seed.

Which is the best description of this poem's formal genre?

A. villanelle

B. dramatic monologue

C. Shakespearean sonnet

D. Petrarchan sonnet

21. **Read the passage from Henry James's *Portrait of a Lady*. Then answer the question that follows.**

> It was her deep distrust of her husband—this was what darkened the world. . . . It had come gradually—it was not till the first year of their life together, so admirably intimate at first, had closed that she had taken the alarm. Then the shadows had begun to gather; it was as if Osmond deliberately, almost malignantly, had put the lights out one by one. The dusk at first was vague and thin, and she could still see her way in it. But it steadily deepened, and if now and again it had occasionally lifted there were certain corners of her prospect that were impenetrably black.

Which of the following statements describes most accurately how a literary or rhetorical device is used in this passage?

A. Hyperbole is used to suggest the protagonist's helplessness in the face of her husband's untrustworthy behavior.

B. Words connoting darkness and blindness are used to hint that the protagonist is misled about the situation with her husband.

C. An extended metaphor of creeping darkness is used to portray how the protagonist's distrust of her husband is ruining her marriage.

D. Irony is used to present the comic absurdity of the protagonist's plight.

22. *The Misanthrope* is an example of which form of drama?

A. Jacobean revenge play

B. Restoration drama

C. Theatre of the Absurd

D. French Neoclassical drama

23. To depict the soul's journey toward God, Dante's *Divine Comedy* mainly employs which of the following literary devices?

A. allegory

B. paradox

C. irony

D. personification

24. Which of the following best describes the characteristics of an epic poem?

A. a long fictional work that is often realistic and tends to address the concerns of the society in which it is produced

B. a brief work in verse that addresses the reader directly and expresses the poet's feelings and perceptions

C. a long narrative poem in a formal or elevated style that relates the adventures of an heroic figure

D. a long poem written in heroic couplets that mocks the pretensions or hypocrisies of some person or group

25. **Read the passage from the story "My Name" by Sandra Cisneros. Then answer the question that follows**

> In English my name means hope. In Spanish it means too many letters. It means sadness, it means waiting. It is like the number nine. A muddy color. It is the Mexican records my father plays on Sunday mornings when he is shaving, songs like sobbing. . . .
>
> At school they say my name funny as if the syllables were made out of tin and hurt the roof of our mouth. But in Spanish my name is made out of a softer something like silver, not quite as thick as sister's name Magdelena, which is uglier than mine. Magdalena, who at least can come home and become Nenny. But I am always Esperanza.

In this passage, the speaker's imaginative images and comparisons most likely reflect which of the following attitudes towards her name?

A. bitter shame and impatience

B. ambivalence yet also a certain pride

C. humility and a deference to family tradition

D. smug superiority and haughtiness

26. **Read the two poems. Then answer the question that follows.**

Ozymandias
by Percy Bysshe Shelley

I met a traveller from an antique land,
Who said—"Two vast and trunkless legs of stone
Stand in the desert. . . . Near them, on the sand,
Half sunk a shattered visage lies, whose frown,
And wrinkled lip, and sneer of cold command,
Tell that its sculptor well those passions read
Which yet survive, stamped on these lifeless things,
The hand that mocked them, and the heart that fed;
And on the pedestal, these words appear:
My name is Ozymandias, King of Kings;
Look on my Works, ye Mighty, and despair!
Nothing beside remains. Round the decay
Of that colossal Wreck, boundless and bare
The lone and level sands stretch far away."

Africa
by Claude McKay

The sun sought thy dim bed and brought forth light,
The sciences were sucklings at thy breast;
When all the world was young in pregnant night

Thy slaves toiled at thy monumental best.
Thou ancient treasure-land, thou modern prize,
New peoples marvel at thy pyramids!
The years roll on, thy sphinx of riddle eyes
Watches the mad world with immobile lids.
The Hebrews humbled them at Pharaoh's name.
Cradle of Power! Yet all things were in vain!
Honor and Glory, Arrogance and Fame!
They went. The darkness swallowed thee again.
Thou art the harlot, now thy time is done,
Of all the mighty nations of the sun.

Which of the following best describes the theme that these two sonnets share?

A.   the importance of traveling to compare cultures and monuments

B.   the decline of the modern world compared to antique splendor

C.   the vanity of great power that inevitably declines and fades

D.   the dangers of allowing rulers to obtain too much power

27. A sixth grade teacher assigns John Steinbeck's novel *The Grapes of Wrath* to her class because various readability ratings suggest it has a text complexity in the grades 2–3 range. Also, a Coh-Metrix analysis indicates it has uncomplicated syntax and a conventional story arc. Yet the class struggles with the sophistication of the novel's theme and inferences. This example shows the limitations of

A.   quantitative measures of text complexity.

B.   qualitative measures of text complexity.

C.   quantitative and qualitative measures of text complexity.

D.   reader-task considerations related to text complexity.

28. **Read the following excerpt from a speech delivered by Abraham Lincoln on June 16, 1858, in Springfield, Illinois. Then answer the question that follows.**

If we could first know where we are, and whither we are tending, we could then better judge what to do, and how to do it.

We are now far into the fifth year, since a policy was initiated, with the avowed object, and confident promise, of putting an end to slavery agitation.

Under the operation of that policy, that agitation has not only not ceased, but has constantly augmented.

In my opinion, it will not cease until a crisis shall have been reached, and passed.

"A house divided against itself cannot stand."

I believe this government cannot endure, permanently half slave and half free.

I do not expect the Union to be dissolved—I do not expect the house to fall—but I do expect it will cease to be divided. It will become all one thing or all the other.

Either the opponents of slavery will arrest the further spread of it, and place it where the public mind shall rest in the belief that it is in the course of ultimate extinction; or its advocates will push it forward, till it shall become alike lawful in all the states, old as well as new—North as well as South. . . .

Which of the following best describes Lincoln's purpose in this speech?

A. express his belief that the slavery question must be reckoned with once and for all

B. express his belief that the United States cannot survive as a unified nation

C. recommend that the United States be divided officially into pro-slavery and anti-slavery states

D. call for the arrest of all those who support slavery in the United States

29. Which of the following Shakespearean characters would probably be of most interest in a postcolonial analysis of *The Tempest*?

A. Caliban

B. Shylock

C. Lady Macbeth

D. Hamlet

30. **Read the paragraph below about the French anthropologist Claude Lévi-Strauss. Then answer the question that follows.**

In a famous essay, Lévi-Strauss pointed out that myths from different cultures around the world are strikingly similar. He also observed that while poetry is a specialized kind of speech that always is distorted in translation, the fundamental meaning of a myth comes through even in the worst translation. As he put it, "A myth is still felt as a myth by any reader anywhere in the world."

The paragraph discusses Lévi-Strauss's important idea about which of the following?

A.   psychological meaning of literature

B.   genre conventions of literature

C.   meaning and structure of language

D.   difficulty of translation

31.   **Read the excerpt below from "Down the Mississippi," an article by George Ward Nichols that appeared in the November 1870 issue of *Harper's Magazine*. Then answer the question that follows.**

> I can not conceive of a more arduous and dangerous business that that of guiding one of these gigantic steamboats along the twisting, shifting, treacherous channel of the river. The ocean steamship, whatever may happen, has the refuge of the open sea. The direction to be pursued is well known, and the compass points the way, while, if the vessel is deprived of the use of steam, she can resort to canvas, and, beyond delay, but little injury occurs. The man who directs the movement of the locomotive may, by the slightest carelessness, cause the death of hundreds of his fellow-beings; yet most accidents by railroad happen from exterior and accidental causes. There are many other stations in life where the safety of human beings and of property is dependent upon the judgment and good conduct of a single man. But in neither one nor all of them is there any such grave responsibility as that resting upon the pilot of the Western river.

In this excerpt, what is the author's primary purpose?

A.   point out the dangers of sailing the ocean

B.   prove that travel by water is safer than travel by rail

C.   warn against giving one person too much responsibility

D.   emphasize the difficult task of piloting a river steamboat

32.   **Read the excerpt below from *Daniel Deronda*, a novel by George Eliot. Then answer the question that follows.**

> Music was soon begun. Miss Arrowpoint and Herr Klesmer played a four-handed piece on two pianos which convinced the company in general that it was long, and Gwendolen in particular that the neutral, placid-faced Miss Arrowpoint had a mastery of the instrument which put her own execution out of the question—though she was not discouraged as to her often-praised touch and style. After this every one became anxious to hear Gwendolen sing: especially

Mr. Arrowpoint; as was natural in a host and a perfect gentleman, of whom no one had anything to say but that he had married Miss Cutler, and imported the best cigars; and he led her to the piano with easy politeness.

Which of the following qualitative aspects of text complexity would most likely add to the difficulty level of this excerpt for eleventh-grade students?

A. multiple layers of meaning

B. demands on background knowledge

C. conventionality of language

D. sentence structure

33. A literary scholar consults versions of Jane Austen's *Pride and Prejudice* both in print and on the Internet. For which task would it be most helpful for the scholar to use the electronic version?

A. to highlight passages for quotation in an article

B. to find out how many times the word "love" appears in the text

C. to study the illustrations that have appeared in different editions of the text

D. to make notes for an examination of Austen's writing style

34. **Read the following poem by Phillis Wheatley, who was sold into slavery in Boston around 1761. Then answer the question that follows.**

On Being Brought from Africa to America

'Twas mercy brought me from my Pagan land,
Taught my benighted soul to understand
That there's a God, that there's a Savior too:
Once I redemption neither fought nor knew,
Some view our sable race with scornful eye,
"Their color is a diabolic die."
Remember, Christians, Negroes, black as Cain,
May be refined, and join the angelic train.

To contexualize this poem most successfully, a secondary school teacher should probably ask which of the following questions?

A. What literary movement does Wheatley's poem represent?

B. How does the attitude that Wheatley displays in the poem reflect her situation as an enslaved person?

C. What are the differences between how this poem would have been received by Wheatley's original readers and how it is received today?

D. How does Wheatley use overtly religious imagery and language to express her feelings?

35. **Read this excerpt from Molly Bloom's soliloquy in James Joyce's *Ulysses*. Then answer the question that follows.**

> …I love flowers I'd love to have the whole place swimming in roses God of heaven there's nothing like nature the wild mountains then the sea and the waves rushing then the beautiful country with fields of oats and wheat and all kinds of things and all the fine cattle going about that would do your heart good to see rivers and lakes and flowers all sorts of shapes and smells and colours springing up even out of the ditches primroses and violets nature it is as for them saying there's no God I wouldn't give a snap of my two fingers for all their learning why don't they go and create something I often asked him . . .

This passage is an example of what literary technique or device?

A. stream of consciousness

B. parody

C. personification

D. flashback

36. Miguel de Cervantes' novel *Don Quixote* is a parody of the popular romances and chivalric tales of his time. What is a parody?

A. a work that ridicules the follies and vices of individuals and society, often through comic exaggeration

B. a work written in imitation of an author's style or of a genre in order to make fun of it and mock its conventions

C. a traditional story that has become part of the collective experience of a nation, ethnic group, or culture

D. a story that features fantasy characters from folklore and usually ends happily

37. *Deus ex machina,* which is a method of solving the characters' problems in a play through divine intervention, was originally a feature of what category of drama?

    A.   Jacobean revenge plays

    B.   Restoration drama

    C.   ancient Greek drama

    D.   Elizabethan drama

38. Narrative point of view is one of the basic elements of fiction and poetry. Which of the following is an example of a third-person omniscient narrator?

    A.   When I walked into the room, I was overcome with a strange feeling of familiarity. Although I'd never been there before, I somehow felt as if I had.

    B.   He walked into the room for the first time, yet he was overcome with a feeling of peculiar familiarity.

    C.   You walk into the room, and immediately are overcome with an odd sensation that you've been here before.

    D.   He walked into the room and was overcome with a strange feeling of familiarity. Meanwhile, the man he'd been seeking for months was crouched behind the sofa, cursing himself for still being there, waiting to spring.

39. **Read the excerpt below from an informational brochure called "Maintaining a Healthy Diet." Then answer the question that follows.**

    It's never too late to pursue healthier eating habits. The key is to decide on a plan and then stick to it. The following ideas can help you improve your diet immediately.

    7 Keys to a Healthy Diet
    · Eat enough calories.
    · Eat your share of protein.
    · Eat healthy fats, not trans-fats.
    · Eat less processed foods and sugars.
    · Eat less candy and drink less soft drinks and juices.
    · Eat enough fruits and vegetables daily.
    · Eat less salt.

Which of the following statements most accurately describes how textual features are used in this excerpt to help convey the brochure's information?

A. Parallel structure is used to aid comprehension, such as introducing what to eat more of or less of.

B. Bullets are used to help the reader locate major details quickly.

C. Boldfaced text is used to call the reader's attention to key words and phrases, such as "Healthy Diet."

D. An introductory paragraph previews important ideas, such as how to approach changing one's diet.

40. The best way for a researcher to locate the name of the cinematographer on the 2008 Clint Eastwood film *Gran Torino* is to

A. consult a biography of Clint Eastwood.

B. look up the name on an Internet database.

C. rent the movie and find the name in the credits.

D. consult an almanac.

Use the information below to answer questions 41 and 42.

A writer has drafted the paragraph below as part of an academic essay on the topic of Hispanic American authors in the United States.

[1] One Hispanic author who achieved great success in the United States is Oscar Hijuelos. [2] The Cuban-American novelist had been writing about the experience of immigrants in America with a sympathetic eye to their daily travails and triumphs. [3] Born in Manhattan in 1951, Hijuelos grew up in the northern Morningside Heights neighborhood, which became a frequent setting in his fiction. [4] Today Morningside Heights remains a popular residential area for many ambitious young Hispanic New Yorkers. [5] Speaking Spanish at home, Oscar ironically strengthened his skills in English only after a 1955 trip to Cuba, where he got a kidney infection and was required to spend a year in a Connecticut hospital upon his return. [6] Hijuelos went to several colleges in New York City before earning his bachelor's degree. [7] He published *Our House in the Last World,* the first of several novels, in 1983. [8] Hijuelos's 1989 novel, *The Mambo Kings Play Songs of Love,* an affectionate look at a flamboyant Cuban-American bandleader and his trumpet-playing brother, won the Pulitzer Prize for fiction.

41. During the revision process, which of the following changes could the writer make to improve the logic and flow of the paragraph?

    A. delete Sentence 4

    B. insert Sentence 7 after Sentence 2

    C. insert Sentence 8 after Sentence 1

    D. delete Sentence 5

42. Which of the following revisions of a sentence from the writer's paragraph has been edited correctly to eliminate an error in verb tense?

    A. Sentence 1: One Hispanic author who will achieve great success in the United States is Oscar Hijuelos.

    B. Sentence 2: The Cuban-American novelist wrote about the experience of immigrants in America with a sympathetic eye to their daily travails and triumphs

    C. Sentence 5: Speaking Spanish at home, Oscar ironically strengthens his skills in English only after a 1955 trip to Cuba, where he got a kidney infection and was required to spend a year in a Connecticut hospital upon his return.

    D. Sentence 8: Hijuelos's 1989 novel, *The Mambo Kings Play Songs of Love,* an affectionate look at a flamboyant Cuban-American bandleader and his trumpet-playing brother, had won the Pulitzer Prize for fiction.

43. A researcher adds to a draft research paper a passage that is a direct quotation from a primary source. The quote requires the researcher to insert a phrase in order to explain a technical term to readers. Which of the following procedures is the best way to show that the inserted phrase is not a part of the original quotation?

    A. Enclose the explanatory phrase in brackets.

    B. Identify the inserted phrase in text of the footnote for the quotation.

    C. Add a footnote after the explanatory phrase.

    D. Put the inserted phrase in italics to differentiate it from the quoted material.

44. Problems with the structure of a piece of writing should usually be addressed during which stage of the writing process?

    A. planning

    B. drafting

    C. revising

    D. editing/proofreading

45. Of the sentences below, which includes an appositive?

    A. In the twentieth century, Henri Matisse was a French painter who favored vivid colors and patterns

    B. Henri Matisse was a great French painter of the twentieth century who filled his canvases with vivid colors and patterns.

    C. The great French painter Henri Matisse—some say the greatest of the century—filled his canvases with vivid colors and patterns.

    D. Henri Matisse, a great French painter of the twentieth century, filled his canvases with vivid colors and patterns.

Read the excerpt from President Franklin D. Roosevelt's "Arsenal of Democracy" speech. Then answer questions 46 and 47.

There are those who say that the Axis powers would never have any desire to attack the Western Hemisphere. That is the same dangerous form of wishful thinking which has destroyed the powers of resistance of so many conquered peoples. The plain facts are that the Nazis have proclaimed, time and again, that all other races are their inferiors and therefore subject to their orders. And most important of all, the vast resources and wealth of this American hemisphere constitute the most tempting loot in all of the round world. . . .

The experience of the past two years has proven beyond doubt that no nation can appease the Nazis. No man can tame a tiger into a kitten by stroking it. There can be no appeasement with ruthlessness. There can be no reasoning with an incendiary bomb. We know now that a nation can have peace with the Nazis only at the price of total surrender. Even the people of Italy have been forced to become accomplices of the Nazis; but at this moment they do not know how soon they will be embraced to death by their allies.

46. Which of the following is the main claim that Roosevelt is making in the excerpt?

    A.   It is wishful thinking to believe that the United States can defeat the Nazis in war.

    B.   Appeasement will not work against the aggressive policies of the Nazi regime.

    C.   The vast wealth and resources of the American continent assures that the Allies will defeat the Nazis.

    D.   The only choice that the United States faces is surrender or destruction.

47. Which of the following best describes the form of Roosevelt's appeal to reason in this passage?

    A.   generalization, where a rule is applied to a specific case

    B.   part-to-whole, where the whole is assumed to be like individual parts

    C.   prediction, where the future is assumed to be like the past

    D.   extrapolation, where areas beyond the area of focus are assumed to be like the focused-on area

48. **Use the information below to answer the question that follows.**

A writer has drafted the paragraph below as part of a narrative about a harrowing experience.

> My most memorable summer job as a teenager was at a small warehouse owned by a local meat-packing company. I worked with another fellow filling orders and moving pallets onto the company trucks with a forklift. Late one afternoon, my co-worker headed out early, leaving me in charge of the warehouse for the first time. Before he left, he reminded me about the tricky freezer door, but I waved him off with a smile. It was a steamy day in July, and as I finished a last few chores on the dock my mind kept turning to that freezer at the back, in which sat a box of cherry popsicles we kept as a reward for each loaded truck. Finally, I could resist no longer. I wrenched open the freezer door. _____ my heart leaped inside my chest. The freezer door had slammed shut behind me! I dropped the popsicle and tried the handle, but as usual it refused to spring the door open. In a panic, I began to pound on the heavy freezer door and shout for help. My flimsy T-shirt would not be much protection against the frigid air in there. After a couple of hours, with things looking fairly hopeless, a secretary from next door popped in and heard my shouting. When she opened the door to the freezer, I felt rather foolish standing there shivering in the middle of July.

To control the flow and pace of the narrative, which of the following clausal modifiers should the writer use in the blank in this paragraph?

A.   Due to my carelessness,

B.   After I thought about the consequences,

C.   When I realized my predicament,

D.   As I headed for the frozen treats,

49. **Read the following statement made by a concerned citizen at a City Council meeting. Then answer the question that follows.**

> At first we were told the Blue Fin Restaurant would be the only eating establishment allowed to be built on the shore of the lake. Today you are voting on whether to allow a second restaurant to be constructed alongside. And next year, a third restaurant and a fourth will be added, just for good measure. And soon developers will submit plans for shops and bars and convenience stores. Where will it end? The peaceful lakeshore that people have enjoyed for years will be ruined!

This statement is an example of what logical fallacy?

A.   slippery slope

B.   red herring

C.   begging the question

D.   bandwagon appeal

50. A local newspaper editor wants to run a review of the local symphony's performance of Edward Elgar's *Enigma Variations*. Given the general newspaper audience, which of the following passages would be most appropriate for the review?

A.   The final selection of the evening was Edward Elgar's remarkable but also somewhat baffling *Enigma Variations,* the actual title of which is *Variations on an Original Theme for Orchestra.* Each section is an affectionate portrait of one of Elgar's friends, and the "enigma" is supposedly a hidden theme in the piece that, according to Elgar himself, is "not played."

B.   The final piece, Elgar's *Enigma Variations,* was the highlight of the evening's performance. The piece, which consists of fourteen variations on a theme, featured a pounding energy in some places and the stately tones of a lovely adagio in others. The orchestra shone particularly in the later sections, when it swirled and dazzled like fireworks against a night sky.

C.   The last song that the symphony played was a little less boring. It was called *Enigma Variations* by Edward Elgar. For some reason, it was divided into lots of separate parts, and the orchestra paused after each one, which was a little annoying. The tunes were good, though, and I could imagine an electric guitar solo adding a lot to the grand finale.

D.   The final performance on the program, Elgar's sublime *Enigma Variations*, disappointed this reviewer for several reasons. Mainly, the deficiency lay with the conductor's deployment of the string section, which not only seemed puzzlingly sluggish on the dynamic Finale, which should soar not plod, but also persistently sounded a bit ragged in the violas—at least to my ears.

Practice Test 1, Subtest I
Answer Key

1.	D	18.	C	35.	A
2.	B	19.	B	36.	B
3.	A	20.	D	37.	C
4.	B	21.	C	38.	D
5.	C	22.	D	39.	B
6.	D	23.	A	40.	B
7.	B	24.	C	41.	A
8.	A	25.	B	42.	B
9.	D	26.	C	43.	A
10.	C	27.	A	44.	C
11.	C	28.	A	45.	D
12.	A	29.	A	46.	B
13.	B	30.	C	47.	C
14.	C	31.	D	48.	D
15.	B	32.	D	49.	A
16.	D	33.	B	50.	B
17.	A	34.	C		

Progress Chart: Multiple-Choice Questions

Below are grids that group questions by subject matter requirement codes. Place a checkmark in the box below each question that you answered correctly and calculate the percentage of correct answers for each area. This will give you an indication of your strengths and weaknesses and show you which topics need further study.

Reading Literature   SMR Code 1.1   11/16

1	3	4	5	6	7	8	12	13	14
	✓	✓	✓	✓	✓	✓			

17	18	19	25	26	34
✓	✓	✓		✓	✓

9?
15

Craft and Structure of Literature   SMR Code 1.2   11/14

2	10	11	16	20	21	22	23	24	29
✓	✓	✓			✓		✓	✓	✓

35	36	37	38
✓	✓	✓	✓

Reading Informational Texts   SMR Code 1.3   2/3

30	31	46
	✓	✓

Craft and Structure of Informational Texts   SMR Code 1.4   3 /4

9	15	39	47
✓	✓	✓	

Integration of Knowledge and Ideas in Informational Texts   SMR Code 1.5   1 /1

28
✓

Text Complexity   SMR Code 1.6   1 /2

27	32
	✓

Writing Processes (Individual and Collaborative)   SMR Code 3.1   1 /2

41	44
	✓

Text Types and Purposes   SMR Code 3.2   1 /2

49	50
	✓

Production and Distribution of Writing   SMR Code 3.3   __1__/2

45	48
	✓

Conventions of Oral and Written Language   SMR Code 3.4   __1__/1

42
✓

Research to Build and Present Knowledge   SMR Code 3.5   __3__/3

33	40	43
✓	✓	✓

Practice Test 1, Subtest I
Detailed Answer Explanations

Reading Literature and Informational Texts

1. **D.**

   A fable often features anthropomorphized animals in a tale that ends by teaching a lesson about life or human nature. This example is translated from the French original of Jean de La Fontaine, who wrote his many fables in French alexandrine verse. The clever Fox teaches the Crow that "every flatterer lives at the expense of the one who listens to him."

2. **B.**

   A *dystopia* is the opposite of a *utopia,* or an imaginary place with ideal laws, government, and social conditions. Thomas More's *Utopia* (1516) describes such a perfect land. In contrast, the books listed here imagine horrible totalitarian states where life is regimented and ordinary citizens have little or no freedom.

3. **A.**

   This passage refers to the rigorous political and social hierarchy of feudalism, in which each person from the ruler to an aristocrat to a farmer has his or her "authentic place." Elizabethans accepted the privileges associated with certain stations in life as a natural feature of the social order.

4. **B.**

   Literature for young adults most often features a teenage protagonist whose experiences and reactions are presented from her or his point of view. In addition, the action tends to be immediate and to take place over a relatively brief period of time.

5. **C.**

   The passage describes the plight of young Native Americans who have been educated in European ways but lack the skills necessary to live effectively as an Iroquois ("were therefore neither fit for hunters, Warriors, nor Counsellors"). It thus expresses a common concern among Native American writers about the dangers of abandoning Native American cultural values and practices.

6. **D.**

   In the ancient Greek theater, the chorus offered background facts and summaries of the action to help audiences understand the drama. In effect, the chorus represented the general populace onstage and guided the audience in how they should react to the events taking place before them.

7. **B.**

    Romantic writers placed a strong emphasis on subjective emotions such as love, terror, pity, and depression. They often tried to convey their powerful feelings when confronted by untamed nature, as in Wordsworth's *The Prelude,* or the conflicts of joy and sorrow, as in Keats's "Ode to a Nightingale" (e.g., "Where palsy shakes a few, sad, last gray hairs,/Where youth grows pale, and spectre-thin, and dies;/Where but to think is to be full of sorrow/And leaden-eyed despairs").

8. **A.**

    The speaker reveals her feelings of being an outsider in the white-dominated culture by describing how "people told me I was dark and I believed my own darkness," and by pointing out that her "sisters with fair skin got praised for their beauty" while she "fell further, crushed between high walls." The speaker feels that to be accepted in the society she needs to attain some ideal look ("blonde movie stars, white skin").

9. **D.**

    In the excerpt, Henri urges the art student to have faith in his or her own impressions and preferences in painting, and not simply try to reproduce paintings that appeal to popular taste. Henri is inferring that the art student should strive to be original in his or her approach to making art.

10. **C.**

    Symbolism as a literary device is the use of an object, place, action, or idea (the symbol) to mean or suggest something other than the ordinary meaning. In the passage, Fitzgerald indicates that the green light on Daisy's dock (which is mentioned several times in the novel) symbolizes Gatsby's dream of being with Daisy and achieving future happiness with her.

11. **C.**

    The dramatic monologue is a poetic form in which a character speaks in his or her own voice and reveals (sometimes inadvertently) his or her true character and motivations. It usually also includes a silent listener and an implied setting. It is often, but not always, written in blank verse. Many critics think the form reached its peak of perfection in such works as Browning's "Andrea Del Sarto" and Tennyson's "Ulysses."

12. **A.**

    Amy Lowell was one of the leading imagist poets. This type of poetry is usually written in free verse, is phrased in common speech, addresses a wide variety of subject matter, and conveys meaning through clear, precisely described images. In "The Pike," Lowell uses plain language ("So the fish passed across the pool/Green and copper") and free verse to describe a fish's movement in sun-dappled water.

13. **B.**

    Everyman is a fine example of a medieval morality play. Written near the end of the fifteenth century, its 900 lines describe a complacent Everyman who is warned by Death of his impending end and progresses from fear to resignation and acceptance. Mystery plays and morality plays of the Middle Ages taught Christian stories and values mainly through the use of allegory and symbolism.

14. **C.**

    The excerpt from Pope's *Essay on Man* displays his witty survey of the contradictions that attend the human condition. Like his neoclassical contemporaries Samuel Johnson and John Dryden, Pope wrote in rhymed heroic couplets and often distilled his insights into detachable aphorisms ("Know then thyself, presume not God to scan;/The proper study of Mankind is Man.").

15. **B.**

    In the first line of the passage, the speaker reveals that the landscape is familiar to her. She goes on to describe with pleasure "the smell of the country night air," and her stomach starts "quivering" when she recalls happy times when she bought candy and comic books in the local town. The exclamation "There it was!" cinches the mood of excitement and expectation.

16. **D.**

    The poem uses personification, which ascribes human qualities to animals or things, to present the point of view of a cow in a field. As the speaker of the poem, the cow comments on humanity's preference for speed ("I know them mostly as flashes . . . Flicking past in metal shells") over simpler pursuits, such as looking for shade. The cow sardonically remarks upon the "restlessness" of human beings, which causes them to "miss the calming satisfactions of all this"—i.e., the slow but reassuring cycles of the natural world.

17. **A.**

    The passage describes how *London Fields* presents ordinary reality as "harsh, confusing, fragmented, and frustrating," and its protagonist thus prefers to concentrate on the fantasy world of television. Postmodern authors often focus on the fragmented nature of the modern world and mirror it in their fragmented, experimental approach to the novel. In addition, postmodernism often deals with the ways in which people can shift consciousness between reality and fantasy.

18. **C.**

    In this excerpt, Ovid wittily advises the suitor to be nimble in praising the object of his desire for whatever she is wearing—and then to show concern ("Beware of chills") if she is wearing very little. For Ovid, such a strategic approach to win favor is one more aspect of "the art of love."

19. **B.**

An autobiographical account of life as a slave, an American slave narrative typically provides harrowing descriptions of the horrors of slavery, including the transatlantic voyage in which African prisoners were chained together ("in fetters") in the hold of a ship. The author of this account, Olaudah Equiano, describes how he expected to "share the fate of my companions, some of whom were almost daily brought upon the deck at the point of death." Equiano remarks of the sea creatures, "I envied them the freedom they enjoyed."

20. **D.**

The fact that the poem has fourteen lines in iambic pentameter indicates that it is a sonnet. Its rhyme scheme (ABBAABBA CDDCEE) is that of a Petrarchan sonnet, with the sestet (last six lines) variously rhymed. A villanelle is a nineteen-line poem consisting of five tercets (three-line stanzas) and one quatrain (four-line stanza). In a dramatic monologue, a character speaks with her or his own voice, but "1914" describes a situation—the beginning of war. A Shakespearean sonnet has the rhyme scheme ABAB CDCD EFEF GG.

21. **C.**

In this passage, James uses an extended metaphor ("darkened the world, the shadows had begun to gather, had put out the lights one by one, certain corners of her prospect that were impenetrably black") to show how the protagonist's "light" or happiness in marriage is being extinguished bit by bit by her untrustworthy husband.

22. **D.**

The Misanthrope, by the actor/playwright Molière, or Jean-Baptiste Poquelin, was a comedy that exemplified the classical values of order and control in its witty verse and clever situations. In the Neoclassical Period in France, Molière dominated comedy, while Corneille and Racine were the leading tragic playwrights.

23. **A.**

The three parts of *The Divine Comedy* make up an allegory representing the soul's upward journey through Hell *(Inferno)* and Purgatory *(Purgatorio)* and finally to Heaven *(Paradiso)*. Each part also uses allegory, as in the *Inferno*'s representation of the Christian soul seeing sin for what it actually is.

24. **C.**

Examples of epic poems include *The Epic of Gilgamesh*, one of the first works of literature to be preserved in writing, and Homer's *Iliad* and *Odyssey*, about the Trojan War and the adventures of the Trojan general Odysseus.

25. **B.**

In this passage, the narrator reveals her ambivalence about her name by comparing its positive meaning in English to its more negative connotations for her in Spanish. Yet she expresses a certain pride that her name as it is pronounced in Spanish "is made out of a softer something like silver."

26. **C.**

Both poems portray a center of power—"Ozymandias, King of Kings" and an Africa that was the "Cradle of Power"—that has declined from ancient splendor into decay and darkness, thus expressing the vanity and fleeting nature of great power ("Nothing beside remains," "Yet all things were in vain!").

27. **A.**

The example demonstrates that quantitative measures of text complexity, such as various readability scales and the Coh-Metrix analysis system, can be misleading when used with texts that, like *The Grapes of Wrath,* have straightforward syntax and vocabulary yet present sophisticated themes and ideas that require higher-level background knowledge and inference skills.

28. **A.**

Lincoln's metaphorical statement that a house divided against itself cannot stand indicates his belief that the United States must settle the question of slavery one way or another or risk being permanently broken apart over the issue. Of course, as president, Lincoln signed the Emancipation Proclamation, bringing an end to slavery in the U.S.

29. **A.**

Postcolonial analysis examines literary works as examples of western colonialism and imperialism and tries to show how these works helped further ideas of racial and cultural inequality. For example, a postcolonial analysis of Shakespeare's *The Tempest* might focus on the character of Caliban and how he represents a culture that has been colonized and oppressed by western Europeans as represented by Prospero.

30. **C.**

The paragraph discusses Lévi-Strauss's idea about the meaning and structure of language. He is a structuralist who believes that genre conventions such as myths are like codes or signs in that they convey meaning independently of the actual words in a written text. Structuralist theory holds that certain underlying patterns and symmetries are common to the literatures of almost all societies and cultures. The quote from Lévi-Strauss in the paragraph comes from his essay "The Structural Study of Myth."

31. **D.**

In this excerpt, the author compares the challenges that a riverboat pilot faces to those faced by an ocean steamship captain or a locomotive conductor. The author's main purpose is to show that the riverboat pilot's task—"guiding one of these gigantic steamboats along the twisting, shifting, treacherous channel of the river"—is more difficult than piloting other modes of transportation.

32. **D.**

The passage from *Daniel Deronda* begins with a simple sentence, but then includes two long, complicated sentences featuring several independent and dependent clauses joined variously by a dash, a colon, and a semicolon. There are no multiple layers of meaning and background knowledge is not necessary to understand the passage. The language is fairly conventional. However, the sentence structure would probably present difficulties for eleventh-grade readers.

33. **B.**

Locating and totaling specific occurrences of words and phrases in a printed text can be very time consuming. An electronic text allows researchers and scholars to use a search engine to locate all the instances in which a specific word or phrase occurs.

34. **C.**

To place the poem in context, a teacher should elicit that Wheatley's first readers would have read the work as a statement of understandable gratitude and surprising assertiveness by a remarkable young woman who, uncharacteristically for African Americans at the time, could write sophisticated poetry. On the other hand, readers of today are probably jarred by a statement of gratitude from a person living in slavery and might assume that the poem is intended to be ironic or can only be read ironically.

35. **A.**

Stream of consciousness is a literary device in which the unfiltered thoughts of a character, often fragmentary or repetitive, are presented in words.

36. **B.**

Cervantes parodies the chivalric romances of his time by having Don Quixote ride off on adventures mounted on an old nag of a horse, tilt at windmills he sees as giants, and choose as his lady fair a village girl renowned for her salted pork.

37. **C.**

The Latin phrase *deus ex machina* means "god from the machine," referring to the method by which gods were lowered onto the stage during a play to rescue characters from a desperate situation. Today, the phrase refers to any unexpected or improbable turn of events brought in by a playwright to solve the problems of the plot.

38. **D.**

In third-person omniscient point of view, an all-knowing narrator reports on the actions, thoughts, and dialogue of all the characters.

39. **B.**

Since the main purpose of the brochure is to describe clearly and concisely how to improve one's eating habits, the bullets are an important text feature because they call attention to the important details and help readers locate and distinguish each point easily.

40. **B.**

While C is a possible source for this information, the easiest method would be to consult a reliable database on the Internet such as IMDb.

Composition and Rhetoric

41. **A.**

The focus of the paragraph is on the life and work of Cuban-American novelist Oscar Hijuelos. The Morningside Heights section in Manhattan is relevant as the place where Hijuelos grew up, but the sentence about its status today is an irrelevant digression. It upsets the logical flow of the paragraph and should be deleted.

42. **B.**

In Sentence 2, the use of the past perfect continuous tense ("had been writing") is unnecessary and incorrect. The simple past tense ("wrote") matches the verb tense used throughout the paragraph.

43. **A.**

In direct quotations, an inserted explanatory phrase should always be enclosed in brackets to signal the reader that it is not a part of the quoted material. For example: "In the interview, Nabokov lamented the *poshlost* [smug philistinism] that he saw everywhere in American popular fiction."

44. **C.**

In revising an essay, the writer should consider whether the structure includes a strong introduction, a clear sequence of main points and supporting details, and a strong conclusion. While structure can be addressed in the drafting and editing stages, it is probably most usefully adjusted in the revising stage.

45. **D.**

An appositive is a noun or noun phrase that renames another noun nearby. Here, the phrase "a great French painter of the twentieth century" renames the noun "Henri Matisse."

46. **B.**

Roosevelt emphasizes that thoughts of appeasement are basically "wishful thinking" and should be abandoned. The price of making peace with the Nazis, he says, is "total surrender."

47. **C.**

Roosevelt gives examples of the failures of appeasement toward the Nazis in the past ("That is the same dangerous form of wishful thinking which has destroyed the powers of resistance of so many conquered peoples") in order to predict that American attempts at appeasement will also fail ("There can be no appeasement with ruthlessness"). Roosevelt's metaphors are vivid and provoke emotional response ("There can be no reasoning with an incendiary bomb"), but they are in service of a logical argument about the foolhardiness of appeasement.

48. **D.**

The clausal modifier "As I headed for the frozen treats," preceding the independent clause "my heart leaped inside my chest," is most effective in setting up a sudden change in the formerly relaxed and confident attitude of the narrator. This modifying clause also makes the most sense chronologically, since the narrator would not be thinking about the consequences or realizing his predicament until after the door has slammed shut and induced his panic.

49. **A.**

The "slippery slope" argument is based on the idea that if a first step is taken, then a second and third step will follow inevitably, until a disaster occurs like a person sliding on a slippery incline until he or she falls to the bottom.

50. **B.**

Since the review is for ordinary newspaper readers rather than classical music aficionados, it should describe the symphony's performance in clear, mostly nontechnical language. Answer choice B gives the best capsule review of the performance; the other versions feature too much history and biography (A), ignorance of the basics of symphonic performance (C), or intellectual self-display (D).

PRACTICE TEST 1

CSET: English Subtest II

Also available at the REA Study Center (*www.rea.com/studycenter*)

This practice test is also available online at the REA Study Center. The CSET: English test is only offered as a computer-based exam; therefore, we recommend that you take the online version of the practice test to receive these added benefits:

- **Timed testing conditions** – helps you gauge how much time you can spend on each question

- **Automatic scoring** – find out how you did on the test, instantly

- **On-screen detailed explanations of answers** – gives you the correct answer and explains why the other answer choices are wrong

- **Diagnostic score reports** – pinpoint where you're strongest and where you need to focus your study

Practice Test 1, Subtest II
Answer Sheet

1. Ⓐ Ⓑ Ⓒ Ⓓ
2. Ⓐ Ⓑ Ⓒ Ⓓ
3. Ⓐ Ⓑ Ⓒ Ⓓ
4. Ⓐ Ⓑ Ⓒ Ⓓ
5. Ⓐ Ⓑ Ⓒ Ⓓ
6. Ⓐ Ⓑ Ⓒ Ⓓ
7. Ⓐ Ⓑ Ⓒ Ⓓ
8. Ⓐ Ⓑ Ⓒ Ⓓ
9. Ⓐ Ⓑ Ⓒ Ⓓ
10. Ⓐ Ⓑ Ⓒ Ⓓ
11. Ⓐ Ⓑ Ⓒ Ⓓ
12. Ⓐ Ⓑ Ⓒ Ⓓ
13. Ⓐ Ⓑ Ⓒ Ⓓ
14. Ⓐ Ⓑ Ⓒ Ⓓ
15. Ⓐ Ⓑ Ⓒ Ⓓ
16. Ⓐ Ⓑ Ⓒ Ⓓ
17. Ⓐ Ⓑ Ⓒ Ⓓ
18. Ⓐ Ⓑ Ⓒ Ⓓ
19. Ⓐ Ⓑ Ⓒ Ⓓ
20. Ⓐ Ⓑ Ⓒ Ⓓ
21. Ⓐ Ⓑ Ⓒ Ⓓ
22. Ⓐ Ⓑ Ⓒ Ⓓ
23. Ⓐ Ⓑ Ⓒ Ⓓ
24. Ⓐ Ⓑ Ⓒ Ⓓ
25. Ⓐ Ⓑ Ⓒ Ⓓ

26. Ⓐ Ⓑ Ⓒ Ⓓ
27. Ⓐ Ⓑ Ⓒ Ⓓ
28. Ⓐ Ⓑ Ⓒ Ⓓ
29. Ⓐ Ⓑ Ⓒ Ⓓ
30. Ⓐ Ⓑ Ⓒ Ⓓ
31. Ⓐ Ⓑ Ⓒ Ⓓ
32. Ⓐ Ⓑ Ⓒ Ⓓ
33. Ⓐ Ⓑ Ⓒ Ⓓ
34. Ⓐ Ⓑ Ⓒ Ⓓ
35. Ⓐ Ⓑ Ⓒ Ⓓ
36. Ⓐ Ⓑ Ⓒ Ⓓ
37. Ⓐ Ⓑ Ⓒ Ⓓ
38. Ⓐ Ⓑ Ⓒ Ⓓ
39. Ⓐ Ⓑ Ⓒ Ⓓ
40. Ⓐ Ⓑ Ⓒ Ⓓ
41. Ⓐ Ⓑ Ⓒ Ⓓ
42. Ⓐ Ⓑ Ⓒ Ⓓ
43. Ⓐ Ⓑ Ⓒ Ⓓ
44. Ⓐ Ⓑ Ⓒ Ⓓ
45. Ⓐ Ⓑ Ⓒ Ⓓ
46. Ⓐ Ⓑ Ⓒ Ⓓ
47. Ⓐ Ⓑ Ⓒ Ⓓ
48. Ⓐ Ⓑ Ⓒ Ⓓ
49. Ⓐ Ⓑ Ⓒ Ⓓ
50. Ⓐ Ⓑ Ⓒ Ⓓ

Practice Test 1, Subtest II
Language, Linguistics, and Literacy

1. Shakespeare apparently pronounced *clean* to rhyme with *lane*, while today it rhymes with *bean*. This is an example of which of the following?

   A. the influence of printed books on English pronunciation

   B. the effect of the Great Vowel Shift

   C. the variations in English pronunciation due to dialect

   D. the shift in English from being a Germanic-based language to a Germanic-Francophone hybrid

2. Which of the following best describes Noam Chomsky's concept of Universal Grammar?

   A. the genetic predisposition or innate capacity of human beings to learn and use language

   B. the grammatical rules that govern subject-verb agreement in a language

   C. the branch of linguistics that deals with syntax and sentence structure

   D. the process by which a person learns a second language

3. Which of the following words contains three phonemes?

   A. thrill

   B. tray

   C. chandelier

   D. ridiculous

4. **Read the sentence below. Then answer the question that follows.**

    What disturbed Trey was being disregarded by everyone.

    Which of the following changes would make this sentence unambiguous?

    A.   Change the word *disturbed* to *seemed to disturb*.

    B.   Insert the words *so thoroughly* after *Trey*.

    C.   Insert the word *not* between *was* and *being*.

    D.   Insert the word *our* between *was* and *being*.

5. Which of the following best exemplifies how grammatical change in the English language occurs over time?

    A.   Derivational affixes that alter the meaning of a base word become standardized.

    B.   The word *weblog* is shortened into the word *blog*.

    C.   Demonstrative pronouns and adjectives such as *this, that, these,* and *those* become gender neutral.

    D.   Thousands of French words such as *bouquet* and *chandelier* are adopted into English.

6. Which of the following is the best definition of a morpheme?

    A.   the smallest unit of sound in a language

    B.   a letter or combination of letters that represent a sound in a language

    C.   the smallest unit of meaning in a language

    D.   another word for the grammar of a language

7. A simplified language that is derived from two or more languages evolves over time into a richer language with a more complex structure and larger vocabulary. What is the term for the new, richer language?

    A.   pidgin

    B.   Creole

    C.   interlanguage

    D.   dialect

8.   The study of pragmatics includes which of the following topics?

   A.   the relationship between the structure of a word and its meaning

   B.   the alteration in a word's meaning over time

   C.   the uses of different types of sentences and phrases in different contexts

   D.   the acquisition of grammatical rules in a second language

9.   Which of the following words contains an overt inflectional ending?

   A.   fastens

   B.   television

   C.   assertive

   D.   knapsack

10.   **Use the diagram below to answer the question that follows.**

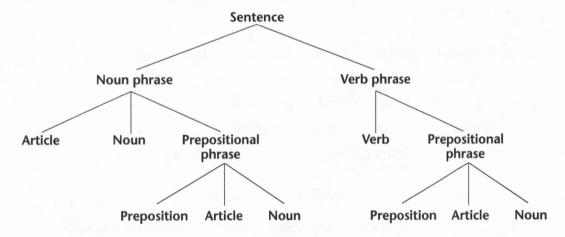

   This diagram represents the structure of which of the following sentences?

   A.   The detective in my story likes to ask questions.

   B.   A cloudy day provided a break from the heat.

   C.   A cat in the alley yowls when it is hungry.

   D.   The shop around the corner opens in the morning.

11. Which of the following nouns is formed by adding a derivational suffix to a verb?

    A.   establishment

    B.   bushy

    C.   happiness

    D.   artistry

12. Which of the words below contain a base word and a prefix?

    I.   tribunal

    II.   relinquish

    III. reapply

    IV.   trilingual

    A.   I, II

    B.   II, III

    C.   III, IV

    D.   I, III, IV

13. **Read the dialogue below. Then answer the question that follows.**

    Nelda: It's so hot outside!

    Richard: I think it's hotter *inside* right now.

    Nelda: I'll turn up the air-conditioning.

    Richard: And it's so dark in here that I can barely see the pages of my book.

    Nelda: Is your arm broken?

    To a person who has a pragmatic knowledge of American English, it's obvious that Nelda's meaning is:

    A.   The light in the room is just fine.

    B.   Let me turn on the lights for you.

    C.   Your arm looks strange to me.

    D.   Turn on the lights yourself.

14. Which of the following words was borrowed from the French language?

    A.   avant-garde

    B.   angst

    C.   ad infinitum

    D.   taboo

15. Which of the following words has a predictable pronunciation based on reliable sound-symbol correspondences?

    A.   know

    B.   mantel

    C.   friction

    D.   wreath

16. Terms such as *firefighter, mail carrier, flight attendant*, and *police officer* represent which of the following developments in contemporary American English usage?

    A.   substituting technical names for job titles with shopworn associations

    B.   employing gender-neutral terms for occupations to reflect modern workplace practices

    C.   using euphemistic job descriptions that make certain occupations sound more impressive

    D.   inventing names for new occupations that did not exist years ago

17. **Read the sentence below. Then answer the question that follows.**

> *Mr. Webster could be irascible in the morning before he'd had his coffee, but later in the day his sunny disposition tended to re-emerge.*

Which group of words in the sentence is most helpful as a context clue to the meaning of *irascible*?

    A.   Mr. Webster could be

    B.   in the morning before he'd had his coffee

    C.   but later in the day

    D.   his sunny disposition tended to re-emerge

18. Which statement is the best example of the influence of an affective factor on the acquisition of a second language?

    A. The second-language learner uses words from his or her first language when speaking the second language but not when writing it.

    B. The adult second-language learner finds it extremely difficult to form second-language sounds that do not occur in his or her first language.

    C. The second-language learner employs familiar vocabulary to mentally form sentences before speaking them.

    D. The second-language learner makes reasoned guesses about word meanings in a text by recognizing cognates.

19. In which of the following aspects of language development are English-speaking children from different social and cultural backgrounds most likely to differ?

    A. style and structure of their oral narratives

    B. inferences they make about a speaker's intentions or desires

    C. use of coordinate structures in their oral language

    D. syntactic structures that they find easiest to learn

20. In which of the following sentences does the word *asked* function as a synonym for the word *inquired*?

    A. Mr. Groves asked his students to submit their term papers on Thursday.

    B. Cheryl asked the cashier if the store accepted a particular credit card.

    C. The price that the diner asked for pancakes was cheap compared to other restaurants nearby.

    D. New government regulations asked employers to file additional paperwork each quarter.

21. During which stage of development did the French language have its greatest effect on English?

    A. Old English

    B. Middle English

    C. Early Modern English

    D. Late Modern English

22. The word *carnivorous* comes from the Latin root *carn-,* meaning "flesh." Which of the following words also derives from this Latin root?

    A.   cardiovascular

    B.   carjacking

    C.   carpenter

    D.   incarnate

23. Which type of second-language learner would probably acquire a second language most easily?

    A.   a businessperson whose chances of career advancement depend on fluency in the second language

    B.   a visitor to a country where the second language is spoken and the person interacts with restaurant personnel in the second language

    C.   an immigrant to the country where the second language is spoken who feels comfortable and accepted by speakers of that language

    D.   a high school student who has been taking mandatory classes in the secondary language since elementary school

24. A student for whom English is the second language says, "I baked a pie and taked it to school." This student is displaying what kind of linguistic behavior?

    A.   transfer

    B.   negative transfer

    C.   hypercorrection

    D.   borrowing

25. To encourage a reader to use visual-imaging skills to better understand a word's meaning, which of the following questions would a teacher most likely ask?

    A.   "How would you use a glossary or dictionary to locate the definition of this word?"

    B.   "In what literary genre are you most likely to see this word?"

    C.   "What features does this word have in common with other words you know or have seen?"

    D.   "Can you describe an incident from your own life that reminds you of this word?"

26. When a person changes dialects or goes from formal to informal speech depending on which group he or she is interacting with, that person is engaging in which of the following?

    A. borrowing

    B. code-switching

    C. hypercorrection

    D. transfer

27. **Use the sentence below to answer the question that follows.**

    > Having built a large lead, the Dodgers were *content* to coast through the late innings of the game.

    Which strategy would be most effective for a reader to use to pronounce the italicized word correctly?

    A. Use content clues and analyze the syntax of the sentence.

    B. Recognize the word as a high-frequency sight word.

    C. Think about the differences between British and American pronunciation.

    D. Compare the word to similar words.

28. A student can use predicting most effectively as a reading comprehension strategy if the student is:

    A. familiar with the content-area vocabulary.

    B. able to refer to a text's introduction and glossary.

    C. able to recognize faulty logic or reasoning.

    D. familiar with different genres and their conventions.

29. **A writer must develop an essay in support of the thesis statement below.**

    The Shakespearean tragedies *Hamlet* and *Othello* would be completely different if the hero of each play became the protagonist of the other.

    Given the writer's purpose, which of the following organizational structures would be most appropriate for this essay?

    A. enumeration and description

    B. comparison and contrast

    C. problem and solution

    D. definition and example

30. A hybrid language such as Spanglish is one usual result of which kind of linguistic behavior?

    A. borrowing

    B. hypercorrection

    C. code-switching

    D. negative transfer

31. Only a student who is able to read on the level of applied comprehension can do which of the following when reading a story?

    A. obtain the basic facts and details of the story

    B. predict the outcome of the story using prior knowledge

    C. move beyond the story to think critically and creatively about its implications

    D. make inferences and draw conclusions about the story

32. Which pre-reading activity would be most helpful for a high school class that is preparing to read a Native American creation myth?

    A. using a dictionary to find the derivation of the word *myth*

    B. analyzing how Native American creation myths reflect the values of Native Americans today

    C. discussing their prior knowledge and past readings of creation stories from other cultures

    D. skimming the text to locate words that are difficult to spell or pronounce

33. Which of the following is the branch of linguistics that deals with the internal structure and form of words?

   A.   etymology

   B.   semantics

   C.   phonology

   D.   morphology

34. Which of the following sentences would be most appropriate for an academic essay about Shakespeare's *A Midsummer Night's Dream*?

   A.   Pretty quick it gets to be obvious that Bottom doesn't have a brain, because he can't even see that his head has been turned into an ass's head and he looks like a fool, which is "what these mortals be."

   B.   For all his bluster and overconfidence, Bottom proves to be a vital character who realizes he has been allowed, by whatever means, to experience something magical.

   C.   The legerdemain that Puck mistakenly imposes upon Bottom emphasizes the hegemony of the fairy world over the world of mere mortals while also demonstrating Bottom's essentially innocent readiness to accept whatever befalls him.

   D.   Bottom (my favorite character by far!) has the funniest spell put on him by Puck (a hilarious mistake!), but even with the head of an ass Bottom keeps his good nature and basic innocence (quite an accomplishment!).

35. Encountering an unfamiliar word in a text, a reader sounds the word out using phonics and syllabication skills. The reader will then probably be able to grasp the word's meaning if:

   A.   the word's part of speech is known to the reader.

   B.   the word is a homophone of a more familiar word.

   C.   the word is in the reader's oral vocabulary.

   D.   the word's language of origin is known to the reader.

36. The words *anachronism, chronicle, chronometer,* and *chronological* can be analyzed as

   A.   words with inflectional affixes.

   B.   borrowed words.

   C.   compound words.

   D.   a word family.

37. Which of the following is the best definition of the term *orthography*?

    A.   a standardized system for writing words with the proper letters according to accepted rules of usage

    B.   a detailed account of a word's origin and derivation

    C.   the process by which people acquire the ability to understand and use words

    D.   the study of meaning in language, both oral and contextual

38. Research indicates that the human brain's capacity to acquire language seems to diminish over time. This apparently occurs most markedly after age five or after a person reaches puberty. Which linguistic theory accounts for this phenomenon?

    A.   the Critical Period hypothesis

    B.   the Acquisition-Learning hypothesis

    C.   the Natural Order hypothesis

    D.   the Affective Filter hypothesis

39. In which reading comprehension activity do readers use a chart to categorize information, analyze ideas, compare items, and make inferences about what they read?

    A.   think-aloud summaries

    B.   central question diagram

    C.   semantic feature analysis

    D.   character report card

40. In which of the following sentences does the underlined word function as a non-count noun?

    A.   I was flattered by my teacher's <u>compliment</u>.

    B.   Her advice always contained much <u>wisdom</u>.

    C.   Each <u>leaf</u> is rendered in great detail.

    D.   Those <u>books</u> must go back to the library.

41. In which of the following sentences does a prepositional phrase modify a verb?

    A.   Today's rainstorm provides an opportunity to work indoors.

    B.   The crowd on the rooftop watched the fireworks.

    C.   Charmed by her accent, the director hired the French actress.

    D.   The band played several songs during the broadcast.

42. **Read the sentence below. Then answer the question.**

    _____ our team scored thirty-five points, we still lost the game.

    Which subordinating conjunction should be used to complete this sentence?

    A. Until

    B. Because

    C. Although

    D. Since

43. In which of the following sentences is the underlined portion a noun phrase?

    A. To those who say writing is too difficult, I recommend attending a writing class.

    B. Writing for five hours every day of the week required great discipline.

    C. To complete the first draft of a novel is the goal of each student in our writing class.

    D. Our teacher made it a priority to offer her encouragement.

44. Read the sentences below. Then answer the question that follows.

    • Toni Morrison is an African American writer.

    • She is the author of *Beloved*.

    Which of the following sentences combines the two sentences using an embedded appositional phrase?

    A. Toni Morrison is an African American writer; she is the author of *Beloved*.

    B. Toni Morrison, the author of *Beloved,* is an African American writer.

    C. An African American writer, Toni Morrison is the author of *Beloved*.

    D. The author of *Beloved* is Toni Morrison, an African American writer.

45. In which of the following sentences is the underlined portion an adverb clause?

    A. The stadium was surrounded by kiosks loaded with T-shirts and souvenirs.

    B. Whoever wanted a ticket to the show was out of luck.

    C. Fans who had waited outside for hours rushed inside to get good seats.

    D. Police officers monitored the crowd when the concert ended.

46. Which of the following suffixes typically changes an adjective into a verb?

    A.   -ize

    B.   -ous

    C.   -ness

    D.   -ence

47. Which of the following word sets is composed of verbs that function as modals?

    A.   winning, reading, coasting

    B.   go, stay, sleep

    C.   could, must, ought

    D.   simmered, boiled, sharpened

48. In which of the following sentences is the underlined portion a verbal phrase?

    A.   We had some time to explore the city after the lecture was over.

    B.   My uncle gave me fifty dollars, a wonderful present.

    C.   On the next block, we found a charming bookstore.

    D.   Browsing in bookstores is Matthew's favorite hobby.

49. Which of the following sentences uses a coordinating conjunction to connect two independent clauses?

    A.   Despite the rain that fell last week, the ground is still dry and cracked.

    B.   Summer temperatures are very warm here, and the grass generally turns brown.

    C.   The weather report predicted more rain for tomorrow, which will certainly help.

    D.   While extremely hot, this is far from the hottest summer we've had in this area.

50. A student has just finished reading a chapter on volcanoes in a science textbook. Which question would be most likely to help the student synthesize the key concepts in the chapter?

    A.   How does the environment change as the result of a volcanic eruption?

    B.   What does a volcanologist do?

    C.   What are three differences between an active and an inactive volcano?

    D.   Which area of the world currently has the most volcanic activity?

Practice Test 1, Subtest II
Answer Key

1.	B	18.	C	35.	C
2.	A	19.	A	36.	D
3.	B	20.	B	37.	A
4.	D	21.	B	38.	A
5.	C	22.	D	39.	C
6.	C	23.	C	40.	B
7.	B	24.	B	41.	D
8.	C	25.	D	42.	C
9.	A	26.	B	43.	C
10.	D	27.	A	44.	B
11.	A	28.	D	45.	D
12.	C	29.	B	46.	A
13.	D	30.	A	47.	C
14.	A	31.	C	48.	D
15.	B	32.	C	49.	B
16.	B	33.	D	50.	A
17.	D	34.	B		

Practice Test 1, Subtest II
Progress Chart: Multiple-Choice Questions

Below are grids that group questions by subject-matter requirement codes. Place a checkmark in the box below each question that you answered correctly and calculate the percentage of correct answers for each area. This will give you an indication of your strengths and weaknesses and show you which topics need further study.

Human Language Structures   SMR Code 2.1   ____/21

1	2	3	4	5	6	8	9	10	11

12	13	14	15	16	20	21	27	33	35

36

Acquisition and Development of Language and Literacy   SMR Code 2.2   ____/18

7	17	18	19	22	23	24	25	26	28

29	30	31	32	34	38	39	50

Grammatical Structures of English   SMR Code 2.3   ____/11

37	40	41	42	43	44	45	46	47	48

49

Practice Test 1, Subtest II
Detailed Answer Explanations

Language, Linguistics, and Literacy

1. **B.**

   In the Great Vowel Shift of the fifteenth century, pronunciation of the long vowels in English slowly changed—although in linguistic terms the changes were relatively rapid. As in this example from Shakespeare, long *e* was originally pronounced like the *e* in *there* or the *a* in *fate*, but after the Great Vowel Shift, long *e* was pronounced like the *e* in *sweep*, as it is today.

2. **A.**

   Universal Grammar is the idea that a facility for language is programmed into every human brain. Chomsky's theory emphasized that people share an innate and universal set of linguistic structures, which accounts for why young children can learn a new language so easily.

3. **B.**

   The phoneme is the smallest unit of speech sound. It combines with other units of speech sound to form a word. For example, the word *tray* contains three phonemes: /t/, /r/, and /a/. The word *thrill* contains four phonemes: /th/, /r/, /i/, and /l/. It is important to remember that a phoneme is *not* the same as a syllable.

4. **D.**

   As it stands, the sentence can mean either "Trey was disturbed at being disregarded by everyone," or "What was disturbing Trey was being disregarded by everyone." Adding *our* between *was* and *being* fixes the meaning as "Our being disregarded by everyone was what disturbed Trey." This is an example of syntax, or the knowledge of sentence structures.

5. **C.**

   In Old English, demonstrative pronouns and adjectives were gender-specific, with each word's gender determined by inflection instead of by meaning. Middle English changed these demonstrative pronouns and adjectives to the fixed, gender-neutral forms *this, that, these,* and *those*.

6. **C.**

   Morphemes are studied in the branch of linguistics called morphology, which deals with the internal structure and forms of words.

7. **B.**

A simplified language that is derived from the merging of two or more languages is called a pidgin. It is a contact language used by people who do not share a common language in a certain area. If the pidgin continues to develop over time and add vocabulary, and acquires native speakers, it becomes a Creole.

8. **C.**

Pragmatics focuses on language as a tool for communication and is concerned with how different types of sentences or phrases are used in different contexts and for different purposes. In other words, pragmatic theory is concerned with a speaker's intended meaning rather than the literal meaning of an utterance. For example, different forms of speech can be used to request something, assert something, or inquire about something.

9. **A.**

The *s* in *fastens* is an overt inflectional suffix that functions as the indicator for the present-tense, third-person singular form of the verb *fasten*. In English, inflectional suffixes never change the base word's part of speech—*fasten* and *fastens* are both verbs. A derivational suffix such as *–ive* changes the part of speech of the word to which it is attached.

10. **D.**

The sentence in choice D has the same structure as the diagram, including the noun phrase ("The shop around the corner") and the verb phrase ("opens in the morning"). The phrases can be divided into the same individual parts of speech as shown in the diagram (e.g., the article *The,* the noun *shop,* and the prepositional phrase *around the corner*). Each level of the diagram corresponds to a level of syntactic structure.

11. **A.**

The noun *establishment* is formed by adding the derivational suffix *–ment* to the verb *establish.*

12. **C.**

The word *reapply* contains the base word *apply* and the prefix *re-*, which means "again." The word *trilingual* contains the base word *lingual* and the prefix *tri-*, which means "three." The *tri-* in *tribunal* and the *re-* in *relinquish* are not prefixes.

13. **D.**

To someone who lacks a pragmatic knowledge of American English, Nelda's last utterance might be puzzling. However, Nelda knows that Richard is asking her to turn on a light without actually making the request. When she asks, "Is your arm broken?" she is telling him to turn on the light himself.

14. **A.**

The French word *avant-garde* means "advance guard or vanguard." In English, it refers to an advanced artistic work or movement.

15. **B.**

The pronunciation of the word *mantel* is simple because of the reliable, predictable sound-symbol correspondences of its letters. Less predictable are the sound-symbol correspondences in the word *know* (the digraph *kn* pronounced as /n/), in the word *friction* (the digraph *ti* pronounced as /sh/), and in the word *wreath* (the digraph *wr* pronounced as /r/).

16. **B.**

All these terms are examples of gender-neutral workplace language. *Firefighter* is the gender-neutral replacement for *fireman*; *mail carrier* for *mailman* or *postman*; *flight attendant* for *stewardess*; and *police officer* for *policeman* or *patrolman*.

17. **D.**

Context clues are the words and sentences around the unfamiliar word that provide clues to its meaning. In the sentence, the words "his sunny disposition tended to re-emerge" indicate that *irascible* means the opposite of a "a sunny disposition, or "irritable or crabby."

18. **C.**

Affective factors are personal qualities such as empathy, self-esteem, extroversion, and ability to imitate that all positively affect the acquisition of language skills. Lack of these qualities can have negative consequences for a second-language learner. For example, a second-language learner who is embarrassed at producing incorrect utterances will try to avoid mistakes by mentally rehearsing known vocabulary and forming sentences before speaking them.

19. **A.**

Research indicates that social class has a major effect on how children use language, and that different social classes employ different language codes. Thus, a child's sociocultural circumstance may determine to a large degree his or her language usage and skills. For example, English-speaking children from different sociocultural backgrounds have been found to differ also in the style and structure of their spoken narratives, with some focusing on open-ended stories developed through free association and others on stories with a central topic or conclusion.

20. **B.**

In choices A and D, the word *asked* functions as a synonym for *required*. In choice C, it functions as a synonym for *charged*.

21. **B.**

Large changes in English vocabulary began about 1250—coinciding with the period of greatest influence regarding the French language and English. As Norman nobles settled into the English court, they brought with them many French words such as *bouquet* and *chandelier*. As Middle English became established among the merchant classes, it incorporated increasing numbers of French words. As a result, some 10,000 French words were adopted into Middle English.

22. **D.**

The word *incarnate,* from the Latin root *carn-,* means "to give bodily form or substance to"—as in "in the flesh."

23. **C.**

Research indicates that a second-language learner who wants to integrate into the culture in which the second language is spoken is more likely to be successful in learning the second language.

24. **B.**

Negative transfer is when a speaker uses skills from a previously learned behavior or topic but applies them incorrectly to a new topic. For example, a student who recalls that the past tense of *fake* is *faked* and then assumes that the past tense of *take* is *taked* is employing negative transfer.

25. **D.**

Visual imaging skills involve the student's ability to use personal images or experiences to comprehend a word's meaning. According to research, the more vivid the images are, the greater the reader's comprehension.

26. **B.**

A person with a good command of Standard English may be able to switch more easily between different modes of speaking or writing. For example, a teacher might employ Standard English in the classroom and use a more relaxed dialect with family members or friends.

27. **A.**

Using content clues and the syntax of the sentence, a reader could determine that *content* here is used as an adjective and refers to a relaxing of intensity, and so is pronounced with the stress on the second syllable.

28. **D.**

Genre expectation is an important part of the skill of predicting. For example, a reader who is approaching a tragedy will know that the hero or heroine is likely to die, and so will be better able to predict the outcome of certain scenes or plot lines.

29. **B.**

The thesis statement calls for the writer to compare and contrast the personal qualities of the characters Hamlet and Othello that would make their respective dramas different if their roles were switched.

30. **A.**

Borrowing is when a speaker switches into his or her first language and borrows single words or entire phrases for which the speaker knows no equivalent in the second language.

31. **C.**

A student reading on the level of applied comprehension might write a brief narrative describing the main character's circumstances ten years after the story's ending or describe the author's philosophy of life based on the story, its characters, and its implications.

32. **C.**

Drawing on the prior knowledge of the characteristics of a particular literary genre, such as creation myths from other cultures, can help with comprehension of a text from that genre.

33. **D.**

Morphology is concerned with the rules for the use of morphemes, or the smallest units of meaning, in a language. For example, the morphology of English allows its speakers to know that plural endings depend on the last sound of the word stem: *spatula/spatulas*; *patch/patches*.

34. **B.**

An academic essay on Shakespeare's *A Midsummer Night's Dream* should follow the conventions of Standard English and should not be stilted, overwrought, or breezy in style.

35. **C.**

A reader who has encountered a word only in the context of speaking the word and hearing it spoken may not immediately recognize the word in print. However, once the reader has sounded out the word, he or she is likely to match its printed form with its spoken equivalent and remember its correct meaning.

36. **D.**

A word family is a category of words built around the same word part. For example, the words *anachronism, chronicle, chronometer,* and *chronological* all include the word part *chron-*, which comes from the Greek word for "time."

37. **A.**

Orthography includes the spelling rules for a language. In English one of the main rules of orthography is "*i* before *e* except after *c*, or when sounded as *ay,* as in *neighbor* and *weigh*."

38. **A.**

Research indicates that second-language learners under the age of 15 tend to achieve greater proficiency in grammar, pronunciation, vocabulary, and comprehension than adult learners. One reason for this difference may be that the brain's language faculty either shuts down or becomes less accessible after a certain age. Thus an adult must use other cognitive mechanisms to learn a second language.

39. **C.**

Semantic feature analysis is a reading activity used primarily to examine how vocabulary words relate to one another and to expand content knowledge.

40. **B.**

A noncount noun, or mass noun, denotes a concept or substance (in this case, wisdom) that is not divisible into countable units. Noncount nouns are usually preceded in indefinite constructions by modifiers such as *some* or *much*.

41. **D.**

A prepositional phrase includes a preposition and its object plus any modifiers. In the sentence "The band played several songs during the broadcast," the word *during* serves as a preposition and the word *broadcast* is the object of the preposition. The entire phrase, "during the game," functions as an adverb modifying the verb *played*.

42. **C.**

The dependent clause in a complex sentence contains the subordinating conjunction. Here the sense is that something happened *despite* something else also happening.

43. **C.**

The infinitive phrase "To complete the first draft of a novel" is a noun phrase and serves as the subject of the sentence.

44. **B.**

An appositional phrase identifies or describes a nearby noun, as shown by the way "the author of *Beloved*" identifies Toni Morrison. An embedded appositional phrase is placed within the body of the sentence rather than coming at the beginning or end.

45. **D.**

Adverb clauses are phrases that begin with subordinating conjunctions and modify verbs, adjectives, and other adverbs. In the sentence "Police officers monitored the crowd when the concert ended," the word *when* serves as a subordinating conjunction and the entire phrase "when the concert ended" is an adverb clause modifying the verb *monitored*.

46. **A.**

The suffix –*ize* is often added to an adjective to create a verb. For example, adding –*ize* to the adjective *tender* creates the verb *tenderize*, meaning "to make tender."

47. **C.**

Modals, or modal auxiliary verbs, are a set of English verbs that are used with other verbs to express capability, possibility, willingness, suggestion, or something similar. Modals include *can, could, may, might, must, ought, shall, should, will,* and *would*.

48. **D.**

Verbals are formed from verbs but are not used as verbs in a sentence. In the sentence "Browsing in bookstores is Matthew's favorite hobby," the phrase "Browsing in bookstores" is a gerund phrase that functions as a noun and the subject of the sentence.

49. **B.**

The sentence "Summer temperatures are very warm here, and the grass generally turns brown" consists of two independent clauses: "Summer temperatures are very warm here" and "the grass generally turns brown." An independent clause is a clause that can stand alone as a sentence. In this sentence, the two independent clauses are joined by the coordinating conjunction *and*.

50. **A.**

One of the best ways to help a reader comprehend and retain the information in a chapter is to ask questions that require the reader to synthesize the facts presented. Questions that simply require the reader to remember specific facts are less effective at improving comprehension.

PRACTICE TEST 1

CSET: English Subtest III

Also available at the REA Study Center (*www.rea.com/studycenter*)

This practice test is also available online at the REA Study Center. The CSET: English test is only offered as a computer-based exam; therefore, we recommend that you take the online version of the practice test to receive these added benefits:

- **Timed testing conditions** – helps you gauge how much time you can spend on each question

- **On-screen detailed analysis of sample essays** – guides you to a 4-point response

SCORING THE CSET: ENGLISH SUBTEST III

In CSET: English Subtest III, you will have 2 hours to respond to two constructed-response writing prompts.

For each constructed-response question in Subtest III, you should write a response of about 800–1,000 words, although you may write longer responses if you prefer. Each response will be assessed according to the subject-matter knowledge and skills they demonstrate, *not* writing ability. You should, however, write clearly enough to allow for a valid judgment of your knowledge and skills regarding the subject matter. You should write for an audience of educators in the field.

Your response essays will be scored by California educators using focused holistic scoring. The scorers will evaluate the overall effectiveness of your essay responses with a focus on the performance characteristics that have been judged most important for CSET: English Subtest III.

These performance characteristics, or writing standards, are established by the California Commission on Teacher Credentialing and include the following:

> **Purpose:** The extent to which the response focuses on and accomplishes the task set by the prompt in relation to relevant CSET: English subject-matter requirements.

> **Subject matter knowledge:** The extent to which the response applies accurate subject matter knowledge as described in the relevant CSET: English subject-matter requirements.

> **Support:** The extent to which the response employs quality, appropriate supporting evidence in relation to CSET: English subject-matter requirements.

> **Depth and breadth of understanding:** the extent to which the response shows understanding of the relevant CSET: English subject-matter requirements.

Your essay responses will be scored based on the following scoring scale:

Scoring Scale

4: To earn a **4-point score**, your response must show that you have a sophisticated grasp of the relevant knowledge and skills as defined in the subject matter requirements for CSET: English. These include:

- The ability to address the specific purpose of the assignment comprehensively and without distractions in order to accomplish the assigned task.

- The ability to select and include relevant supporting evidence and examples that demonstrate your overall understanding of the subject matter.

A 4-point essay demonstrates that you have a thorough understanding of the assignment and the relevant subject matter.

3: To earn a **3-point score**, your response must show that you have an overall or general understanding of the relevant knowledge and skills as defined in the subject matter requirements for CSET: English. These include:

- The ability to recognize the overall purpose of the assignment in order to accomplish the assigned task adequately.

- The ability to recognize and apply some accurate information and relevant supporting evidence to the given subject matter.

A 3-point essay demonstrates that you have an adequate or sufficient understanding of the assignment.

2: To earn a **2-point score**, your response will show that you have a basic, partial, or insufficient understanding of the knowledge and skills as defined in the subject-matter requirements for CSET: English. These include:

- The ability to address the assignment's purpose only partially or not at all.

- The ability to recognize and apply only a limited amount, if any, of relevant supporting evidence, demonstrating only a partial understanding of the subject matter.

A 2-point essay demonstrates that you have a limited, partial, or unsatisfactory understanding of the assignment.

1: To earn a **1-point score**, your response will show that you have little or no understanding of the knowledge and skills as defined in the subject-matter requirements for CSET: English. These include:

- The lack of ability to recognize or achieve the most basic elements and goals of the assignment.

- The lack of ability to recognize or apply basic relevant supporting evidence, demonstrating little or no understanding of the subject matter.

A 1-point essay demonstrates that you have a limited, partial, or unsatisfactory understanding of the assignment.

U: A grade of **"U" (Unscorable)** is given to essays that are completely unrelated to the assignment, illegible, written in a language other than English, and/or lack a sufficient amount of your own original writing. Most problems that cause an essay to earn a "U" are solvable by simply slowing down and pacing yourself as you systematically respond to each question or prompt.

B: A grade of **"B" (Blank)** is given to essay responses left blank. Never leave a test question blank if at all possible.

Practice Test 1, Subtest III Composition and Rhetoric; Reading Literature and Informational Texts

Practice Question 1

Read the two selections below; then complete the exercise that follows.

Selection I: "Laziness," a poem
by Robert Service

1 Let laureates sing with rapturous swing
2 Of the wonder and glory of work;
3 Let pulpiteers preach and with passion impeach
4 The indolent wretches who shirk.
5 No doubt they are right: in the stress of the fight
6 It's the slackers who go to the wall;
7 So though it's my shame I perversely proclaim
8 It's fine to do nothing at all.

9 It's fine to recline on the flat of one's spine,
10 With never a thought in one's head:
11 It's lovely to lie staring up at the sky
12 When others are earning their bread.
13 It's great to feel one with the soil and the sun,
14 Drowned deep in the grasses so tall;
15 Oh it's noble to sweat, pounds and dollars to get,
16 But—it's grand to do nothing at all.

17 So sing to the praise of the fellows who laze
18 Instead of lambasting the soil;
19 The vagabonds gay who lounge by the way,
20 Conscientious objectors to toil.
21 But lest you should think, by this spatter of ink,
22 The Muses still hold me in thrall,
23 I'll round out my rhyme, and (until the next time)
24 Work like hell—doing nothing at all.

Selection II: Excerpt from *Bleak House*, a novel
by Charles Dickens

[1] I gathered from the conversation, that Mr. Skimpole had been educated for the medical profession, and had once lived in his professional capacity, in the household of a German prince. [2] He told us, however, that as he had always been a mere child in points of weights and measures, and had never known anything about

them (except that they disgusted him), he had never been able to prescribe with the requisite accuracy of detail. [3] In fact, he said, he had no head for detail. [4] And he told us, with great humour, that when he was wanted to bleed the prince, or physic any of his people, he was generally found lying on his back, in bed, reading the newspapers, or making fancy sketches in pencil, and couldn't come. [5] The prince, at last objecting to this, "in which," said Mr. Skimpole, in the frankest manner, "he was perfectly right," the engagement terminated, and Mr. Skimpole having (as he added with delightful gaiety) "nothing to lie upon but love, fell in love, and married, and surrounded himself with rosy cheeks." [6] His good friend Jarndyce and some other of his good friends then helped him, in quicker or slower succession, to several openings in life; but to no purpose, for he must confess to two of the oldest infirmities in the world: one was, that he had no idea of time; the other, that he had no idea of money. [7] In consequence of which he never kept an appointment, never could transact any business, and never knew the value of anything! [8] Well! [9] So he had got on in life, and here he was! [10] He was very fond of reading the papers, very fond of making fancy sketches with a pencil, very fond of nature, very fond of art. [11] All he asked of society was, to let him live. [12] *That* wasn't much. [13] His wants were few. [14] Give him the papers, conversation, music, mutton, coffee, landscape, fruit in the season, a few sheets of Bristol-board, and a little claret, and he asked no more. [15] He was a mere child in the world, but he didn't cry for the moon. [16] He said to the world, "Go your several ways in peace! [17] Wear red coats, blue coats, lawn sleeves, put pens behind your ears, wear aprons; go after glory, holiness, commerce, trade, any object you prefer; only—let Harold Skimpole live!"

Write a critical essay in which you analyze the two selections, supporting your conclusions with specific evidence from the texts. Assume that you are writing for an educated audience knowledgeable about literary criticism. In your essay:

- identify a significant theme that the two texts share;

- compare and contrast the two writers' perspectives on the theme you have identified;

- examine how the two writers employ literary techniques, including genre features, literary elements, and rhetorical devices, to express their perspectives on this theme; and

- draw a conclusion that explains how the literary techniques you have identified affect the ideas conveyed in the texts.

Practice Question 2

Read "I Sing the Car Electric," an editorial written for a large metropolitan newspaper. After reading the editorial, complete the exercise that follows.

There's a silent revolution about to take place in the auto industry—silent because you can barely hear the new engines revving up. The revolution is in electric vehicles, or EVs. It won't be long before these sleek, silent automobiles are dominating American streets and highways.

EVs have long enjoyed the support of environmentalists, who seek to limit the carbon dioxide emissions that affect climate change as well as the harmful pollution from traditional engines that run on fossil fuels. Those concerned about energy security and world petroleum markets are also longtime fans. But increasingly the ranks of EV enthusiasts are being joined by ordinary drivers who don't have much of a political or environmental agenda.

Why are these drivers fired up about EVs? It comes down to the old standbys of car buying: performance and value. As the technology for EVs improves, they become more competitive with traditional vehicles that use an internal combustion engine (ICE). Soon the advantages that ICE vehicles have enjoyed over EVs will melt away completely.

The basic facts about EVs are simple enough. An EV features an electric motor for propulsion and a battery pack for storing electricity charged from the power grid. There are also many kinds of hybrid EVs, which mostly employ some combination of an electric motor and an ICE-powered generator for electricity.

The first thing one notices about an EV is its silence. Once the motor is started it makes almost no noise (and produces no noxious fumes). On a first test drive, drivers often question whether the motor is running. Even when it accelerates, the EV seems quiet as if it is coasting. The second thing one notices is the incredible response of the motor and power train. Pressing the gas pedal—or let's say, the power pedal—produces immediate acceleration. The motor doesn't have to shift through gears, so the EV accelerates much more rapidly and smoothly. One model from the EV company Tesla goes from zero to sixty in a quick 4.2 seconds. Reportedly, Tesla engineers had some concerns about the vehicle being too powerful.

So what are the drawbacks to this remarkable automobile? Admittedly, cost is one of them—for now. Prices of EVs are indeed higher for ICE vehicles of comparable size, but they are competitive and starting to come down. Generous government subsidies already make up some of the difference. And purchase price is only part of the EV story. The simpler mechanical setup of EVs often requires fewer replacement parts and less maintenance, which saves money over the lifetime of the vehicle. And electricity remains much less expensive than gasoline or diesel.

Then there is the issue of driving range. Most of today's EVs and hybrids have ranges on electric power of less than 100 miles. However, studies suggest that eighty percent of daily driving covers distances of 50 miles or less—well within the EV's capability. And prospective EV purchasers should not be deterred by lack of infrastructure for high-speed battery charging. It seems inevitable that reliable, standardized charging stations will soon become a common sight on American roadways.

Technology changes can occur with amazing speed in today's world, as proven by the now-ubiquitous smartphone. Electric vehicles are on the verge of just such a breakthrough in the United States. And with EVs' powerful but silent engines, the public may not even hear them coming.

Write a critical essay in which you analyze the editorial "I Sing the Car Electric." Assume that you are writing for an educated audience, and make sure to support your conclusions with evidence from the text. In your essay:

- summarize, in your own words, the author's main argument in this editorial;

- evaluate the author's reasoning;

- describe the author's methods of persuasion and use of rhetorical devices;

- identify the audience for which the author is most likely writing; and

- describe the extent to which the passage is likely to be effective in persuading this audience, and explain why.

Practice Test 1, Subtest III
Written Response Answer Sheets

Although the actual CSET: English test is computer-based and you will input your responses on a computer screen, use the answer sheets that follow to write your responses. For Subtest III, you will have 2 hours to complete the two constructed-response questions.

_____

_____

_____

_____

_____

_____

_____

_____

_____

_____

_____

_____

_____

_____

_____

Written Response Answer Sheets (cont'd)

_____

_____

_____

_____

_____

_____

_____

_____

_____

_____

_____

_____

_____

_____

_____

_____

_____

_____

_____

Written Response Answer Sheets *(cont'd)*

Written Response Answer Sheets *(cont'd)*

Practice Test 1, Subtest III
Sample Essays

Sample Response for Practice Question #1

4-Point Response

Robert Service's comic poem "Laziness" and the excerpt from Charles Dickens' novel *Bleak House* both explore the idea of being not just lazy but irresponsible. The speaker in "Laziness" and Mr. Skimpole as described in the scene from *Bleak House* would agree that, as Service writes, "It's lovely to lie staring up at the sky/When others are earning their bread." Both Service and Dickens make the satirical point that much of the satisfaction from being indolent and irresponsible comes from knowing that others are hard at work.

Service's poem bounces along merrily with its strong ballad-like rhythms, internal rhymes, and alliterations, which serve to emphasize the humor. The tone throughout the poem is light and satirical, even when it veers into more serious objections to laziness, such as the slackers in wartime. The speaker quite candidly agrees that his preference for not working could be considered perverse. He refers to people like himself as "indolent wretches," and admits "So though it's my shame I perversely proclaim/It's fine to do nothing at all." But he also invites the reader to sing the praises of lazy people, or as he describes them—in a playful metaphor—those "conscientious objectors to toil." By the end of each stanza, the speaker comes around to the same conclusion: it feels good to do nothing at all.

Obviously Service is having fun by creating a lazybones persona. This device allows him to satirize the earnest poets and preachers (or "laureates" and "pulpiteers") who extol the glories of work. The whole poem seems to mock society's attitude toward working hard and making money ("Oh it's noble to sweat, pounds and dollars to get"). Service even makes fun of his own poetic work as a mere "spatter of ink." He insists that he is not in thrall to the Muses, those goddesses of inspiration, but instead is free to work or not work as he pleases.

Like Service, Dickens focuses on a lazy character in the excerpt from *Bleak House*. In Dickens' episode, the lazy person is not the narrator, but a character that the narrator is describing. Mr. Skimpole is presented with well-chosen details as a sort of lazy child. Although Skimpole is trained in medicine, he "had never been able to prescribe with the requisite accuracy of detail," and he claims to have "no head for detail." Skimpole even admits—"with great humour," says the narrator—that "he was generally found lying on his back, in bed, reading the newspapers, or making fancy sketches in pencil." Skimpole does manage to fall in love and get married, but apparently has no ambition to improve the lot of his family. When Skimpole's friends try to find a position for him, he prefers instead to pursue his carefree, indolent life. Skimpole seems to think that his inability to deal responsibly with issues of time and money in transacting business makes him superior to others, since he only wants to be left alone to indulge his fondness for nature and art and the finer things in life.

Service and Dickens both hint that laziness is often irresponsible. Service mentions the "slackers" in the midst of a battle, who in effect are letting their comrades down. The reader can infer that slackers often bring disaster down upon the people who are counting on them. In a similar vein, Dickens has his narrator note that Skimpole shirks his duties as physician to a German prince and his household in order to lie around. Any sense of obligation to his employer is completely foreign to Skimpole. In the end Skimpole pleads only to be left alone by the world—"All he asked of society was, to let him live"—but he still depends on other people for his upkeep. Thus Dickens, like Service, casts a satirical eye on those who would justify their laziness and irresponsibility as being perfectly natural.

Analysis:

The writer deftly responds to each requirement of the prompt with clear and penetrating ideas. The writer analyzes how Service and Dickens use certain literary techniques and rhetorical devices to develop the common theme. The writer displays a thorough understanding of the assignment.

Sample Response for Practice Question #1

3-Point Response

"Laziness" by Robert Service and the excerpt from *Bleak House* by Charles Dickens both examine the very human failing of indolence, but they use different literary tools and devices. Service employs the resources of poetry and colorful rhetoric in his mock celebration of laziness. Dickens, by contrast, expresses his ideas about laziness through the words of a narrator describing a character who freely admits to his laziness and inability to be responsible. Both passages use humor and irony but the ultimate effect is very different in each.

Service's comic poem uses meter, rhyme, and internal rhyme to carry the reader along. At one point he even rhymes "praise" with "laze," thus expressing succinctly the theme of his tongue-in-cheek poem—in praise of laziness. Service's narrator admits that society's representatives are right to support "the wonder and glory of work," but he then goes on to express his "perverse" view that "It's fine to do nothing at all." He agrees that "it's noble to sweat, pounds and dollars to get," but then praises the alternative. Service expresses this idea in different forms at the end of each stanza to emphasize his humorous point.

Dickens examines laziness through the device of a narrator describing a lazy person, Mr. Skimpole. The narrator notes that Skimpole "had been educated for the medical profession," which would lead one to think he is an industrious person. But the narrator then reveals that Skimpole has "no head for detail," in a metaphor that indicates Skimpole is simply not fit for complicated work. When Skimpole is sacked for "lying on his back, in bed, reading the newspapers," he himself agrees that the decision is "perfectly right." Throughout the passage, the narrator seems to present Skimpole in a positive light. He describes him as someone who just wants to be left alone: "He said to the world, 'Go your several ways in peace! . . . only let Harold Skimpole live!'" Meanwhile Dickens lets the reader make up her or his own mind about Skimpole's lazy character.

Overall, Service and Dickens both use irony to skewer lazy people. Service seems to praise his "conscientious objectors to toil," but admits that they are actually "indolent wretches." Dickens offers an ironical portrait of a man who defends his laziness by claiming to have no aptitude for practical life. Nevertheless, the reader can guess these industrious authors' true feelings about the value of work.

Analysis:

The writer responds to the prompt with a sound appraisal of the texts and the rhetoric and literary devices used by the authors. The writer shows a basic knowledge of the subject matter. One possible weakness is that the writer does not follow through with an explanation of how the ultimate effect of each piece is different.

Sample Response for Practice Question #1

2-Point Response

Robert Service's poem "Laziness" and the excerpt from Charles Dickens' novel *Bleak House* share the significant theme of laziness. Service draws a contrast between "the wonder and glory of work" and the joy of doing nothing. Since he is writing in poetical form, he uses rhyme, rhythm, and poetic language. For example, Service writes "Let pulpiteers preach and with passion impeach/The indolent wretches who shirk." This basically means that fine, upstanding citizens will be quick to criticize those who don't work as being lazy. Throughout his poem, Service draws this contrast between those who "are earning their bread" and sweating to make money and those who "lie staring up at the sky" and "feel one with the soil and sun." The poem should probably be called "Work and Laziness."

The excerpt by Charles Dickens actually tells about a lazy person. The narrator describes Mr. Harold Skimpole, whose name is typical of Dickens' amusing characters. As a young man, Skimpole had enough ambition to become a doctor, but while working for a German prince he decided "he had no head for detail." Instead of doing his job for the prince and his people, Skimpole "was generally found lying on his back, in bed, reading the newspapers, or making fancy sketches in pencil." After being fired by the prince, Skimpole settles down to a lazy life. Skimpole just wants to live and not be bothered. Dickens doesn't explain any more than that.

Together these two texts tell you all you need to know about laziness. As Robert Service writes: "It's fine to recline on the flat of one's spine,/With never a thought in one's head." I think Mr. Skimpole would agree.

Analysis:

The writer displays some understanding of the prompt and the required skills and subject matter associated with it. The writer addresses the Service poem fairly effectively, but does less well with the Dickens excerpt. The methods of the two texts are not compared and contrasted sufficiently.

Sample Response for Practice Question #1

1-Point Response

Robert Service in his poem called "Laziness" makes fun of lazy people while he admits to being lazy himself. His poem is like a tribute to laziness. It is very funny in places, but it also has some obscure words that make it hard to understand. When he says "It's fine to recline on the flat of one's spine,/ with never a thought in one's head," I thought of those long summer afternoons when I used to take a nap in a hammock and just chill out. Sometimes everybody is a little bit lazy, but that doesn't make them "wretches" or "slackers" necessarily. While I like the humor of Service's poem, I don't think he adds much to the theme of laziness and why it occurs. And all the fancy language and clever rhymes take away from the overall effect of the poem.

The piece by Charles Dickens doesn't have much in common with Robert Service's poem. Dickens' character Mr. Skimpole describes a friend who is educated to be a doctor but would rather lie around and read and draw pictures instead of practicing medicine. This friend is not really a bad person; he just prefers to keep to himself and do his own thing, like many people do. In fact, I'm not sure that Mr. Skimpole's friend is actually an example of anything. He is more of an individual who lives his own life his own way. Mr. Skimpole says "all he asked of society was, to let him live." This friend does not understand much about work, or being on time, or making money. Maybe he wasn't lazy so much as just immature. Dickens needed to explain the friend's character in more detail.

Analysis:

The writer does not respond effectively to the prompt or show much understanding of the texts. The writer does not identify literary devices and has scant analysis of rhetoric. The writer also fails to develop any connection between the texts and confuses Mr. Skimpole and the narrator in the excerpt from Dickens.

Sample Response for Practice Question #2

4-Point Response

The editorial "I Sing the Car Electric" argues that electric vehicles are on the verge of dominating the American market, replacing automobiles with traditional internal combustion engines. According to the author, the reasons for this coming revolution include the improved value and performance of electric vehicles.

This piece was written for a metropolitan newspaper, meaning that its intended audience is mostly adults who are reasonably well-educated and informed about current events but not experts or academics. The author writes with clarity and vigor. The opening sentence imaginatively links the "silent revolution" of electric vehicles—or EVs, as the author abbreviates them—with the silent motors of the actual cars. Throughout, the writer uses sentences and paragraphs that are concise without being abrupt or choppy. For example, in paragraph 4 the writer lays out the basic facts about EVs as briefly and straightforwardly as possible.

Twice the writer opens a paragraph with a question that a curious reader might ask. This allows for an explanation of important points, such as why EVs are gaining in popularity and what drawbacks there are to EVs. In paragraph 5, the writer practically places the reader in the driver's seat of an EV, describing the sound and feel of driving one of these vehicles. The author also employs a sly sense of humor, suggesting in an aside that the "gas pedal" of an EV should be renamed the "power pedal." Overall, the editorialist makes a rapid, but not too detailed, case for EVs as an improvement over cars with internal combustion engines (ICEs).

Unfortunately, the argument presented is less effective than the writing itself. The author claims that "Soon the advantages that ICE vehicles have enjoyed over EVs will melt away completely." Yet the remainder of the piece fails to support this contention. The writer admits that the higher price of EVs is a significant drawback for them right now, although supposedly government subsidies and lower maintenance and fuel costs will offset this problem. The writer also mentions the problem of limited driving range. This apparently refers to the distance an EV can travel on a full battery charge, but the author does not make this point clear.

Surprisingly the writer fails to address one of the most important issues about EVs: the quest to build more efficient batteries. This is a major failing in a piece that presents itself as a candid look at the potential for electric vehicles in the United States. The editorial is an interesting overview, but it mostly skims over the genuine problems that EVs face before they have any chance of replacing ICE vehicles.

Analysis:

The writer displays a thorough understanding of the prompt and answers each of its requirements with style and clarity. Each of the writer's points is supported with evidence, and the writer deftly identifies the strong and weak points of the editorial.

Sample Response for Practice Question #2

3-Point Response

In the newspaper editorial "I Sing the Car Electric," the author claims that electric vehicles (EVs) are about to take over the American automobile industry. It is a "silent revolution," in the author's words, not only because the EVs themselves make very little noise but also apparently because most people do not realize this revolution is taking place. And on the evidence of this article, the electric car revolution may be silent because it really doesn't exist.

The author's main argument seems to be that EVs are on the verge of a breakthrough because they not only are better and cleaner for the environment, they also are becoming more competitive in the areas of concern for most car buyers: value and performance. In writing that is clear and straightforward, the author compares EVs to automobiles with internal combustion engines (ICEs) and tries to make the case that

EVs are rapidly improving and are now better than ICEs in many ways. "Soon the advantages that ICE vehicles have enjoyed over EVs will melt away completely," according to the article. I don't think the article makes this case very well, however.

The author structures the editorial by listing the positive things about EVs up front, then following with possible drawbacks or faults, which the article then attempts to explain. In two paragraphs, the author begins with questions, asking "Why are these drivers fired up about EVs?" and "So what are the drawbacks to his remarkable automobile?" This is an effective device, as the author tries to anticipate actual questions that the reader might have. The problem is that the author's is too intent on minimizing any problems with EVs. After all, if EVs were really the future of the American auto industry, we would already be seeing many more of them on the road.

According to the writer, EVs are not only quiet because of their electric motors, but they also have great acceleration and performance. But is this the same for all EVs? Or are there major differences between models as with any other car line in America? The writer tries to explain away the question of the high price of EVs also. The problem of how far EVs can go without recharging is also skimmed over. No one wants to be stranded in a car without power. I am afraid that most readers will not be "singing the praises of the car electric" anytime soon.

Analysis:

The writer shows a sufficient understanding of the assignment, but neglects to identify the audience for which the editorial is written. Overall, the writer's analysis of the editorialist's approach is good.

Sample Response for Practice Question #2

2-Point Response

"I Sing the Car Electric" is an editorial about the exciting field of electric vehicles, or EVs for short. The author of this article, like me, is very excited about the potential for this new technology. I believe that we will soon see EVs on every street in America. It is a "silent revolution" that is very welcome indeed.

The author is writing for newspaper readers. So the editorial can only say so much. It would be pointless to go into too much detail about how EVs operate. No one would understand it anyway.

It is exciting news that ordinary drivers are growing interested in driving EVs. The author explains that ordinary drivers like the performance and value of EVs more and more. There is a section explaining the basics of how EVs work, which is just enough for this piece. Then the author describes how it feels to drive an electric car. I would love to drive one myself, and maybe buy one in the future.

There are certainly problems with EVs, and the writer goes over some of them. The writer names a problem and then gives the actual facts that back up the argument that EVs are high-quality vehicles. It seems like the writer is trying to anticipate what the reader wants to know. One thing is that EVs cost more than regular cars, at least they do right now. But the writer points out that EV prices "are competitive and starting to come down." I certainly agree that the price will fall. Look how the price of computers came down. I would love it if electric cars became as common a sight as the personal computer. I agree that things change today with amazing speed, as the author says, so maybe the silent revolution is right around the corner. This editorial explains why so many people are excited about EVs.

Analysis:

The writer shows some understanding of the assignment, for example identifying the target audience of the editorial. The writer discusses the editorialist's methods of persuasion, but not in much detail, and he/she devotes too much space to his/her own opinions about electric vehicles.

Sample Response for Practice Question #2

1-Point Response

The author of "I Sing the Car Electric" (and what is that supposed to mean?) seems to be against the whole idea of a cleaner, healthier environment. He claims that electric cars will save the world because they use electricity, but lots of things use electricity and our air and water are still getting dirtier and our planet is still getting warmer every day. Doesn't this writer know that electricity has to come from somewhere? And if it comes from fossil fuels, it is still dirty.

An article like this is trying to fool newspaper readers by presenting only part of the story. Yes, electric cars, or EVs, as the author calls them, have some potential. But they also have big problems. I read somewhere that they are so quiet that pedestrians walking the street cannot sometimes hear them coming and can't get out of the way, which is of course very dangerous. Of course, the author doesn't mention this as a problem, but just jokes about it.

If an electric car can only go fifty miles at a time, it will never be the dominant car on the American road. And I still haven't seen a single charging station for electricity anywhere. This writer thinks the basic facts about so-called EVs are simple and straightforward, but there is a lot more going on that is never covered in this article.

Analysis:

The writer's response is off-topic and the essay rambles without a clear focus. The writer does not understand the prompt and shows limited knowledge of the subject matter.

PRACTICE TEST 1

CSET: English Subtest IV

Also available at the REA Study Center (*www.rea.com/studycenter*)

This practice test is also available online at the REA Study Center. The CSET: English test is only offered as a computer-based exam; therefore, we recommend that you take the online version of the practice test to receive these added benefits:

- **Timed testing conditions** – helps you gauge how much time you can spend on each question

- **On-screen detailed analysis of sample essays** – guides you to a 3-point response

SCORING THE CSET: ENGLISH SUBTEST IV

In CSET: English Subtest IV, you will have 1 hour and 30 minutes to respond to four constructed-response writing prompts.

For each constructed-response question in Subtest IV, you should write a response of about 75–125 words, although you may write longer responses if you prefer. Your responses will be assessed according to the subject-matter knowledge and skills they demonstrate, *not* writing ability. You should, however, write clearly enough to allow for a valid judgment of your knowledge and skills regarding the subject matter. You should write for an audience of educators in the field.

Your response essays will be scored by California educators using focused holistic scoring. The scorers will evaluate the overall effectiveness of your essay responses with a focus on the performance characteristics that have been judged most important for CSET: English Subtest IV.

These performance characteristics, or writing standards, are established by the California Commission on Teacher Credentialing and include the following:

Purpose: The extent to which the response focuses on and accomplishes the task set by the prompt in relation to relevant CSET: English subject-matter requirements.

Subject-matter knowledge: The extent to which the response applies accurate subject-matter knowledge as described in the relevant CSET: English subject-matter requirements.

Support: The extent to which the response employs quality, appropriate supporting evidence in relation to CSET: English subject-matter requirements.

Your essay responses will be scored based on the following Scoring Scale:

Scoring Scale

3: To earn a **3-point score**, your response must show that you have a sophisticated grasp of the relevant knowledge and skills as defined in the subject-matter requirements for CSET: English. These include:

- The ability to address the specific purpose of the assignment comprehensively and without distractions in order to accomplish the assigned task.

- The ability to select and include relevant supporting evidence and examples that demonstrate your overall understanding of the subject matter.

A 3-point essay demonstrates that you have a thorough understanding of the assignment and the relevant subject matter.

2: To earn a **2-point score**, your response must show that you have an overall or general understanding of the relevant knowledge and skills as defined in the subject-matter requirements for CSET: English. These include:

- The ability to recognize the overall purpose of the assignment in order to accomplish the assigned task adequately.

- The ability to recognize and apply some accurate information and relevant supporting evidence to the given subject matter.

A 2-point essay demonstrates that you have an adequate or sufficient understanding of the assignment.

1: To earn a **1-point score**, your response will show that you have a basic, partial, or insufficient understanding of the knowledge and skills as defined in the subject-matter requirements for CSET: English. These include:

- The ability to address the assignment's purpose only partially or not at all.

- The ability to recognize and apply only a limited amount, if any, of relevant supporting evidence, demonstrating only a partial understanding of the subject matter.

A 1-point essay demonstrates that you have a limited, partial, or unsatisfactory understanding of the assignment.

U: A grade of **"U" (Unscorable)** is given to essays that are completely unrelated to the assignment, illegible, written in a language other than English, and/or lack a sufficient amount of your own original writing. Most problems that cause an essay to earn a "U" are solvable by simply slowing down and pacing yourself as you systematically respond to each question or prompt.

B: A grade of **"B" (Blank)** is given to essay responses left blank. Never leave a test question blank if at all possible.

CSET: English Practice Test 1, Subtest IV Communications: Speech, Media, and Creative Performance

Practice Question 1

Complete the exercise that follows.

The interaction between a speaker and an audience is an important component of an effective oral presentation. A speaker should maintain eye contact with the audience as much as possible during the speech. Write a response in which you:

- identify two positive elements of maintaining direct eye contact with an audience; and

- describe a negative outcome of not maintaining direct eye contact during a speech or oral presentation.

In your response, be sure to address both of the tasks described above.

Practice Question 2

Complete the exercise that follows.

A discriminating reader, viewer, or listener routinely assesses the reliability and credibility of news reports in the media. Write a response in which you:

- briefly describe one quality (e.g., balance, objectivity, depth) that is characteristic of reliable and credible news reporting; and

- describe how a reader, viewer, or listener can determine whether a particular news story demonstrates this quality.

In your response, be sure to address both of the tasks described above.

Practice Question 3

Complete the exercise that follows.

When a stage director wants to focus the audience's attention on a particular character or object, he or she can either place the character or object in motion or use a shift in lighting to create the same effect. Write a response in which you:

- explain why this technique of motion is such an effective directing tool; and

- describe what happens when more than one actor or object is moving simultaneously.

In your response, be sure to address both of the tasks described above.

Practice Question 4

Complete the exercise that follows.

For an assignment in her high school speech class, Janice must plan and deliver a reflective narrative that examines the significance of a personal experience. The speech should compare the experience to a broader theme while using narrative techniques and sensory language. Janice's preliminary draft for her presentation appears below.

> [1]When I was ten years old, my mom made me go to a birthday party that I really didn't want to attend. [2]Caitlin, the birthday girl, was the meanest girl in my class. [3]No one liked her. [4]She was always causing trouble or mouthing off. [5]However, my mom said if Caitlin's folks were nice enough to invite me to her party I should go. [6]Well, I thought to myself, at least there will be other kids from our class to keep me company.
>
> [7]So there I was, present in hand, watching Mom drive away after dropping me off. [8]Caitlin came out to tell me I was the first guest to arrive. [9]She led me inside into the kitchen, and her mom handed me a cup of punch and told me how nice I looked. [10]There were decorations everywhere—it was a big production—and through the back window I could see a long table outside all set with plates and fancy decorations. [11]As the minutes went by, it became obvious no one else was coming. [12]Despite Caitlin's annoying behavior in class, I began to feel sorry for her. [13]And truthfully she seemed like a different person that day. [14]We laughed together, ate ice cream and cake, played some games, and had a pretty good time. [15]On Monday morning Caitlin was mostly back to her old ways, but she no longer was mean to me. [16]From that day, every time Caitlin mouthed off or played a mean prank on somebody in class, I thought about her standing in her yard waiting for someone to come to her party. [17]I realized that this was a life lesson I would never forget.

Using your knowledge of oral communication, write a response in which you:

- describe one type of revision Janice could make to improve the draft; and

- explain why this type of revision would enhance the audience appeal and effectiveness of the presentation.

In your response, be sure to address both of the tasks described above.

Written Response Answer Sheets for CSET: English Practice Test 1, Subtest IV

Although the actual CSET: English test is computer-based and you will input your responses on a computer screen, use the answer sheets that follow to write your responses. For Subtest IV, you will have 1 hour and 30 minutes to complete the four short-response questions.

_____

_____

_____

_____

_____

_____

_____

_____

_____

_____

_____

_____

_____

_____

_____

_____

Practice Question 1

Practice Question 2

_____

_____

_____

_____

_____

_____

_____

_____

_____

_____

_____

_____

_____

_____

_____

_____

_____

_____

Practice Question 3

_____

_____

_____

_____

_____

_____

_____

_____

_____

_____

_____

_____

_____

_____

_____

_____

_____

_____

Practice Question 4

Sample Responses for Practice Test 1, Subtest IV

Sample Response for Practice Question #1

3-Point Response

Maintaining eye contact with an audience is a critical component of effective speaking because it lets the audience know that the speaker is interested in them as individuals rather than merely as an undifferentiated group. If the speaker shows a genuine interest in the audience, it is more likely that the audience will respond in kind, by showing a more genuine interest in the material being presented. Conversely, a speaker who avoids eye contact with the audience can appear nervous or self-absorbed, and, perhaps worse, apathetic, leading the audience to respond with boredom and indifference.

Direct eye contact with an audience also conveys the speaker's knowledge of and confidence in the materials that he or she is presenting. A speaker's lack of familiarity with the material being presented will be reflected in the speaker's eyes, as a less confident speaker is more likely to avoid eye contact with the audience by nervously shifting his or her gaze from one random vantage point to another. On the other hand, a confident speaker who is well versed in the material being presented will make direct eye contact with as many audience members as possible.

Analysis:

The writer, in fully addressing the assignment, demonstrates a comprehensive understanding of the question and the relevant subject matter. The writer includes both positive and negative elements, as required by the prompt.

Sample Response for Practice Question #1

2-Point Response

With direct eye contact you can let the audience know that you are there for them. You want them to know that you are there to share your information with them and that you like what you're talking about. So for the listeners, the speech seems more exciting and engaging if the speaker looks them directly in the eyes, rather than just looking at his or her note pages, or gazing into space, or anxiously checking the clock on the wall.

Since the listeners will be more involved if the speaker looks at them directly, the speech will seem interactive and not tedious. Time won't drag on for the speaker or the listener. Nothing is worse than a lackluster lecture where the topic is dull and the orator is bored also. Time drags when instead of looking at the audience with excitement, the speaker is looking off and thinking about someplace he or she would rather be, and this shows in the speaker's eyes.

Analysis:

The writer shows a general understanding of the assignment, but is repetitive and rambling, and addresses the negative examples that the prompt requires only indirectly.

Sample Response for Practice Question #1

1-Point Response

Eye contact is important because it means that you like talking to people. Some people like talking to people and some don't. So, if you do, you'll look at them. It makes a big difference if you look at someone or not. Even in school or with friends you should look at people when you talk to them. It's just courteous. It lets people know that you're polite and have good manners. Good manners are important wherever you go, and it doesn't matter if you're at home or giving a speech you should still be polite and give people respect and you can show people respect when you look at them in the eyes.

Analysis:

The writer rambles and barely addresses the tasks in the prompt. The writer does not understand the assignment.

Sample Response for Practice Question #2

3-Point Response

One of the most important characteristics of reliable and credible news reporting is balance, or presenting multiple perspectives about a topic. When a news story is balanced, it allows the reader, viewer, or listener to form an independent opinion based on different perspectives. For example, a news story about a controversial Supreme Court decision would be more reliable and credible if it devoted roughly the same amount of space to different views about the issue, including those of political leaders, legal experts, and voters.

A strategy that a reader, viewer, or listener can employ to assess whether a news story is balanced is to compare how it is covered by several different news organizations. Balanced coverage of a story will present facts from reliable sources clearly and thoroughly and will not favor one viewpoint or political faction over others.

Analysis:

The writer shows a comprehensive understanding of the assignment, succinctly describing balance as a characteristic of reliable and credible news reporting and explaining how one can evaluate whether a news story is balanced. The writer demonstrates excellent knowledge of the subject matter.

Sample Response for Practice Question #2

2-Point Response

A reliable and credible news report should have objectivity. That means taking an unbiased look at each issue or news event. If a reporter allows his or her own opinions to slant a report, that reporter could reasonably be accused of not being objective. Lots of people believe that today's news reporting in general lacks objectivity. But that might be a function of how polarized our politics have become.

There are lots of ways that a reader, viewer, or listener can test for objectivity in news reports. It is important to do this so that a person understands whether or not a news report is slanted one way or another.

Analysis:

The writer shows a general understanding of the required subject matter knowledge and skills in answering the first part of the prompt. However, the writer does not explain how a reader or viewer can determine if a news report exhibits objectivity.

Sample Response for Practice Question #2

1-Point Response

Readers, viewers, and listeners aren't capable of determining how reliable or credible a news report is. The media is expert at fooling most of the people most of the time, and the average viewer doesn't even realize he or she is being fed a lot of slanted nonsense. What is offered up as balanced reporting is actually daily propaganda. Balance and objectivity in the news media are just a pipe dream, I'm afraid.

Analysis:

The writer shows limited understanding of what the prompt requires. Instead of responding to the prompt, the writer expresses irrelevant opinions related to the topic of reliability and credibility in news reporting.

Sample Response for Practice Question #3

3-Point Response

Based on instincts, when one's eye senses a moving object on a stage or elsewhere, it will instinctively follow and focus on that movement. So if the director wants to emphasize a particular character or object, he or she can simply put the character or object in motion and rely on the audience to collectively follow the movement. Likewise, if there are multiple characters or objects already in motion on the stage and the director does not want to stop the action already taking place, he or she can rely on our instincts to follow the most recently animated character or object.

The same principle holds true for shifts in lighting. The appearance or shifting of a stage light will appear to the audience as another form of movement and thus will have the same effect as far as directing the audience's focus. Since the eye perceives the shifting light as a new movement, the audience is instinctively compelled to follow that movement and focus on the character or object that the director wants them to look at.

Analysis:

The writer addresses the assignment thoroughly, showing a clear and complete understanding of the prompt. An apt use of supporting evidence and examples rounds out a well-constructed response.

Sample Response for Practice Question #3

2-Point Response

Unlike a movie theater, where all the action takes place within the confines of a flat, rectangular screen, a theater stage contains numerous nooks and crannies, offering many visual distractions. So, to attract the audience's attention to a particular object, area, or character on stage, the director should use movement, because movement is so "eye-catching" that the audience cannot help but follow it, as they attempt to focus on what is causing the movement. It doesn't matter if it's a person moving or some stage prop, the movement itself is enough to grab the audience's attention.

Several props or people in motion indicate that important action is taking place on stage. Moving the lights from one prop or person to another is like the person or prop moving itself, and has the same effect on the audience, causing their eyes to focus on the alternating spots of light on the stage.

Analysis:

The writer demonstrates a sufficient knowledge of the subject matter but does not explain or support the response very effectively. All parts of the assignment are only adequately addressed.

Sample Response for Practice Question #3

1-Point Response

When it comes to moving things or people around on stage a director should be careful not to move too many things too fast or else the audience won't be able to follow what's going on in the play. Sometimes a comedy can have rapid stage movements, but it can be confusing and hard to follow. So a good director should plan each stage movement that the actors make just like planning a dance.

Lights can also be distracting if not used correctly. Like if they are flashing too fast or blaring into the audience's eyes. You can lose track of what you're supposed to be following on the stage. So using moving or shifting lights should be using only sometimes, so it is not too distracting for the audience and even for the actors.

Analysis:

The writer displays a limited understanding of the assignment and of the relevant subject matter. Instead of focusing on why the technique of using motion is an effective directing tool, the writer focuses on its possible drawbacks.

Sample Response for Practice Question #4

3-Point Response

One type of revision Janice could make to improve her presentation would be to add more specific details about the characters and setting. For example, instead of settling for the general word "decorations" in describing the party setting, Janice could paint a picture of balloons, streamers, glitter, and colorful plates to bring the scene to life. She might also provide other details that appeal to the audience's senses, such as a description of the weather; the sounds that she heard, such as party music or even the awkward silence of no guests; and the scents of the party, such as a smoky grill or baking cupcakes. Janice could also describe Caitlin's voice and attitude when she first meets her in the yard, so the audience could determine if Caitlin felt sad, irritated, grateful, or embarrassed. Adding concrete details would make Janice's narrative more vivid for the audience and convey more clearly the conflicting emotions she felt about Caitlin and her birthday party. Janice should also specify what life lesson she learned from the incident so that the audience understands how the narrative expresses a certain theme.

Analysis:

The writer displays a thorough understanding of the task in the prompt and provides excellent examples to support the response. The writer obviously knows the relevant subject matter and employs it effectively.

Sample Response for Practice Question #4

2-Point Response

> The problem with Janice's preliminary draft is that she is too vague about the details of the narrative. She needs to describe in greater detail what the party was like, how Caitlin reacted when Janice first showed up and when they played games together, and how Caitlin's mother responded to the absence of guests. When Janice says the party was supposed to be a big production, she needs to follow up with details to support that idea. When facing an audience, the speaker must focus on details that bring the story to life.

Analysis:

The writer shows a general understanding of the required task and of the relevant subject matter in responding to the first part of the prompt. However, the writer does not address the second part of the prompt adequately.

Sample Response for Practice Question #4

1-Point Response

> Janice's draft is already very effective and would engage an audience's attention very easily. She has included plenty of details about the party and about Caitlin. We don't need to know anything about Caitlin, just that she is supposed to be mean. We have all met people like Caitlin, so details are not so necessary here. One thing Janice might focus on more is why the other children stayed away from the party so that the audience understands the point of the story.

Analysis:

The writer shows a very limited understanding of the assignment. Instead of describing a type of revision to improve Janice's presentation, the writer claims it is already very effective. The writer also demonstrates limited knowledge of the relevant subject matter.

PRACTICE TEST 2

CSET: English Subtest I

Also available at the REA Study Center (*www.rea.com/studycenter*)

This practice test is also available online at the REA Study Center. The CSET: English test is only offered as a computer-based exam; therefore, we recommend that you take the online version of the practice test to receive these added benefits:

- **Timed testing conditions** – helps you gauge how much time you can spend on each question

- **Automatic scoring** – find out how you did on the test, instantly

- **On-screen detailed explanations of answers** – gives you the correct answer and explains why the other answer choices are wrong

- **Diagnostic score reports** – pinpoint where you're strongest and where you need to focus your study

Practice Test 2, Subtest I
Answer Sheet

1. Ⓐ Ⓑ Ⓒ Ⓓ		26. Ⓐ Ⓑ Ⓒ Ⓓ	
2. Ⓐ Ⓑ Ⓒ Ⓓ		27. Ⓐ Ⓑ Ⓒ Ⓓ	
3. Ⓐ Ⓑ Ⓒ Ⓓ		28. Ⓐ Ⓑ Ⓒ Ⓓ	
4. Ⓐ Ⓑ Ⓒ Ⓓ		29. Ⓐ Ⓑ Ⓒ Ⓓ	
5. Ⓐ Ⓑ Ⓒ Ⓓ		30. Ⓐ Ⓑ Ⓒ Ⓓ	
6. Ⓐ Ⓑ Ⓒ Ⓓ		31. Ⓐ Ⓑ Ⓒ Ⓓ	
7. Ⓐ Ⓑ Ⓒ Ⓓ		32. Ⓐ Ⓑ Ⓒ Ⓓ	
8. Ⓐ Ⓑ Ⓒ Ⓓ		33. Ⓐ Ⓑ Ⓒ Ⓓ	
9. Ⓐ Ⓑ Ⓒ Ⓓ		34. Ⓐ Ⓑ Ⓒ Ⓓ	
10. Ⓐ Ⓑ Ⓒ Ⓓ		35. Ⓐ Ⓑ Ⓒ Ⓓ	
11. Ⓐ Ⓑ Ⓒ Ⓓ		36. Ⓐ Ⓑ Ⓒ Ⓓ	
12. Ⓐ Ⓑ Ⓒ Ⓓ		37. Ⓐ Ⓑ Ⓒ Ⓓ	
13. Ⓐ Ⓑ Ⓒ Ⓓ		38. Ⓐ Ⓑ Ⓒ Ⓓ	
14. Ⓐ Ⓑ Ⓒ Ⓓ		39. Ⓐ Ⓑ Ⓒ Ⓓ	
15. Ⓐ Ⓑ Ⓒ Ⓓ		40. Ⓐ Ⓑ Ⓒ Ⓓ	
16. Ⓐ Ⓑ Ⓒ Ⓓ		41. Ⓐ Ⓑ Ⓒ Ⓓ	
17. Ⓐ Ⓑ Ⓒ Ⓓ		42. Ⓐ Ⓑ Ⓒ Ⓓ	
18. Ⓐ Ⓑ Ⓒ Ⓓ		43. Ⓐ Ⓑ Ⓒ Ⓓ	
19. Ⓐ Ⓑ Ⓒ Ⓓ		44. Ⓐ Ⓑ Ⓒ Ⓓ	
20. Ⓐ Ⓑ Ⓒ Ⓓ		45. Ⓐ Ⓑ Ⓒ Ⓓ	
21. Ⓐ Ⓑ Ⓒ Ⓓ		46. Ⓐ Ⓑ Ⓒ Ⓓ	
22. Ⓐ Ⓑ Ⓒ Ⓓ		47. Ⓐ Ⓑ Ⓒ Ⓓ	
23. Ⓐ Ⓑ Ⓒ Ⓓ		48. Ⓐ Ⓑ Ⓒ Ⓓ	
24. Ⓐ Ⓑ Ⓒ Ⓓ		49. Ⓐ Ⓑ Ⓒ Ⓓ	
25. Ⓐ Ⓑ Ⓒ Ⓓ		50. Ⓐ Ⓑ Ⓒ Ⓓ	

Practice Test 2, Subtest I
Reading Literature and Informational Texts; Composition and Rhetoric

1. Which of the following verse forms originated in Italy, was adapted into English literature during the 1500s, and includes fourteen lines?

   A. limerick

   B. sonnet

   C. ballad

   D. dramatic monologue

2. James Joyce's *A Portrait of the Artist as a Young Man* and Charles Dickens' *David Copperfield* are examples of *bildungsroman*. Which of the following best describes this novelistic form?

   A. a novel that describes the development of a young person from childhood to maturity

   B. a novel that describes a nightmarish, totalitarian future

   C. a novel is which the story is told entirely through letters written by the characters

   D. a novel that critiques a society's social, moral, and political makeup

3. **Read the passage below. Then answer the question that follows.**

   > Anansi the spider was hungry so he went to Elephant's melon patch, chose the largest, ripest melon, and bored a little hole inside, just right for eating. Anansi ate so much, however, that he grew round as a berry and found himself trapped inside the melon. When Elephant returned to his melon patch, Anansi decided to play a clever trick on him.
   >
   > "Hello, Mr. Elephant!" he said.
   >
   > Elephant was astonished at this talking melon. "Why that's as preposterous —"
   >
   > "—as a graceful elephant!" finished the talking melon.
   >
   > Stung by the joke, Elephant decided to take this insolent melon to the King. Arriving at the royal abode, Elephant explained to the King that the melon could talk.

The King stared at the melon. "Why that's as preposterous as —"

"— as a wise king!" said the talking melon.

Well, the King became enraged and threw the melon out the window, where it struck a rock and broke apart, freeing Anansi. And the clever spider laughed all the way home.

This passage is most characteristic of which of the following literary forms associated with the oral tradition?

A.   fable

B.   trickster tale

C.   legend

D.   fairy tale

4.   **Read the passage below from *To Kill a Mockingbird* by Harper Lee. Then answer the question that follows.**

People moved slowly then. They ambled across the square, shuffled in and out of the stores around it, took their time about everything. A day was twenty-four hours long but seemed longer. There was no hurry, for there was nowhere to go, nothing to buy, and no money to buy it with, nothing to see outside the boundaries of Maycomb County.

Which is the main literary or rhetorical technique used in this passage?

A.   oxymoron

B.   extended metaphor

C.   hyperbole

D.   personification

5.   **Read the passage below by the West African poet Mabel Segun. Then answer the question that follows.**

Here we stand
infants overblown
poised between two civilizations
finding the balance irksome
itching for something to happen
to tip us one way or the other
groping in the dark for a helping hand
and finding none.
I'm tired, O my God, I'm tired,

I'm tired of hanging in the middle way —
but where can I go?

This passage is indicative of which of the following issues facing African writers in the mid-twentieth century?

A. the attempt to reach a worldwide readership while still appealing to African readers

B. the conflict between pre-colonial and post-colonial generations in Africa

C. the efforts by urban African elites to improve conditions in rural areas

D. the clash between traditional African culture and the encroaching civilization of the West

6. **Read the poem "The Passionate Shepherd to His Love" by Christopher Marlowe. Then answer the question that follows.**

Come live with me and be my Love,
And we will all the pleasures prove
That hills and valleys, dale and field,
And all the craggy mountains yield.

There will we sit upon the rocks
And see the shepherds feed their flocks,
By shallow rivers, to whose falls
Melodious birds sing madrigals.

This is an example of what genre of poetry?

A. pastoral

B. epic

C. metaphysical

D. symbolist

7. **Read the excerpt from Walt Whitman's poem "Crossing Brooklyn Ferry." Then answer the question that follows.**

Crowds of men and women attired in the usual costumes! How curious you are to me!
On the ferry-boats, the hundreds and hundreds that cross, returning home, are more curious to me than you suppose, ...
Just as you feel when you look on the river and sky, so I felt,
Just as any of you is one of a living crowd, I was one of a crowd,
Just as you are refreshed by the gladness of the river, and the bright flow, I was refreshed.

This is an example of the new style that Whitman brought to nineteenth-century American poetry, which was based on which of the following?

A.   the alliterative verse of old Norse epics

B.   the long lines and repetitive cadences of biblical verses

C.   the versatile iambic pentameter of Shakespeare's drama

D.   the closed, difficult forms of French poetry

8.   The epic allegory in Italian that was written by Dante Alighieri in the fourteenth century is called:

A.   *Beowulf*

B.   *The Divine Comedy*

C.   *The Iliad*

D.   *The Decameron*

9.   **Read the excerpt from Alexander Pope's *The Dunciad*. Then answer the question that follows.**

> Thus at her [Dullness's] felt approach, and secret might,
> Art after Art goes out, and all is Night.
> See skulking Truth to her old Cavern fled,
> Mountains of Casuistry heap'd o'er her head!
> Philosophy, that lean'd on Heav'n before,
> Shrinks to her second cause, and is no more… .
> Lo! thy dread Empire, CHAOS! is restor'd;
> Light dies before thy uncreating word:
> Thy hand, great Anarch! lets the curtain fall;
> And Universal Darkness buries All.

How is this excerpt representative of the literary approach in the Neoclassical Period?

A.   It expresses ideas in an impressionistic, indirect style that alludes to literature of the past and makes great demands upon the reader.

B.   It focuses on the absurdity of man's situation in a chaotic, godless universe and the impossibility of achieving peace and happiness.

C.   It employs satire and ridicule in heroic couplets that are witty and intellectual.

D.   It is concerned mainly with the author's subjective thoughts and feelings about the world and expresses these thoughts in heavily emotional language.

10. **Read the excerpt below from "The Peculiar Weakness of Mr. Hoover," an article that appeared in *Harper's Magazine* in June 1930. Then answer the question that follows.**

> The triangle of fate, character, and reputation is peculiarly important in considering Mr. [Herbert] Hoover's first year of office. For to a greater degree than would be true, I think, of any other President, his reputation is a work of art. Mr. Hoover's ascent to the Presidency was planned with great care and assisted throughout by a high-powered propaganda of the very latest model. He is, in fact, the first American President whose whole public career has been presented through the machinery of modern publicity. The Hoover legend, the public stereotype of an ideal Hoover, was consciously contrived. By arousing certain expectations, the legend has established a standard by which the public judgment has estimated him; if, as I think most observers would admit, his first year ended in an atmosphere of mild disappointment, the cause in some measure at least was the inability of the real Hoover to act up to the standards of the ideal Hoover. Thus Mr. Hoover is blamed for not achieving things which nobody would ever have expected Mr. Coolidge to do.
>
> In saying that Mr. Hoover's reputation was a work of art, I do not mean, of course, that it is a lie. I mean that it is an idealization ...

This excerpt primarily expresses the point of view that:

A.   the public always prefers to know the truth about a politician rather than a contrived legend.

B.   there often is a sizable gap between the media image of a politician and the actual person.

C.   it is always better for a politician to make bold promises than to promise too little and seem too cautious.

D.   the public always sees through the propaganda surrounding a politician and focuses on the person's actual performance in office.

11. **Read the passage below from *Elegy*, a poem by Edna St. Vincent Millay. Then answer the question that follows.**

> But your voice,—never the rushing
> Of a river underground,
> Not the rising of the wind
> In the trees before the rain,
> Not the woodcock's watery call,
> Not the note the white-throat utters,
> Not the feet of children pushing
> Yellow leaves along the gutters
> In the blue and bitter fall,

> Shall content my musing mind
> For the beauty of that sound
> That in no new way at all
> Ever will be heard again.

Which of the following statements describes most accurately how a literary or rhetorical technique is used in this passage?

A. The careful repetition of certain phrases conveys a calm and confident outlook.

B. The descriptions of sounds in nature are presented through imaginative onomatopoeia.

C. The rushing river and rising wind are used as symbols of spiritual discontent.

D. The flood of precisely described images presents the poet's tumultuous state of mind.

12. "Daedalus and Icarus," "King Midas," and "Pandora's Box" are all stories from:

A. Greek mythology.

B. Native American mythology.

C. Anglo-Saxon epics.

D. *Aesop's Fables*.

13. **Read the following poem by Ralph Waldo Emerson, which he used as the epigraph for the 1849 version of his essay "Nature." Then answer the question that follows.**

> A subtle chain of countless rings
> The next unto the farthest brings;
> The eye reads omens where it goes,
> And speaks all languages the rose;
> And, striving to be man, the worm
> Mounts through all the spires of form.

Which tenet of the Transcendentalist movement is presented in this poem?

A. the spark of divinity in all human beings

B. the urgent need to end the practice of slavery in America

C. the interconnectedness of all things

D. the importance of rugged individualism to the American spirit

14. Which of the following are important elements that Mary Shelley's novel *Franken-stein* shares with other works of Romantic literature?

   A. a rejection of the modern industrial age and a celebration of imagina-tion and creativity

   B. a concentration on personal emotions and the language spoken by ordinary people

   C. an infatuation with the ruins of the past and an ecstatic reaction to nature

   D. an atmosphere of gothic horror and questions about the limits of science in the modern world

15. **Read the excerpt from the Nigerian novelist Chinua Achebe's** *Things Fall Apart.* **Then answer the question that follows.**

   "Does the white man understand our custom about land?"

   "How can he when he does not even speak our tongue? But he says that our customs are bad; and our own brothers who have taken up his religion also say that our customs are bad. How do you think we can fight when our own brothers have turned against us? The white man is very clever. He came quietly and peaceably with his religion. We were amused at his foolishness and allowed him to stay. Now he has won our brothers, and our clan can no longer act like one. He has put a knife on the things that held us together and we have fallen apart."

   This excerpt is typical of postcolonial literature in the twentieth century because of its focus on which of the following themes?

   A. political revolution

   B. cultural imperialism

   C. economic imperialism

   D. political tyranny

16. **Read the excerpt from W. B. Yeats's poem "Lines Written in Dejection." Then answer the question that follows.**

   When have I last looked on
   The round green eyes and the long wavering bodies
   Of the dark leopards of the moon?
   All the wild witches, those most noble ladies ...

Which of the following best describes Yeats's use of rhyme in these lines?

A. He uses perfect rhymes.

B. He uses slant rhymes.

C. He uses internal rhymes.

D. He uses free verse that does not rhyme.

17. Authors of literature for young adults tend to focus on:

A. humor and satire, hypocrisy in society, and a mocking style.

B. fate and coincidence, tricky prose, and the absurdity of life in general.

C. immediacy, brisk action, simple prose, and familiar societal problems.

D. psychological depth, complex characters, and difficult moral questions.

18. **Read the following excerpt from the poem "To Walt Whitman" by Angela de Hoyos. Then answer the question that follows.**

> — here's a guitar for you
> — a chicana guitar so
> you can spill out a song
> for the open road
> big enough for my people …
> that I can't seem to find
> in your poems

In this excerpt, de Hoyos is using which of the following literary elements?

A. allusion

B. personification

C. metonomy

D. irony

19. **Read the poem "The Red Wheelbarrow" by William Carlos Williams. Then answer the question that follows.**

> so much depends
> upon
> a red wheel
> barrow
> glazed with rain
> water
> beside the white
> chickens

The style and subject matter of this poem are most characteristic of which literary movement?

A.   Symbolist

B.   new formalist

C.   imagist

D.   Metaphysical

20.   Which of the following best describes the theme of John Milton's *Paradise Lost*?

A.   mankind's journey from the City of Destruction to the Celestial City

B.   mankind's fall from grace and God's banishment of Satan from heaven

C.   God's accounting of the good and evil deeds in the life of Everyman

D.   a poet's journey upward through the circles of hell, purgatory, and heaven

21.   **Read the excerpt from the story "Cecilia Rosas" by Amado Muro. Then answer the question that follows.**

> ... I went on speaking English even though my mother and my uncle did not understand it. This shocked my sisters as well. When they asked me to explain my behavior, I parroted Miss Rosas, saying, "We're living in the United States now."
>
> My rebellion against being a Mexican created an uproar. Such conduct was unorthodox, if not scandalous, in a neighborhood where names like Burciaga, Rodriguez, and Castillo predominated. But it wasn't only the Spanish language that I had lashed out against.
>
> "Mother, why do we always have to eat sopa, frijoles, refritos, mondongo, and pozole?" I complained. "Can't we ever eat roast beef or ham and eggs like Americans do?"

In this excerpt, Muro explores which of the following aspects of immigrant experience?

A.   the disillusionment felt by immigrants when the reality of the new country does not meet expectations

B.   the animosity felt among immigrants when one person abandons their cultural heritage

C.   the satisfaction an immigrant feels when he or she is accepted by the new community

D.   the ambivalence an immigrant experiences when replacing one cultural tradition with another

22. **Read the passage from Shakespeare's *Romeo and Juliet*. Then answer the question that follows.**

> Why then, O brawling love, O loving hate,
> O anything of nothing first create!
> Oh, heavy lightness, serious vanity,
> Misshapen chaos of well-seeming forms,
> Feather of lead, bright smoke, cold fire, sick health,
> Still-waking sleep, that is not what it is.

Which of the following literary devices does Shakespeare use in this passage?

A. paradox

B. malapropism

C. oxymoron

D. antithesis

23. **Read this stanza by the English poet and novelist Rudyard Kipling. Then answer the question that follows.**

> "What are the bugles blowin' for?" said Files-on-Parade.
> "To turn you out, to turn you out," the Colour-Sergeant said.
> "What makes you look so white, so white?" said Files-on-Parade.
> "I'm dreadin' what I've got to watch," the Colour-Sergeant said.
> "For they're hangin' Danny Deever, you can hear the Dead March play,
> The regiment's in 'ollow square—they're hangin' him to-day;
> They've taken of his buttons off an' cut his stripes away,
> An' they're hangin' Danny Deever in the mornin'."

This stanza is an example of what form of poetry?

A. ballad

B. dramatic monologue

C. limerick

D. ode

24. In Vladimir Nabokov's novel *Pale Fire*, the narrator, Charles Kinbote, is a college professor who believes that he is actually the exiled king of a mythical land called Zembla. This description would indicate that *Pale Fire* is an example of:

A. Romanticism.

B. modernism.

C. postmodernism.

D. neoclassicism

25. Which of the following passages is an example of the literary technique called stream of consciousness?

   A.   Whether I shall turn out to be the hero of my own life, or whether that station will be held by anybody else, these pages must show. To begin my life with the beginning of my life, I record that I was born (as I have been informed and believe) on a Friday, at twelve o'clock at night. It was remarked that the clock began to strike, and I began to cry, simultaneously.

   B.   The point in Elfride Swancourt's life at which a deeper current may be said to have permanently set in, was one winter afternoon when she found herself standing, in the character of hostess, face to face with a man she had never seen before—moreover, looking at him with a Miranda-like curiosity and interest that she had never yet bestowed on a mortal.

   C.   Boys are playing basketball around a telephone pole with a backboard bolted to it. Legs, shouts. The scrape and snap of Keds on loose alley pebbles seems to catapult their voices high into the moist March air blue above the wires.

   D.   Such fools we all are, she thought, crossing Victoria Street. For Heaven only knows why one loves it so, how one sees it so, making it up, building it round one, tumbling it, creating it every moment afresh; but the veriest frumps, the most dejected of miseries sitting on doorsteps (drink their downfall) do the same; can't be dealt with, she felt positive, by Acts of Parliament for that very reason: they love life.

26. The "local color" approach to writing, which typically features detailed descriptions of a certain region and its inhabitants' unique customs, habits, and manner of dressing and speaking, includes which of the following groups of writers?

   A.   Ezra Pound, Amy Lowell, H. D. (Hilda Doolittle)

   B.   Willa Cather, Kate Chopin, Sarah Orne Jewett

   C.   Richard Wright, James Baldwin, Zora Neale Hurston

   D.   Ernest Hemingway, F. Scott Fitzgerald, William Faulkner

27. **Read the passage from Shakespeare's *Tempest*, which is spoken by the magician Prospero. Then answer the question that follows.**

   > Our revels now are ended. These our actors,
   > As I foretold you, were all spirits, and
   > Are melted into air, into thin air;
   > And, like the baseless fabric of this vision,
   > The cloud-capped towers, the gorgeous palaces,
   > The solemn temples, the great globe itself,

Yea, all which it inherit, shall dissolve;
And, like this insubstantial pageant faded,
Leave not a rack behind. We are such stuff
As dreams are made on, and our little life
Is rounded with a sleep.

In this passage, what is Shakespeare primarily emphasizing?

A.   the insubstantial and meaningless nature of life

B.   the artificial and theatrical qualities of the performance

C.   the ultimate reckoning for both imperialists and native peoples

D.   the vanity of those who take life too seriously

28.   **Read the excerpt below from Frederick Douglass's autobiography,** *Narrative of the Life of Frederick Douglass.* **Then answer the question that follows.**

The plan which I adopted, and the one by which I was most successful, was that of making friends of all the little white boys whom I met in the street. As many of these as I could, I converted into teachers. With their kindly aid, obtained at different times and in different places, I finally succeeded in learning to read. When I was sent on errands, I always took my book with me, and by going one part of my errand quickly, I found time to get a lesson before my return. I used also to carry bread with me, enough of which was always in the house, and to which I was always welcome; for I was much better off in this regard than many of the poor white children in our neighborhood. This bread I used to bestow upon the hungry little urchins, who, in return, would give me that more valuable bread of knowledge. I am strongly tempted to give the names of two or three of those little boys, as a testimonial of the gratitude and affection I bear them; but prudence forbids—not that it would injure me, but it might embarrass them; for it is almost an unpardonable offence to teach slaves to read in this Christian country.

According to the Common Core State Standards, *Narrative of the Life of Frederick Douglass* belongs in the grade 6–8 text complexity band. Which of the following would be the biggest challenge to sixth-grade students' comprehension of this text?

A.   inferred meanings in the text

B.   text structure

C.   vocabulary and syntax

D.   background knowledge

29. **Read the excerpt from *Invisible Man* by Ralph Ellison. Then answer the question that follows.**

> Or again, you often doubt if you really exist. You wonder whether you aren't simply a phantom in other people's minds. Say, a figure in a nightmare which the sleeper tries with all his strength to destroy. It's when you feel like this that, out of resentment, you begin to bump people back.

Which of the following best describes the dominant mood of the excerpt?

A. alienation leading to anger

B. puzzlement resulting in resignation

C. fear progressing to helpless anxiety

D. outrage subsiding to restful anonymity

30. **Read the following passage from *Roughing It* by Mark Twain. Then answer the question that follows.**

> There is no end of wholesome medicine in such an experience. That morning we could have whipped ten such people as we were the day before—sick ones at any rate. But the world is slow, and people will go to "water cures" and "movement cures" and to foreign lands for health. Three months of camp life on Lake Tahoe would restore an Egyptian mummy to his pristine vigor, and give him an appetite like an alligator. I do not mean the oldest and driest mummies, of course, but the fresher ones. The air up there in the clouds is very pure and fine, bracing and delicious. And why shouldn't it be?—it is the same the angels breathe.

What is the author's primary purpose in writing this passage?

A. inform his audience about Lake Tahoe

B. persuade his audience to adopt a healthy lifestyle

C. mock his audience for succumbing to health fads

D. amuse and entertain his audience

31. In Shakespeare's *Julius Caesar*, Mark Antony says:

    Friends, Romans, countrymen, lend me your ears.

    This line contains an example of which of the following literary devices?

    A.   metaphor

    B.   metonymy

    C.   euphemism

    D.   synechdoche

32. **Read the excerpt from *The Flea* by John Donne. Then answer the question that follows.**

    > Mark but this flea, and mark in this,
    > How little that which thou deniest me is;
    > It suck'd me first, and now sucks thee,
    > And in this flea our two bloods mingled be.
    > Thou know'st that this cannot be said
    > A sin, nor shame, nor loss of maidenhead;
    > > Yet this enjoys before it woo,
    > > And pamper'd swells with one blood made of two;
    > > And this, alas! is more than we would do.

    What aspect of this poem makes it typical of the metaphysical school of poetry?

    A.   It examines the natural world minutely to express a religious sense.

    B.   It employs an outrageous metaphor in an extended comparison.

    C.   It satirizes the social conventions of romantic love.

    D.   It expresses the absurdity and meaninglessness of love and romance.

33. **Read the passage from *The Law of the Great Peace*, which originated with the Iroquois Confederacy. This is part of a ceremony to install new members of the tribal council.**

    > We now do crown you with the sacred emblem of the deer's antlers, the emblem of your chieftainship. You shall now become a mentor of the people of the Five Nations. The thickness of your skin shall be seven spans, which is to say that you will be proof against anger, offensive actions, and criticism. Your heart shall be filled with peace and good will. Your mind shall be filled with a yearning for the welfare of the people of the League. With endless patience you shall carry out your duty and your firmness shall be tempered with tenderness for your people. Neither anger nor fury shall find lodging in your mind. All your words and actions shall be marked with calm deliberation... .

Which of the following is the best paraphrase of the sentence "Neither anger nor fury shall find lodging in your mind"?

A.   A chief does not recognize anger.

B.   A chief does not display anger under any circumstances.

C.   A chief does not tolerate anger in others.

D.   A chief does not let anger rule him.

34.   To successfully read and analyze a literary text, a student must employ metacognition. Which of the following best describes this skill?

A.   The student strives to be always aware of his or her thinking processes while reading.

B.   The student decodes unfamiliar words by analyzing word parts and using context clues.

C.   The student skims a text to help decide on a purpose for reading.

D.   The student makes and verifies predictions while reading a text.

35.   **Read the excerpt from Homer's epic poem *The Odyssey*, in which the enchantress Circe warns Odysseus about the hypnotic voices of the Sirens. Then answer the question that follows.**

> Then royal Circe said, "So, it all came to pass.
> Listen well to what I tell you now,
> And let some God remind you of it later.
> Next, you will come to the Sirens
> Who beguile all men who encounter them.
> Whoever shall approach them unawares
> And listen to their sweet, enchanting voices
> Will never know the joy of reaching home
> And the greetings of a loving wife and children!
> Instead the Sirens will tempt him with their song
> As they sit there in the meadow
> Surrounded by a heap of moldering corpses,
> Bones on which hangs the shriveled skin.
> Plug your comrades' ears with softened beeswax
> Lest they should hear, and bid them row past swiftly.
> And if you must hear, then first instruct your men
> To bind you to the mast, and keep you bound there
> No matter how you beg them to release you.

This passage includes a reference to what important theme of *The Odyssey*?

A.   the theme of the gods' revenge

B.   the theme of mutiny and revolt

C.   the theme of returning home

D.   the theme of women's treachery against men

36.   Which of the following is a consumer document that provides information about returning a defective product?

A.   service contract

B.   warranty

C.   coupon

D.   instruction manual

37.   A researcher is studying Shakespearean drama for a thesis paper. In which of the following situations would it be most helpful for the researcher to use the electronic versions of texts?

A.   The researcher wants to examine how Shakespeare's plays were typeset by the compositors of the First Folio.

B.   The researcher wants to compare Shakespeare's ideas about science to those of modern physicists.

C.   The researcher wants to compare the number of times certain words appear in the works of Shakespeare compared to the works of Thomas Middleton.

D.   The researcher wants to examine early drawings and paintings depicting Shakespeare's plays in performance.

38.   **Read the excerpt from Thomas Middleton and William Rowley's play *The Changeling*. Then answer the question that follows.**

Beatrice: Why, 'tis impossible thou canst be so wicked,
Or shelter such a cunning cruelty,
To make his death the murderer of my honour.
Thy language is so bold and vicious,
I cannot see which way I can forgive it
With any modesty.

Deflores: Push, you forget your self —
A woman dipt in blood, and talk of modesty?

> *Beatrice:*   O misery of sin! Would I had been bound
> Perpetually unto my living hate
> In that Piracquo, than to hear these words.
> Think but upon the distance that Creation
> Set 'twixt thy blood and mine, and keep thee there.
>
> *Deflores:*   Look but into your conscience, read me there,
> "Tis a true book, you'll find me there your equal:
> Push, fly not to your birth, but settle you
> In what the act has made you …

This excerpt has elements that are characteristic of which form of drama?

A.   the Medieval miracle play

B.   Restoration drama

C.   ancient Greek drama

D.   the Jacobean revenge play

39.   Which of the following is most likely to be written in the first-person point of view?

A.   a fable

B.   a biography

C.   a dramatic monologue

D.   an historical essay

40.   **Read the workplace safety poster below. Then answer the question that follows.**

WHAT TO DO IN CASE OF FIRE:

If the fire is *inside* your space:

- Call *911* from a safe location.
- Use an extinguisher only if the fire is small and it is safe to do so.
- Warn others in immediate area and on your entire floor.
- Evacuate using stairwells—DO NOT use elevators.
- Close all doors behind you.
- Notify Security.

If the fire is *outside* your space:

- Feel the door before evacuating—DO NOT open hot doors.
- If trapped, seal the bottom of the door to help prevent smoke from entering.
- Call *911* to report your exact location in the building.
- If the door is cool, open it carefully and evacuate if it is safe to do so.
- If you encounter heavy smoke, drop to your hands and knees—stay near the floor and follow the wall to the nearest exit.

Which of the following textual features is used to differentiate procedures for inside and outside the worker's space?

A.   capital letters and parallel structure

B.   italicized words and parallel structure

C.   boldfaced words and capital letters

D.   bulleted list and capital letters.

Use the information below to answer questions 41 and 42.

A writer develops the paragraph below as part of an op-ed piece about the National Park System.

> [1] As Americans, we should be proud of our National Park System, and particularly of the jewel of that system: Yellowstone National Park. [2] Its history as a place of pride and preservation is worth reviewing. [3] In 1872 the U.S. Congress indeed passed a measure setting aside land for Yellowstone National Park. [4] Covering parts of what is now Wyoming, Montana, and Idaho, Yellowstone's magnificent vistas, natural rock formations, and hot springs left its earliest

visitors awestruck at its beauty. [5] In 1871, the third of three major expeditions, led by Ferdinand Vandiveer Hayden and including scientists, two artists, and a photographer, traveled to the area to see it for themselves. [6] After viewing the magnificent mountain ranges and the mud springs and geysers, among other features, the group agreed that the area should be set aside so that all people could enjoy its natural wonders. [7] Upon returning to the capital, Hayden detailed his findings in a long report and launched a campaign lobbying Congress to establish the area as a park. [8] Over the years and to our nation's enduring benefit, Congress has added other parks to our magnificent national system. [9] It is important that these areas remain pristine and protected forever.

41. In revising the draft, the writer should make which of the following changes to improve the logic and flow of the paragraph?

   A.   delete Sentence 2

   B.   insert Sentence 4 before Sentence 1

   C.   insert Sentence 3 after Sentence 7

   D.   delete Sentence 8

42. Which of the following best describes the author's main purpose in writing this passage?

   A.   to educate readers about the history of how Yellowstone became a national park

   B.   to entertain readers with poetic descriptions of Yellowstone and its beautiful natural features

   C.   to inform readers about the legislative process by which Congress can create a national park

   D.   to persuade readers that the National Park System should be preserved and protected forever

43. Which of the following is most appropriate for the closing of a business letter?

   I.   Sincerely,

   II.   With warmest wishes,

   III.   Respectfully,

   IV.   Wishing you the best,

   A.   I and IV

   B.   I and III

C.   II and IV

D.   III and IV

44. **Read the excerpt from a 1963 speech by Martin Luther King, Jr. Then answer the question that follows.**

In a sense we have come to our nation's capital to cash a check. When the architects of our republic wrote the magnificent words of the Constitution and the Declaration of Independence, they were signing a promissory note to which every American was to fall heir. This note was a promise that all men would be guaranteed the inalienable rights of life, liberty, and the pursuit of happiness.

It is obvious today that America has defaulted on this promissory note insofar as her citizens of color are concerned. Instead of honoring this sacred obligation, America has given the Negro people a bad check which has come back marked "insufficient funds." But we refuse to believe that there are insufficient funds in the great vaults of opportunity of this nation.

What method has King used to develop his idea?

A.   analogy

B.   problem and solution

C.   cause and effect

D.   compare and contrast

45. **Read the following sentence. Then answer the question that follows.**

Not long after he takes a job at a warehouse, Melvin began to pay off his creditors.

The sentence above contains which of the following errors?

A.   incorrect use of subordinate conjunction

B.   inconsistent use of verb tense

C.   incorrect use of punctuation

D.   dangling modifier

46. The role of revision in the writing process can best be described as which of the following?

    A.   a discrete task that should be completed by the second-draft stage of the writing process

    B.   a recursive task that may be done at any or all stages of the writing process

    C.   a discrete task that should be done only after the first-draft stage of the writing process

    D.   a task that should be divided between the drafting and the editing stages of the writing process

47. **Use the information below to answer the question that follows.**

A writer is developing an essay on recycling in the United States. Through research, the writer constructs the outline shown below.

    1.   Thesis: Recycling has become necessary because landfills are rapidly being closed and causing more damage to the environment.

    2.   Americans do not do their share in recycling.

        a.   The United States recycles only about 11 percent of its waste.

        b.   Recycling is required in only 15 percent of American communities.

    3.   Most everything in a trash bag can be reclaimed through recycling.

        a.   _____

        b.   _____

    4.   Wise consumer habits can help with problems related to trash and recycling.

        a.   A consumer should precycle when shopping.

        b.   Recycled goods are usually not more expensive than non-recycled products.

Given the outline for the essay, which details should be included in the blanks in section 3?

A.   a.   Landfills that leak pollution can contaminate groundwater.

       b.   Decomposition of waste in landfills releases methane, which can kill vegetation and spread disease.

B.   a.   Recycling saves energy and reduces pollution.

       b.   Japan recycles nearly 50 percent of its consumer waste.

C.   a.   Paper constitutes the largest portion of recycled material.

       b.   Plastic recycling is a relatively new idea, but is growing rapidly.

D.   a.   Consumers should learn what is recyclable and what is not.

       b.   Many manufacturers now label their products with information about recycling.

48. **Read the following sentence. Then answer the question that follows.**

He was taken to the hospital, and the examination was performed there.

Which of the following is the best description of this sentence?

A.   a simple sentence in the active voice

B.   a simple sentence in the passive voice

C.   a compound sentence in the active voice

D.   a compound sentence in the passive voice

49. **Read the following two sentences. Then answer the question that follows.**

Jorge worked very hard. He made his deadline.

Which of the following sentences shows a logical connection between the ideas?

A.   Despite the fact that Jorge worked very hard, he made his deadline.

B.   Because Jorge worked very hard, he made his deadline.

C.   Jorge worked very hard, although he made his deadline.

D.   Even though Jorge worked very hard, he made his deadline.

50. What is the name for the underlined part of the following sentence?

    <u>The guests having departed in twos and threes</u>, we decided the party was at an end.

    A.   a subordinate clause

    B.   an appositive

    C.   a verbal phrase

    D.   an absolute phrase

Practice Test 2, Subtest I
Answer Key

1.	B	18.	A	35.	C
2.	A	19.	C	36.	B
3.	B	20.	B	37.	C
4.	C	21.	B	38.	D
5.	D	22.	C	39.	C
6.	A	23.	A	40.	B
7.	B	24.	C	41.	C
8.	B	25.	D	42.	D
9.	C	26.	B	43.	B
10.	B	27.	B	44.	A
11.	D	28.	D	45.	B
12.	A	29.	A	46.	B
13.	C	30.	D	47.	C
14.	D	31.	B	48.	D
15.	B	32.	B	49.	B
16.	B	33.	D	50.	D
17.	C	34.	A		

Practice Test 2, Subtest I
Progress Chart: Multiple-Choice Questions

Below are grids that group questions by subject matter requirement codes. Place a checkmark in the box below each question that you answered correctly and calculate the percentage of correct answers for each area. This will give you an indication of your strengths and weaknesses and show you which topics need further study.

Reading Literature   SMR Code 1.1   ____/18

3	5	6	7	8	9	12	13	14	15

17	19	20	21	24	26	32	35

Craft and Structure of Literature   SMR Code 1.2   ___/14

1	2	4	16	18	22	23	25	27	29

31	34	38	39

Reading Informational Texts   SMR Code 1.3   ___/2

33	36

Craft and Structure of Informational Texts   SMR Code 1.4   ___/4

10	30	40

Integration of Knowledge and Ideas in Informational Texts   SMR Code 1.5   ___/1

44

Text Complexity   SMR Code 1.6   ___/1

28

Writing Processes (Individual and Collaborative)   SMR Code 3.1   ___/3

41	46	47

Text Types and Purposes   SMR Code 3.2   ___/1

11	42

Production and Distribution of Writing   SMR Code 3.3   ___/1

49

Conventions of Oral and Written Language   SMR Code 3.4   ___/4

43	45	48	50

Research to Build and Present Knowledge   SMR Code 3.5   ___/1

37

Practice Test 2, Subtest I
Detailed Answer Explanations

Reading Literature and Informational Texts

1. **B.**

   While the earliest sonnets probably were written in Sicily during the 1200s, the Italian poet Petrarch brought the form to a peak of perfection in the next century. In the 1500s, Sir Thomas Wyatt and Henry Howard, Earl of Surrey, adapted the form into English literature, and Shakespeare later mastered it. Its fourteen-line structure has the rhyme scheme *abbaabba, cdecde (*or *cdcdcd)* in Italian and *abba, cdcd, efef, gg* in English (the Shakespearian sonnet).

2. **A.**

   A *bildungsroman,* or "novel of formation," traces the moral, spiritual, or intellectual development of a young person as he or she faces various life experiences and develops a distinct personality and identity. Other examples of the *bildungsroman* in world literature include Gustave Flaubert's *Sentimental Education* (1869) and Thomas Mann's *The Magic Mountain* (1924).

3. **B.**

   In a trickster tale, the hero is usually an anthropomorphized animal and is mischievous, deceptive, or even treacherous in his behavior. In this tale, the hero is Anansi the spider, a common trickster hero in African and Jamaican folktales, who delights in eating Elephant's melons and insulting the King.

4. **C.**

   In this passage, Lee uses hyperbole, or exaggerated statements ("There was no hurry, for there was nowhere to go, nothing to buy, and no money to buy it with, nothing to see outside the boundaries of Maycomb County") to suggest that the townspeople complacently accept the circumscribed lives they lead.

5. **D.**

   The passage indicates that Segun, like many African intellectuals, feels "poised between two civilizations," which are African civilization and the West, and finds the balance difficult and "irksome." Attempts to deal with this clash of cultures and values formed an important theme for mid-twentieth century African writers.

6. **A.**

   Marlowe's poem is one of the famous examples of the pastoral genre, in which rural life or the life of shepherds is depicted in an idealized form.

7. **B.**

Whitman did not write formal verse, but instead wrote in long free-verse lines with repeated constructions ("Just as you feel … Just as any of you … Just as you are refreshed") that are influenced by biblical verses.

8. **B.**

The Divine Comedy is an allegory divided into three parts *(Inferno, Purgatorio, Paradiso)* that narrate Dante's journey through hell, purgatory, and heaven with first the poet Virgil and then the lovely Beatrice as his guides. The work, which employs an intricate structure based on the number three, is written in terza rima, or rhymed stanzas of three lines.

9. **C.**

In the Neoclassical period, poets used elegant heroic couplets and satirical humor to mock the pretensions and hypocrisies of society. Pope was one of the era's leading figures, whose essays and satires in heroic couplets included the mock-epic *Rape of the Lock, An Essay on Man, Epistle to Dr. Arbuthnot,* and one of the landmark satires in English literature, *The Dunciad.* In witty, aphoristic couplets, the poem ridicules those who pretend to have wit, culture, or knowledge but achieve only dullness.

10. **B.**

This non-literary text from 1930 expresses a point of view that is commonly heard today: the media image, or "propaganda," of a politician may differ markedly from the person's actual character and achievements. The article points out that Hoover ascended to the presidency "through the machinery of modern publicity," which is much the same way that many of today's politicians are carefully promoted and presented through elaborate media campaigns. The author goes on to observe that Hoover is suffering from overinflated expectations that he can't possibly live up to and would have been better off had he not presented the public with an ideal image of himself.

11. **D.**

Imagery is the use of descriptive language to enlist the senses in evoking a scene, situation, or state of mind. Here the poet clearly is presenting a fusillade of complementary images from nature to show its inadequacy to "content my musing mind."

12. **A.**

These stories all come from the traditional myths of the ancient Greeks. In "Daedalus and Icarus," the son of the inventor Daedalus flies on manmade wings too close to the sun. In "King Midas," a gold-loving ruler gains the ability to turn anything to gold at his touch. "Pandora's Box" tells of a young woman who disobeys Zeus and opens a box containing all the evils of the world.

13. **C.**

As a leader of the Transcendentalist movement, Emerson expounded the idea of the interconnectedness of all things, or the Great Chain of Being. The concept is similar to that of evolution, which Charles Darwin would present in his *Origin of Species* in 1859.

14. **D.**

The novel *Frankenstein* tells the story of a man of science who brings to life a stitched-together corpse that eventually takes revenge upon him. Its dark atmosphere of horror surrounds a morality tale about the limits of science.

15. **B.**

In the passage, the speaker insists that "the white man" "does not even speak our tongue" yet he "says that our customs are bad." He has also used religion as a divisive weapon: "Now he has won our brothers, and our clan can no longer act like one." This is an example of cultural imperialism, or forcing or insinuating one's own culture onto another people.

16. **B.**

Rhyme is the matching of end sounds in lines of verse. In this excerpt, Yeats employs slant rhymes, which match end sounds that are similar but not exactly the same: *on/moon, bodies/ladies*.

17. **C.**

Writers of fiction for young adults tend to employ these features to attract readers who might otherwise resist reading novels. Most fiction for young adults features adolescent characters who are trying to negotiate the problems and emotions of leaving childhood for the adult world. The novels tend to be short, brisk, and have a tight focus on a main character's thoughts and actions.

18. **A.**

An allusion is a reference in a literary work to some famous person, place, event, artwork, or other literary work. Writers use allusion to enrich their work with shared cultural markers. In this excerpt, de Hoyos is alluding to Walt Whitman's poem "Song of the Open Road," and wistfully imagining Whitman delivering his song on a guitar so that it would be "big enough for my people."

19. **C.**

Imagist poems were generally written in free verse and phrased in common speech while addressing a wide variety of subject matter and conveying meaning through clear, precisely described images. In Williams' brief poem consisting of one sentence, he uses precise words to present the red wheelbarrow, the glaze of the rain, and the white chickens in an almost painterly image.

20. **B.**

    Published in 1667, Milton's long poem in ten books was written, in his words, to "justify the ways of God to man." The other choices also refer to the themes of religious works: *Pilgrim's Progress* (A), *Everyman* (C), and *The Divine Comedy* (D).

21. **B.**

    In this excerpt, Muro points out that when the hero speaks English in the Mexican household, his sisters are "shocked," and his behavior "created an uproar" and was "unorthodox, if not scandalous." As a result, the hero lashes out further, complaining about eating Mexican dishes instead of American ones. The pressures to conform to the larger culture create animosity and tension at home.

22. **C.**

    An oxymoron is a phrase made up of words that seem contradictory when placed together but may actually express a special meaning, such as here with "heavy lightness," "serious vanity," "misshapen chaos of well-seeming forms," "feather of lead," "bright smoke," "cold fire," "sick health," and "still-waking sleep." Here Shakespeare is expressing Romeo's contradictory (and exuberant) feelings about life and love.

23. **A.**

    A ballad is a songlike poem that tells a story and often has a refrain, or repeated line or lines. Many ballads are in iambic form with alternating lines of four stresses and three stresses. (This example has seven stresses in each of the first four lines.) Popular in Europe from the Middle Ages down to the nineteenth century, ballads often were lurid accounts of murders, revenge, and violence—e.g., "An' they're hangin' Danny Deever in the mornin'."

24. **C.**

    Postmodernism as a literary movement presents a fragmented view of reality that draws on parody, pastiche, unreliable narrators, irony, black humor, and a general feeling of cultural exhaustion. Postmodern protagonists, like Nabokov's Charles Kinbote in *Pale Fire*, often create their own versions of reality to compete with or replace the reality of everyday experience.

25. **D.**

    In this passage from her novel *Mrs. Dalloway*, Virginia Woolf uses the device of stream of consciousness to present the unfiltered, free-associative thoughts of a character. This device was used by several modernist writers, including James Joyce in *Ulysses*.

26. **B.**

    "Local color" or regional literature focuses on the characters, dialect, customs, topography, and other features unique to a particular region of the United States. Willa Cather wrote about life on the Nebraska prairie. Kate Chopin set her most famous novel, *The Awakening*, in her native New Orleans. Sarah Orne Jewett described her home region of New England.

27. **B.**

Prospero's speech emphasizes the artificial nature of the play and its performance by referring to "our revels," "our actors," "the baseless fabric of this vision," and "this insubstantial pageant faded." Shakespeare's audience would also have noticed the reference to "the great globe itself," since the name of the theater where Shakespeare's dramas were performed was the Globe.

28. **D.**

Background knowledge about slavery and the state of racial relations in mid-nineteenth century America would present the biggest challenge for sixth-grade readers. The teacher would probably have to provide information on these topics to enhance the students' comprehension. The reader is not required to make difficult inferences while reading this text. The text does not have a complicated structure, since it is written as a fairly straightforward narrative. Vocabulary and syntax are not a major problem, as Douglass writes with great clarity.

29. **A.**

In this excerpt, Ellison expresses the frustration and alienation that results from being a black man ignored or marginalized in the society at large. His alienation then leads him to feel resentment against society, to the point where he begins "to bump people back."

30. **D.**

While Twain lightheartedly assumes the tone of a tour guide extolling the healthful virtues of Lake Tahoe, his real purpose is to entertain the reader. Thus he explains that "Three months of camp life on Lake Tahoe would restore an Egyptian mummy to his pristine vigor, and give him an appetite like an alligator," and describes the mountain air as "the same the angels breathe."

31. **B.**

Metonymy is a figure of speech in which a word is substituted for another word with which it is somehow linked or closely associated. Here Antony is using "ears" for "the ability to hear." Thus "lend me your ears" means "listen to me."

32. **B.**

The metaphysical poets of the early to mid-1600s used outrageous metaphors, extended comparisons, and subtle wit to explore the fundamental nature of reality and humanity's place in it. Their imagination and obscurity made them favorites of the modernist poets of the twentieth century.

33. **D.**

This is a test of reading comprehension and closely interpreting a text. If anger shall not "find lodging in [a chief's] mind," then that means the chief does not allow angry emotions to control him or guide his decisions.

34. **A.**

Metacognition is the skill of self-monitoring in reading, or striving to be always aware of one's thinking processes while reading. This helps readers monitor their level of engagement with the text, whether they understand what they are reading, and how they might use other strategies to improve their understanding.

35. **C.**

Since *The Odyssey* relates the adventures of Odysseus, a general striving to return home to his wife and family from the wars, one of the major themes of the epic is returning home. Circe warns Odysseus that the beguiling song of the Sirens may prevent his homecoming if he is not careful.

36. **B.**

A warranty is a legally binding assurance by a manufacturer that any problems caused by manufacturing defects during a set period will be repaired or else the item will be replaced. By contrast, a service contract is an agreement to have all repairs done during a certain period for a specified fee.

37. **C.**

Modern researchers often use the Internet or special databases to perform rapid detailed analyses of authors' word use and characteristic writing style.

38. **D.**

Middleton and Rowley's *The Changeling* is one of the greatest examples of a category of drama called the Jacobean revenge play. The play tells the story of Deflores, a henchman who commits a murder for Beatrice, a lady at court, then demands her love as payment for the deed. Like other plays in the genre, it is a dark exploration of human psychology, with a crowd-pleasing penchant for violence and sex (i.e., "cunning cruelty," "to make his death the murderer of my honor," "A woman dipt in blood," "O misery of sin!")

39. **C.**

A dramatic monologue is written from the point of view of the character who is speaking, so it would be in the first person: *I, me, mine.*

40. **B.**

Both the parallel structure (two groups of bulleted instructions) and the italicized words *inside* and *outside* emphasize the different procedures for a worker to follow in case of fire when inside the work space or outside the work space.

Composition and Rhetoric

41. **C.**

To improve the logical flow of the paragraph, the fact that Congress did indeed finally set aside the Yellowstone area as a national park should come after the steps describing the expedition and the lobbying campaign.

42. **D.**

While the passage does describe the process by which Yellowstone became a national park as well as describing the park's natural features and beauties, its main purpose is to urge that the National Park System be preserved. The author states that Americans "should be proud" of the park system and concludes with the author's opinion that "It is important that these areas remain pristine and protected forever." Another clue to the author's purpose is that the passage comes from an "op-ed piece" or opinion piece in a newspaper.

43. **B.**

The closing of a business letter should be formal, impersonal, and dignified. "With warmest wishes" and "Wishing you the best" are more appropriate for letters to friends or family members.

44. **A.**

King creates an analogy between a check or a promissory note and the promise of freedom for all Americans contained in the U.S. Constitution and the Declaration of Independence. As he puts it: "We have come to our nation's capital to cash a check."

45. **B.**

To make the use of verb tense consistent, the sentence should read: "Not long after he took a job at a warehouse, Melvin began to pay off his creditors."

46. **B.**

A recursive task or procedure is one that can repeat itself indefinitely. For successful writing, revision should occur at any or every stage of the writing process in which changes are necessary or desirable, from the planning stage to the editing and presentation stages.

47. **C.**

The topic of section 3 is the variety of types of material that can be recycled. So the most helpful details would be those about the recycling potential of paper and plastic.

48. **D.**

The sentence has two independent clauses, "He was taken to the hospital" and "the examination was performed there," which makes it a compound sentence. Also, both clauses are in the passive voice.

49. **B.**
Answer choice B is the only one of the sentences that shows the logical connection between Jorge working hard and making his deadline.

50. **D.**
An absolute phrase is made up of a noun followed by a participle or a participial phrase. It is called an "absolute" phrase because it does not modify any single word in the sentence but rather has a logical relationship to the entire sentence or part of it.

PRACTICE TEST 2

CSET: English Subtest II

Also available at the REA Study Center (*www.rea.com/studycenter*)

This practice test is also available online at the REA Study Center. The CSET: English test is only offered as a computer-based exam; therefore, we recommend that you take the online version of the practice test to receive these added benefits:

- **Timed testing conditions** – helps you gauge how much time you can spend on each question

- **Automatic scoring** – find out how you did on the test, instantly

- **On-screen detailed explanations of answers** – gives you the correct answer and explains why the other answer choices are wrong

- **Diagnostic score reports** – pinpoint where you're strongest and where you need to focus your study

Practice Test 2, Subtest II
Answer Sheet

1. (A) (B) (C) (D)
2. (A) (B) (C) (D)
3. (A) (B) (C) (D)
4. (A) (B) (C) (D)
5. (A) (B) (C) (D)
6. (A) (B) (C) (D)
7. (A) (B) (C) (D)
8. (A) (B) (C) (D)
9. (A) (B) (C) (D)
10. (A) (B) (C) (D)
11. (A) (B) (C) (D)
12. (A) (B) (C) (D)
13. (A) (B) (C) (D)
14. (A) (B) (C) (D)
15. (A) (B) (C) (D)
16. (A) (B) (C) (D)
17. (A) (B) (C) (D)
18. (A) (B) (C) (D)
19. (A) (B) (C) (D)
20. (A) (B) (C) (D)
21. (A) (B) (C) (D)
22. (A) (B) (C) (D)
23. (A) (B) (C) (D)
24. (A) (B) (C) (D)
25. (A) (B) (C) (D)

26. (A) (B) (C) (D)
27. (A) (B) (C) (D)
28. (A) (B) (C) (D)
29. (A) (B) (C) (D)
30. (A) (B) (C) (D)
31. (A) (B) (C) (D)
32. (A) (B) (C) (D)
33. (A) (B) (C) (D)
34. (A) (B) (C) (D)
35. (A) (B) (C) (D)
36. (A) (B) (C) (D)
37. (A) (B) (C) (D)
38. (A) (B) (C) (D)
39. (A) (B) (C) (D)
40. (A) (B) (C) (D)
41. (A) (B) (C) (D)
42. (A) (B) (C) (D)
43. (A) (B) (C) (D)
44. (A) (B) (C) (D)
45. (A) (B) (C) (D)
46. (A) (B) (C) (D)
47. (A) (B) (C) (D)
48. (A) (B) (C) (D)
49. (A) (B) (C) (D)
50. (A) (B) (C) (D)

Practice Test 2, Subtest II
Language, Linguistics, and Literacy

1. Which of the following words has a predictable pronunciation based on reliable sound-symbol correspondences?

    A. photography

    B. knife

    C. global

    D. tension

2. Which of the following English words was borrowed from the German language?

    A. chandelier

    B. kindergarten

    C. dollar

    D. canyon

3. **Read the dialogue below. Then answer the question that follows.**

    Dolores: We're going to need chicken for tonight's dinner.

    Ricardo: What are we having?

    Dolores: Chicken tortilla soup.

    Ricardo: Yes, we will need chicken to make chicken tortilla soup.

    Dolores: Why are you still here?

    To a person who has a pragmatic knowledge of American English, it's obvious that Dolores means:

    A. Why don't you go to the store and get the chicken?

    B. Why are you bothering me?

    C. You don't belong in this house.

    D. Why don't you make the chicken tortilla soup yourself?

4. Which of the following nouns is formed by adding a derivational suffix to a verb?

    A. generosity

    B. employer

    C. truthfulness

    D. dentistry

5. Which of the words below contains a base word and a prefix?

    A. president

    B. premium

    C. presentable

    D. prearrange

6. **Use the diagram below to answer the question that follows.**

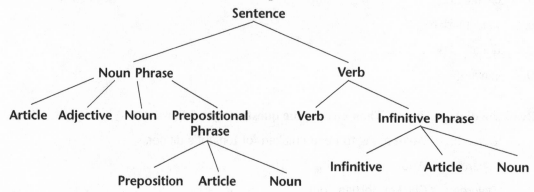

    This diagram represents the structure of which of the following sentences?

    A. A sunny afternoon at the ballpark attracts a big crowd for the game.

    B. The excited fans had gathered for the game several hours early.

    C. A hopeful fan outside the ballpark wanted to buy a ticket.

    D. The tickets to see this ballgame are going to be expensive.

7. Which of the following words contains an overt inflectional ending?

    A. encouragement

    B. improves

    C. wallboard

    D. sensational

8. What is another name for a simplified contact language made up of two or more languages?

    A. pidgin

    B. Creole

    C. interlanguage

    D. dialect

9. Which area of linguistic study is concerned with a speaker's intended meaning rather than his or her literal meaning?

    A. pragmatics

    B. semantics

    C. morphology

    D. etymology

10. Which branch of linguistics allows an English speaker to know that plural endings depend on the last sound of the word stem, as in *spatula/spatulas* and *patch/patches*?

    A. phonology

    B. semantics

    C. morphology

    D. syntax

11. Which of the following describes the most significant effect that the Great Vowel Shift had on the English language?

    A. Regional variations of vowel sounds arose within England and also in Scotland and Wales.

    B. The vowel sounds of "British" English no longer corresponded to the vowel sounds of "American" English.

    C. The spellings of certain words in Great Britain diverged from the spellings used in the American colonies.

    D. The spelling of certain vowel sounds in English no longer corresponded to the pronunciation of those sounds.

12. Which of the following words contains four phonemes?

    A. combination

    B. show

    C. throat

    D. unusual

13. Rules of grammar are generally too complex for young children to figure out, yet they still are able to use language grammatically. This is an example of:

    A. Ferdinand de Saussure's Structuralist Theory of Language.

    B. Stephen Krashen's Affective Filter Hypothesis.

    C. Eric Lenneberg's Critical Period Hypothesis.

    D. Noam Chomsky's Theory of Universal Grammar.

14. A reader is using decoding skills when he or she does which of the following?

    A. applies phonics and syllabication skills to sound out an unfamiliar word

    B. rereads a difficult passage in a story to understand it better

    C. skims a story to find unfamiliar words before actually reading the text

    D. looks up the meaning of an unfamiliar word in a dictionary

15. Which of the following sentences is unambiguous with regard to its meaning?

    A. The landlord gave her cat food.

    B. The lady hit the man with the umbrella.

    C. She put on her robe and went downstairs.

    D. I cannot recommend this candidate too highly.

16. An office worker, told that his use of the pronoun *who* is often incorrect, says to a caller on the phone, "Whom should I say is on the line?" This type of linguistic behavior is an example of which of the following?

    A. borrowing

    B. negative transfer

    C. code-switching

    D. hypercorrection

17. Which of the following terms has entered contemporary American English usage as a result of workplace concerns about gender neutrality?

    A.   blogger

    B.   mail carrier

    C.   ballplayer

    D.   editor

18. Which of the following statements is true about Stephen Krashen's Acquisition-Learning hypothesis?

    A.   The "acquisition" system is significantly more important than the "learning" system.

    B.   The "learning" system is significantly more important than the "acquisition" system.

    C.   The "learning" system uses a subconscious process much like the one that children go through in learning a first language.

    D.   The "acquisition" system is the traditional process of formal instruction in a language.

19. Old English is closely identified with which of the following?

    A.   Anglo-Norman

    B.   The Great Vowel Shift

    C.   Anglo-Saxon

    D.   The English Renaissance

20. The word *lustrous* comes from the Latin root *lustrare,* meaning "purify, polish, or make bright." This information is part of the word's:

    A.   orthography

    B.   etymology

    C.   morphology

    D.   grammar

21. A reader of Shakespeare's *Julius Caesar* understands that Mark Antony's repeated claim that Brutus is "an honorable man" is meant ironically. This is an example of which of the following?

    A.   pragmatic competence

    B.   code-switching

C. total immersion

D. semantic mapping

22. **Use the sentence below to answer the question that follows.**

> There was widespread concern that the villagers might *contract* malaria from the mosquitoes.

Which strategy would be most effective for a reader to use to pronounce the italicized word correctly?

A. Compare the word to similar words that the reader knows.

B. Think about the differences between British and American pronunciation.

C. Use content clues and analyze the syntax of the sentence.

D. Recognize the word as a high-frequency sight word.

23. A student is reading aloud from *Roughing It* by Mark Twain. Occasionally the student pauses to "think aloud" when confronted by an unfamiliar word.

> (Reading aloud)
> We found the small skiff belonging to the Brigade boys, and without loss of time set out across a deep bend of the lake—
>
> [Thinking aloud]
> What's a skiff? If they are setting out across the lake, it must be some kind of small boat.

The student is mainly using which of the following metacognitive strategies for constructing meaning?

A. paraphrasing

B. visualizing

C. recalling prior knowledge

D. using context clues

24. Which of the following would be characteristic of a person exhibiting the linguistic behavior called borrowing?

A. speaking a hybrid language like Spanglish

B. speaking formal English to one group and informal slangy English to another group

C. importing grammatical structures from a first language into a second

D. speaking a rudimentary contact language like pidgin

25. **Read the sentence below. Then answer the question that follows.**

    Many houses were damaged in the hailstorm, but luckily the village glazier was able to replace the windows early the next day.

    Which group of words in the sentence is most helpful as a context clue to the meaning of *glazier*?

    A.   Many houses were damaged

    B.   in the hailstorm

    C.   was able to replace the windows

    D.   early the next day

26. Which of the following is an example of negative transfer?

    A.   "The coach told he and I to do the drill again."

    B.   "The girl I met yesterday had eyes blue and very beautiful."

    C.   "I lighted the fire in the stove and fighted back the urge to sneeze."

    D.   "Someday I plan to travel *todo el mundo*."

27. In which of the following sentences does the underlined word function as a non-count noun?

    A.   Today's <u>move</u> has been in the planning stages for weeks.

    B.   Have you wrapped all the kitchen <u>items</u> in newspaper?

    C.   It should only take one <u>session</u> to move everything.

    D.   Orlando helped us move the <u>furniture</u> into the truck.

28. To clarify a confusing passage, a reader turns to other passages in the same article. Which of the following describes this reading comprehension skill?

    A.   visual imaging

    B.   cohesion analysis

    C.   repeated oral reading

    D.   semantic mapping

29. Which of the following groups of words is part of a word family based on a common root?

    A.   post, impostor, posterior

    B.   word, worthy, worth

C.   mortician, immortal, mortality

D.   unfamiliar, family, famous

30.   Which of the following is the best definition of the term *semantics*?

A.   a standardized system for writing words with the proper letters according to accepted rules of usage

B.   a detailed account of a word's origin and derivation

C.   the process by which people acquire the ability to understand and use words

D.   the study of meaning in language, both oral and contextual

31.   Research indicates that variables such as motivation, self-confidence, and anxiety play an important role in language acquisition. Which linguistic theory accounts for this phenomenon?

A.   the Affective Filter hypothesis

B.   the Acquisition-Learning hypothesis

C.   the Natural Order hypothesis

D.   the Critical Period hypothesis

32.   Which of the following passages would be most appropriate for an academic essay about Mark Twain's *The Adventures of Huckleberry Finn*?

A.   Mischievously yet magisterially, Twain plays the literary ventriloquist through his homely narrator, Huckleberry Finn, to express his own animosity towards the abominable system of slavery that he abhors.

B.   With a mixture of humor and pathos, Twain allows his narrator, Huck, to come to his own conclusions about Jim's humanity and the foolishness of racial bias.

C.   Twain writes Huck's dialogue like he is just an ignorant boy, but he shows how Huck figures out how wrong racism and slavery are all the same.

D.   Huck is a great creation. He talks like a bumpkin, but often he makes sense. He comes to love and respect Jim. Huck sees how stupid racism is. That makes it a great book.

33. While infants start out able to discriminate between all the phonemes occurring in human language, they soon lose the ability to distinguish between phonemes that they do not hear being used in their own environment. This finding helps to explain which of the following?

    A. the tendency for some second-language learners to use the second language in school or work situations and the first language at home or among friends

    B. the internalized set of rules for speaking and understanding a second language used by new speakers

    C. the inflected third-person singular -s becomes one of the last features learned by a speaker of English as a second language

    D. the tendency for adult learners of a second language to retain an accent

34. **Read the sentence below. Then answer the question that follows.**

    Although I never watch comic book movies, I saw *The Avengers: Age of Ultron* last night, and I absolutely loved it!

    What type of sentence is this?

    A. simple sentence

    B. compound sentence

    C. complex sentence

    D. compound-complex sentence

35. A writer would like to develop an essay in support of the thesis statement below.

    Running is a sport for all ages that provides a number of excellent lifelong benefits.

    Given the writer's purpose, which of the following organizational structures would be most appropriate for this essay?

    A. comparison and contrast

    B. definition and example

    C. enumeration and description

    D. problem and solution

36. A teacher writes the word *courage* in a large circle on the blackboard and solicits responses from the class through brainstorming or free association. This exercise is an example of which of the following?

    A. note taking

    B. semantic mapping

    C. word analogies

    D. cohesion analysis

37. Which of the following sentences uses a prepositional phrase to modify a noun?

    A. The old gentleman in a top hat and tuxedo stood up when the orchestra launched into *The Star-Spangled Banner.*

    B. The orchestra began the concert before most of the audience had taken their seats.

    C. During the last piece, the oboe player outdid herself with a beautiful interlude.

    D. At the concert's conclusion, the conductor bowed amidst the deafening cheers.

38. **Read the sentences below. Then answer the question that follows.**

    • Preston Sturges is my favorite Hollywood filmmaker.

    • He wrote and directed *The Lady Eve* and *The Palm Beach Story.*

    Which of the following sentences combines the two sentences above using a subordinate clause?

    A. Preston Sturges is my favorite Hollywood filmmaker, and he wrote and directed *The Lady Eve* and *The Palm Beach Story.*

    B. Preston Sturges, my favorite Hollywood filmmaker, wrote and directed *The Lady Eve* and *The Palm Beach Story.*

    C. Preston Sturges, who wrote and directed *The Lady Eve* and *The Palm Beach Story,* is my favorite Hollywood filmmaker.

    D. My favorite Hollywood filmmaker, Preston Sturges, wrote and directed *The Lady Eve* and *The Palm Beach Story.*

39. In which of the following sentences do the underlined words function as a verb complement?

    A. If you join a health club, tell me how you like it.

    B. To exercise in the morning, I get up at six.

    C.   <u>To find time to exercise every day</u> is my goal.

    D.   Akira considered <u>joining a health club</u>.

40.   Which word set is composed of verbs that function as modals?

    A.   shall, might, can

    B.   fix, inflict, inspect

    C.   thinking, reading, running

    D.   bailed, lost, ran

41.   A teacher wants her students to evaluate the effectiveness of an author's technique. Which of the following questions should she ask?

    A.   Based on the events in the story so far, what do you think will happen at the end?

    B.   What is the setting of this story?

    C.   How well does the author develop the main conflict in this story?

    D.   What experience in your own life is similar to the situation described in the story?

42.   Which of the following is a British spelling of an English word?

    A.   flour

    B.   organise

    C.   honor

    D.   traveler

43.   While reading F. Scott Fitzgerald's *The Great Gatsby* for the first time, a student makes a note about the passage describing a billboard with an enormous pair of eyes. Later, the student connects this image with a description of the eyes keeping a "watchful vigil." Which strategy for understanding a text is the student employing here?

    A.   questioning

    B.   word analysis

    C.   predicting

    D.   concept formation

44. Which of the following sentences consists of two independent clauses connected by a coordinating conjunction?

    A. My dog Hannibal refuses to fetch a stick, nor will he run after a rubber ball.

    B. Hannibal is a stubborn creature, which is quite an understatement.

    C. Despite my best efforts, he simply sits in the shade all day.

    D. Hannibal occasionally trots to his food bowl or chases a squirrel without enthusiasm.

45. In which of the following sentences is the underlined portion a verbal phrase?

    A. My grandmother was sitting on the front porch <u>when I got home</u>.

    B. <u>Sitting on the front porch</u> is my grandmother's favorite way to relax.

    C. <u>After dinner</u>, we all gathered on the porch.

    D. A cool breeze <u>blows across the porch</u> in the evening.

46. A student understands that in the following sentence, the underlined portion is an adverb clause modifying the verb *had left*.

    Most of the crowd had left the arena <u>before the game ended</u>.

    The student's ability to recognize this is an example of:

    A. inferential comprehension

    B. semantic mapping

    C. pragmatic competence

    D. syntactical knowledge

47. Which of the following sentences uses a prepositional phrase to modify a verb?

    A. Working as a set designer in films can be a rewarding career.

    B. Brimming with ideas, a good set designer creates a fantasy world.

    C. My sister designed a space station set during her vacation.

    D. Working with a familiar crew, she loves her job.

48. In the word *rationalize* the suffix *-ize* does which of the following?

    A.   changes a noun into an adjective

    B.   changes an adjective into a verb

    C.   changes a verb into an adjective

    D.   changes a verb into a noun

49. Nouns, verbs, and adjectives are found in languages that have never interacted or influenced each other. This fact supports which of the following?

    A.   the ability of adults to learn languages as easily as children

    B.   the need for total immersion language classes

    C.   Chomsky's theory of a Universal Grammar

    D.   Krashen's Theory of Second Language Acquisition

50. Learning to recognize prefixes, suffixes, and roots as well as their meanings is a part of:

    A.   orthographic analysis

    B.   syntactical analysis

    C.   pragmatic competence

    D.   morphemic analysis

Practice Test 2, Subtest II
Answer Key

1. C	18. A	35. C
2. B	19. C	36. B
3. A	20. B	37. A
4. B	21. A	38. C
5. D	22. C	39. D
6. C	23. D	40. A
7. B	24. A	41. C
8. A	25. C	42. B
9. A	26. C	43. D
10. C	27. D	44. A
11. D	28. B	45. B
12. C	29. C	46. D
13. D	30. D	47. C
14. A	31. A	48. B
15. C	32. B	49. C
16. D	33. D	50. D
17. B	34. D	

Practice Test 2, Subtest II
Progress Chart: Multiple-Choice Questions

Below are grids that group questions by subject-matter requirement codes. Place a checkmark in the box below each question that you answered correctly and calculate the percentage of correct answers for each area. This will give you an indication of your strengths and weaknesses and show you which topics need further study.

Human Language Structures   SMR Code 2.1   ____/23

1	2	3	4	5	6	7	9	10	11
12	15	17	19	20	21	22	29	30	36
46	48	50							

Acquisition and Development of   SMR Code 2.2   ____/17
Language and Literacy

8	13	14	16	18	23	24	25	26	28
31	32	33	35	41	43	49			

Grammatical Structures of English   SMR Code 2.3   ____/10

27	34	37	38	39	40	42	44	45	47

Practice Test 2, Subtest II
Detailed Answer Explanations

Language, Linguistics, and Literacy

1. **C.**

   The pronunciation of the word *global* is simple because of the reliable, or predictable, sound-symbol correspondences of its letters. Less predictable are the sound-symbol correspondences in the word *photography* (the digraph *ph* pronounced as /f/), in the word *knife* (the digraph *kn* pronounced as /n/), and in the word *tension* (the digraph *si* pronounced as /sh/).

2. **B.**

   The German word *kindergarten* literally means "garden of children." In English, it refers to a school class that precedes the first grade.

3. **A.**

   A person who lacks a pragmatic knowledge of American English usage might not understand Dolores's last remark. Dolores is indicating that Ricardo should quit joking and go get the chicken for the soup.

4. **B.**

   The noun *employer* is formed by adding the derivational suffix *–er* to the verb *employ*.

5. **D.**

   The word *prearrange* contains the base word *arrange* and the prefix *pre-*, which means "before." In the words *president, premium,* and *presentable,* the letters *pre* are not used as a prefix.

6. **C.**

   The sentence in choice C has the same structure as the diagram, including the noun phrase ("A hopeful fan outside the ballpark") and the verb with an infinitive phrase ("wanted to buy a ticket"). The phrases can be divided into the same individual parts of speech as shown in the diagram (e.g., the article *A,* the adjective *hopeful,* the noun *fan,* and the prepositional phrase *outside the ballpark*). Each level of the diagram corresponds to a level of syntactic structure.

7. **B.**

   The *s* in *improves* is an overt inflectional suffix that functions as the indicator for the present-tense, third-person singular form of the verb *improve*. In English, inflectional suffixes never change the base word's part of speech—*improve* and *improves* are both verbs. A derivational suffix such as *–ment* changes the part of speech of the word to which it is attached, as in *encouragement*.

8. **A.**

Makeshift languages, or pidgins, were originally employed by traders, plantation workers and overseers, and Europeans in their contacts with various indigenous peoples. The term *pidgin* apparently came from the Chinese word for "business." Pidgin is characterized by a small vocabulary and simple grammatical structures.

9. **A.**

Pragmatics focuses on language as a tool for communication. It looks at how different types of sentences or phrases are used in different contexts and for different purposes. In general, pragmatic theory is concerned with a speaker's intended meaning rather than the literal meaning of an utterance. For example, it would examine how different forms of speech can be used to request something, assert something, or inquire about something.

10. **C.**

Morphology is the branch of linguistics that deals with the internal structure and forms of words. It is concerned with the rules for the use of morphemes, or the smallest units of meaning, in a language.

11. **D.**

In the Great Vowel Shift of the fifteenth century, pronunciation of the long vowels in English slowly changed. For example, long *e* was originally pronounced like the *e* in *there* or the *a* in *fate*, but by the sixteenth century, after the Great Vowel Shift, the long *e* was pronounced like the *e* in *sweep*, as it is today. Since English spelling did not alter to reflect the Great Vowel Shift, vowel symbols still correspond to their former sounds. The result has been that English spelling is one of the most difficult systems in the world.

12. **C.**

The phoneme, the smallest unit of speech sound, combines with other units of speech sound to form a word. For example, the word *grow* contains three phonemes: /g/, /r/, and /ō/. The word *throat* contains four phonemes: /th/, /r/, /ō/, and /t/. It is important to remember that a phoneme is *not* the same as a syllable.

13. **D.**

Chomsky noticed that toddlers move quickly from forming single words to speaking in complete sentences. He explained this capacity for acquiring language skills with his theory of Universal Grammar or the Language Acquisition Device. He reasoned that this capacity must be genetically endowed or innate, since it can't have been learned in the ordinary way.

14. **A.**

Decoding, or the ability to translate the symbols of letters and words into meaningful information, is an important tool for comprehension. Students invariably find many unfamiliar words in their reading, and they must be prepared to decode these words in various ways. Students should use language sounds (phonics) and the meanings of word parts (morphemes) to analyze and decode unfamiliar words. They may also use context clues, or the words and sentences around an unfamiliar word, to decode the word.

15. **C.**
Ambiguity results when a word or phrase can be understood to have more than one possible function in a sentence. In choice A, the landlord could be giving her cat some food or giving her cat-food. In choice B, did the lady hit the man with her umbrella or did she hit the man who was carrying the umbrella? In choice D, does the speaker mean to praise the candidate or admit that he or she cannot offer a high recommendation?

16. **D.**
Hypercorrection is when a person who has been corrected for a mistake in usage makes further mistakes in trying to avoid the original error.

17. **B.**
Mail carrier is the gender-neutral term that has replaced *postman, mailman,* or *mailwoman.*

18. **A.**
Krashen's research indicated that the "acquisition" system depends on natural, meaningful communication in the target language, and so is a more fundamental process for new speakers than the "learning" system.

19. **C.**
Old English or Anglo-Saxon developed from the Germanic dialects spoken by tribes migrating from northern Europe about 500 CE. By about 730 CE, the Venerable Bede, an early historian, was referring to invaders from the north as Angles, Saxons, and Jutes.

20. **B.**
In a dictionary, the etymology, or word origin, appears in square brackets after the pronunciation key and part of speech of the word.

21. **A.**
Pragmatic competence is the ability to understand the true meaning or insinuated meaning of an utterance or passage of writing.

22. **C.**
By using context clues and examining the syntax of the sentence, a reader could determine that *contract* here is used as a verb meaning "catch or get an illness," and so is pronounced with the stress on the second syllable.

23. **D.**

The student is using the metacognitive strategy of using context clues to construct meaning. The student uses words from the passage—"set out across a deep bend of the lake"—to guess that the narrator must be traveling in a boat; therefore a "small skiff" must be a small boat.

24. **A.**

Borrowing is when a speaker switches into his or her first language and borrows single words or entire phrases for which he or she knows no equivalent in the second language. The result often is the formation of a hybrid language such as Spanglish.

25. **C.**

A *glazier* is a tradesperson who sells and replaces glass; thus, the phrase "was able to replace the windows" is the best context clue to the word's meaning.

26. **C.**

This is an example of negative transfer, which is when a speaker uses skills from a previously learned behavior or topic but applies them incorrectly to a new topic. For example, a student who recalls that the past tense of *fake* is *faked* and then assumes that the past tense of *take* is *taked* is employing negative transfer.

27. **D.**

A noncount noun, or mass noun, refers to things that cannot be counted because they are not divisible into parts. It often names an abstraction or has a collective meaning, as in *furniture*.

28. **B.**

Cohesion analysis is a method of analyzing how all the parts of a work come together to create an overall effect or convey a message. For example, a reader faced with a difficult passage might read ahead or review previous sections to see how the unfamiliar part fits into the whole.

29. **C.**

These three words—*mortician, immortal,* and *mortality*—all share the common Latin root *mort-*, which means "death."

30. **D.**

Semantics deals with word meanings, sentence meanings, and contextual understanding for oral and written communications.

31. **A.**

Krashen's theory says that a number of "affective variables," such as motivation, self-confidence, and anxiety, play an important "facilitative but non-causal" role in language acquisition. Low motivation, lack of self-esteem, and high levels of anxiety function as filters that create a mental block, preventing the learner from using comprehensible input for acquisition.

32. **B.**

An academic essay on Mark Twain's *The Adventures of Huckleberry Finn* should follow the conventions of Standard English and should be written in a formal style that is clear without being stilted, choppy, or breezy.

33. **D.**

Research indicates that second-language learners have difficulty in recognizing certain phonemes in the second language because there is a limited developmental period during which infants and children can discriminate between all phonemes in speech. Thus, older learners of a second language may retain an accent due to their inability to distinguish and properly reproduce certain phonemes.

34. **D.**

This is a compound-complex sentence with two independent clauses ("I saw *The Avengers* last night" and "I loved it") connected by a coordinating conjunction ("and") and with a dependent clause ("Although I never watch comic book movies").

35. **C.**

The best organizational structure for this essay would be one that provides a list and descriptions of facts and examples supporting the thesis statement about the lifelong benefits of running as a sport. The writer could explain how a regular regime of distance running improves cardiovascular health, keeps weight problems in check, and helps provide a positive mental outlook. The writer could also describe social benefits such as joining running clubs, participating in running events, and forming neighborhood running groups on weekends.

36. **B.**

Semantic mapping is a method of gathering responses to a word or phrase through a process of brainstorming or free association. The teacher usually writes a word or phrase on the blackboard and asks students to suggest other words they think of as a result. Graphic organizers such as Venn diagrams, clusters, or word trees can also be used.

37. **A.**

The prepositional phrase "in a top hat and tuxedo" modifies the noun *gentleman*.

38. **C.**

A group of related words that contains a subject and a predicate is called a clause. A subordinate clause is one that cannot stand alone. In answer choice C, the subordinate clause is "who wrote and directed *The Lady Eve* and *The Palm Beach Story*."

39. **D.**

The phrase "joining a health club" is a verb complement serving as the object of the verb *considered*.

40. **A.**

Also called auxiliary verbs, modals are a set of English verbs that are used with other verbs to express capability, possibility, willingness, suggestion, or something similar.

41. **C.**

To evaluate any part of an author's performance, a reader must judge its effect. Therefore, a question that asks "how well" the author did something encourages the reader to make an evaluation.

42. **B.**

American spelling employs *–ize* in place of *–ise* in certain words, such as *organize/organise*. The British spelling of *honor* is *honour*, and the British spelling of *traveler* is *traveller*.

43. **D.**

Concept formation is a metacognitive reading strategy used during and after a reading to connect and categorize ideas and reflect on the material's overall meaning and effect.

44. **A.**

The two independent clauses are "My dog Hannibal refuses to fetch a stick" and "will he run after a rubber ball." (The complete verb in the second clause is *will run.*) The coordinating conjunction *nor* joins the two clauses.

45. **B.**

The phrase "Sitting on the front porch" is a gerund phrase that functions as a noun and the subject of the sentence.

46. **D.**

Syntax refers to the arrangement and relationship of words in phrases and sentences. The ability to analyze a sentence and its various parts of speech shows syntactical knowledge.

47. **C.**

A prepositional phrase consists of a preposition and its object plus any modifiers. In the sentence "My sister designed a space station set during her vacation," the preposition is the word *during* and the word *vacation* is the object of the preposition. The phrase "during her vacation" serves as an adverb modifying the verb *designed*.

48. **B.**

The suffix *–ize* is often added to an adjective to create a verb. For example, adding *–ize* to the adjective *rational* creates the verb *rationalize* meaning "to make something seem reasonable or rational."

49. **C.**

Chomsky's concept of Universal Grammar is a set of principles that apply to all languages and are unconsciously accessible to every human language user. Universal Grammar includes the fundamental qualities shared by all languages—which include the equivalents of nouns, verbs, and adjectives. Similarities between languages may be due to common aspects of human experience, common patterns of descent, and contact between cultures and the borrowing of words and sentence structures.

50. **D.**

Morphemic analysis is used to decode unfamiliar words by identifying word parts (roots and affixes) and their meanings.

PRACTICE TEST 2

CSET: English Subtest III

Also available at the REA Study Center (*www.rea.com/studycenter*)

This practice test is also available online at the REA Study Center. The CSET: English test is only offered as a computer-based exam; therefore, we recommend that you take the online version of the practice test to receive these added benefits:

- **Timed testing conditions** – helps you gauge how much time you can spend on each question

- **On-screen detailed analysis of sample essays** – guides you to a 4-point response

SCORING THE CSET: ENGLISH SUBTEST III

In CSET: English Subtest III, you will have 2 hours to respond to two constructed-response writing prompts.

Your response essays will be scored by California educators using focused holistic scoring. The scorers will evaluate the overall effectiveness of your essay responses with a focus on the performance characteristics that have been judged most important for CSET: English Subtest III. These performance characteristics, or writing standards, are established by the California Commission on Teacher Credentialing and include the following:

> **Purpose:** The extent to which the response focuses on and accomplishes the task set by the prompt in relation to relevant CSET: English subject-matter requirements.

> **Subject-matter knowledge:** The extent to which the response applies accurate subject matter knowledge as described in the relevant CSET: English subject-matter requirements.

> **Support:** The extent to which the response employs quality, appropriate supporting evidence in relation to CSET: English subject-matter requirements.

> **Depth and breadth of understanding:** the extent to which the response shows understanding of the relevant CSET: English subject-matter requirements.

Your essay responses will be scored based on the following scoring scale:

Scoring Scale

4: To earn a **4-point score**, your response must show that you have a sophisticated grasp of the relevant knowledge and skills as defined in the subject-matter requirements for CSET: English. These include:

- The ability to address the specific purpose of the assignment comprehensively and without distractions in order to accomplish the assigned task.

- The ability to select and include relevant supporting evidence and examples that demonstrate your overall understanding of the subject matter.

A 4-point essay demonstrates that you have a thorough understanding of the assignment and the relevant subject matter.

3: To earn a **3-point score**, your response must show that you have an overall or general understanding of the relevant knowledge and skills as defined in the subject-matter requirements for CSET: English. These include:

- The ability to recognize the overall purpose of the assignment in order to accomplish the assigned task adequately.

- The ability to recognize and apply some accurate information and relevant supporting evidence to the given subject matter.

A 3-point essay demonstrates that you have an adequate or sufficient understanding of the assignment.

2: To earn a **2-point score**, your response will show that you have a basic, partial, or insufficient understanding of the knowledge and skills as defined in the subject-matter requirements for CSET: English. These include:

- The ability to address the assignment's purpose only partially or not at all.

- The ability to recognize and apply only a limited amount, if any, of relevant supporting evidence, demonstrating only a partial understanding of the subject matter.

A 2-point essay demonstrates that you have a limited, partial, or unsatisfactory understanding of the assignment.

1: To earn a **1-point score**, your response will show that you have little or no understanding of the knowledge and skills as defined in the subject-matter requirements for CSET: English. These include:

- The lack of ability to recognize or achieve the most basic elements and goals of the assignment.

- The lack of ability to recognize or apply basic relevant supporting evidence, demonstrating little or no understanding of the subject matter.

A 1-point essay demonstrates that you have a limited, partial, or unsatisfactory understanding of the assignment.

U: A grade of **"U" (Unscorable)** is given to essays that are completely unrelated to the assignment, illegible, written in a language other than English, and/or lack a sufficient amount of your own original writing. Most problems that cause an essay to earn a "U" are solvable by simply slowing down and pacing yourself as you systematically respond to each question or prompt.

B: A grade of **"B" (Blank)** is given to essay responses left blank. Never leave a test question blank if at all possible.

Practice Test 2, Subtest III
Composition and Rhetoric;
Reading Literature and Informational Texts

Practice Question 1

Read the two selections below, then complete the exercise that follows.

Selection I: "Sonnet LXXIII"
by William Shakespeare

That time of year thou mayst in me behold
When yellow leaves, or none, or few, do hang
Upon those boughs which shake against the cold,
Bare ruin'd choirs, where late the sweet birds sang.

In me thou see'st the twilight of such day
As after sunset fadeth in the west,
Which by and by black night doth take away,
Death's second self, that seals up all in rest.

In me thou see'st the glowing of such fire
That on the ashes of his youth doth lie,
As the death-bed whereon it must expire,
Consumed with that which it was nourished by.

This thou perceivest, which makes thy love more strong,
To love that well which thou must leave ere long.

Selection II: "An Old Man's Winter Night"
by Robert Frost

All out of doors looked darkly in at him
Through the thin frost, almost in separate stars,
That gathers on the pane in empty rooms.
What kept his eyes from giving back the gaze
Was the lamp tilted near them in his hand.
What kept him from remembering what it was
That brought him to that creaking room was age.
He stood with barrels round him — at a loss.
And having scared the cellar under him
In clomping there, he scared it once again
In clomping off; — and scared the outer night,
Which has its sounds, familiar, like the roar
Of trees and crack of branches, common things,
But nothing so like beating on a box.
A light he was to no one but himself

Where now he sat, concerned with he knew what,
A quiet light, and then not even that.
He consigned to the moon, such as she was,
So late-arising, to the broken moon
As better than the sun in any case
For such a charge, his snow upon the roof,
His icicles along the wall to keep;
And slept. The log that shifted with a jolt
Once in the stove, disturbed him and he shifted,
And eased his heavy breathing, but still slept.
One aged man — one man — can't fill a house,
A farm, a countryside, or if he can,
It's thus he does it of a winter night.

Write a critical essay in which you analyze the two selections above, supporting your conclusions with specific evidence from the texts. Assume that you are writing for an educated audience knowledgeable about literary criticism. In your essay:

- identify a significant theme that the two texts share;

- compare and contrast the two texts' perspectives on the theme you have identified;

- examine how the two texts employ literary techniques, including genre features, literary elements, and rhetorical devices, to express their perspectives on this theme; and

- draw a conclusion that explains how the literary techniques you have identified affect the ideas conveyed in the texts.

Practice Question 2

Read the op-ed article "A Word of Advice for the Fracking Industry." Then complete the exercise that follows.

A Word of Advice for the Fracking Industry

A "Golden Age of Gas" — that's what we're living in, according to the gurus at the International Energy Agency. Trillions of cubic feet of unconventional natural gas have been discovered in shale-rock formations around the world. And what's more, drillers today have the know-how to harvest this energy bonanza. We're talking a treasure trove of cheap fuel — and, emissions-wise, it's lower in carbon than that *bete noire* of the Greens, nasty old coal.

So let's have at it, right?

Well, there's a kicker. The technology employed to extract all that natural gas from shale rock — a process known as hydraulic fracturing, or "fracking" — involves certain side effects, some generally acknowledged, others more speculative. For example, drillers use gallons of chemicals in the process that potentially could contaminate nearby drinking wells. Disposal of the wastewater has been blamed for earthquakes in places like Ohio and Oklahoma. And some environmentalists worry that leaking methane from fracking sites could be more dangerous for global warming than coal (that *bête noire,* etc., etc.).

These concerns have led to today's thorny debate over fracking and exactly how, and how much, it should be regulated. Industry representatives, with dollar signs floating in their eyes, insist that burdensome regulation will stifle this fledgling technology in the nest. Or at least make it way more costly.

However, a recent IEA report suggests that reasonable up-front regulations might be the best thing that ever happened to all those fretful frackers. In fact it might end up being cheaper than no regulations at all. Why, you ask? Because "Fracking Gone Wild" might well produce exactly the massive political opposition that could threaten use of the new technology worldwide.

The IEA estimates that even stiff environmental regulations on fracking would increase the cost of production by only 7 percent or so. True, some experts expect actual compliance costs to be double that figure — but that's still looks relatively cheap when compared to potential profits.

Should governments and drillers reach agreement on a set of rules, the result, according to the IEA, would be a boom in natural gas production, leading to natural gas replacing coal as the world's second-largest energy source by 2035. All of this depends, of course, on a global shrug regarding carbon emissions; natural gas would be cheap but it would also still be a fossil fuel. And the Sierra Club isn't going out of business anytime soon.

The IEA has even come up with a list of "golden rules" for the fracking industry: everything from choosing drilling sites with care to spending extra on the construction of well-sites and disposal areas to minimize the leaks and seismic shocks. In addition, the IEA urges careful monitoring of drinking water. Pretty vanilla stuff, really.

And what's the alternative? Think hordes of anti-fracking protesters roaming outside the headquarters of the energy behemoths, making the nightly news on a nightly basis, waving their snide signs, and generally making life miserable for the poor honest fracker. With no regulations, or even a watered-down version, the anti-frackers would have an ideological field day.

I think most players in the fracking field would agree: Better to help write the rules than be blind-sided somewhere down the road. They could even call it "green-fracking" for PR appeal. Couldn't hurt.

Write a critical essay in which you analyze the op-ed article above. Assume that you are writing for an educated audience, and make sure to support your conclusions with evidence from the text. In your essay:

- summarize, in your own words, the author's main argument in this passage;

- evaluate the author's reasoning;

- describe the author's methods of persuasion and use of rhetorical devices;

- identify the audience for which the author is most likely writing; and

- describe the extent to which the passage is likely to be effective in persuading this audience, and explain why.

Practice Test 2, Subtest III
Written Response Answer Sheets

Although the actual CSET: English test is computer-based and you will input your responses on a computer screen, use the answer sheets that follow to write your responses. For Subtest III, you will have 2 hours to complete the two constructed-response questions.

_____

_____

_____

_____

_____

_____

_____

_____

_____

_____

_____

_____

_____

_____

_____

Written Response Answer Sheets (cont'd)

Written Response Answer Sheets *(cont'd)*

_____

_____

_____

_____

_____

_____

_____

_____

_____

_____

_____

_____

_____

_____

_____

_____

_____

_____

_____

Written Response Answer Sheets *(cont'd)*

Practice Test 2, Subtest III
Sample Essays

Sample Response for Practice Question #1

4-Point Response

Both Shakespeare's Sonnet LXXIII and Frost's "An Old Man's Winter Night" deal with the emptiness and dissatisfactions of old age. Both poems begin with an image of winter as a (well-worn) analogy to the condition of growing old, yet the effects produced are fresh and powerful. Shakespeare refers to "That time of year thou mayst in me behold," when there are few leaves, or none, left hanging "upon those boughs which shake against the cold." Perhaps the leaves are also the sheets of Shakespeare's poetry, blowing away in the wind. He then adds the beautifully desolate image of "Bare ruin'd choirs, where late the sweet birds sang" — an image of a church in ruins, and of a long-lost springtime.

Frost's poem also opens with an image from nature, as "all out of doors looked darkly in at him," yet his aged old man can only see his own reflection in the frosty windowpane due to the lamp tilted in his hand. His age affects his memory and leaves him standing there at a loss.

Shakespeare next compares his aging to a fading sunset, "which by and by black night doth take away, Death's second self." The speaker seems resigned to this incursion of the night, since indeed it "seals up all in rest." In his fading condition, restfulness appears as a comforting thought, as the word **rest** firmly ends the eighth line. Frost also refers to the night, but his protagonist has "scared the outer night" with his clomping footfalls. The old man's solitary condition — "A light he was to no one but himself" — emphasizes the idea of loneliness that all the imagery suggests.

Shakespeare's last analogy for age is a fire "That on the ashes of his youth doth lie," like a "death-bed." His life, he admits, has been "consumed with that which it was nourished by," like the fire consuming the fuel.

(Is he referring to poetry, which nourished and consumed him?) A note of regret and decay enters in here, but there is also a hint of having once in youth burned brightly. Frost too refers to a fire — "The log that shifted with a jolt/Once in the stove." The old man shifts like the log but does not awaken. "His snow upon the roof," like a description of white hair, is kept by the cold moon instead of the sun, as is appropriate to this wintry scene.

The poems diverge in their final lines. Shakespeare's, more anxious at the thought of approaching death and the loss of a once-great vitality, addresses again the unnamed "thou" who perceives his plight and loves him well, knowing that death will soon take him away. Frost's poem, on the other hand, reverts to the idea of loneliness, that "One aged man — one man — can't fill a house, a farm, a countryside." The sounds of the night previously mentioned, "the roar of trees and crack of branches," hint at a vitality the old man might once have had, but now he is reduced to sleeping alone by the fire.

Analysis:

The writer deftly compares Shakespeare and Frost in this review of both poets' poems about old men. Well-selected quotes carry the theme of the writer's opinion. Several analogies from each piece also give supporting evidence to this opinion. The writer has evidenced a comprehensive and complex understanding of the assignment.

Sample Response for Practice Question #1

3-Point Response

While Shakespeare's Sonnet LXXIII and Robert Frost's "An Old Man's Winter Night" are both superficially about aging, the two poems leave very different impressions about that theme. One of the main differences is that Shakespeare's poem is written in the first-person point of view, presenting the problems of aging in an immediate way. Frost's poem, on the other hand, is written in the third-person point of view, describing an old man's lonely life from the outside. In fact, the first words of Frost's poem are: "All out of doors looked darkly in at him." The reader is put in the position of looking in also.

Shakespeare's poem begins in a tone that sounds halfway between self-pity and acceptance. He says that he is in the autumn or even winter

PRACTICE TEST 2 – SUBTEST III – SAMPLE ESSAYS

of his life, "when yellow leaves, or none, or few, do hang." Then he compares the boughs of his tree to "Bare ruin'd choirs," like an empty church where no more singing happens. In the second stanza, the speaker is even more morose, comparing himself to a fading sunset "which by and by black night doth take away." He sounds like he is prepared for death to arrive soon.

By contrast, we don't know what Frost's old man thinks about his situation. We only see him clomping around what seems to be a cabin or small house, and he can't even remember what it was that made him enter the room. While Shakespeare's aging speaker is a fading sunset, Frost's old man is a light "to no one but himself." He's a "quiet light, and then not even that." Frost gives the scene subtle pathos by simply describing it and leaving the reader to feel the emotion produced.

By the end of Sonnet LXXIII, Shakespeare's speaker is only "the glowing of such fire" that burns on the ashes of his youth. It sounds like he feels remorse for some things in his life, or maybe he simply is regretful that his life is almost over. Whoever he is speaking to knows that the end is near, but this "makes thy love more strong." At least he has someone who cares for him. At the end of Frost's poem, the old man is asleep by the stove, and perhaps when he "eased his heavy breathing," Frost intends this to mean he dies. At any rate, as Frost says, one man "can't fill a house." As Frost says in another poem, one must "provide, provide" for oneself to keep the end from being hard.

Analysis:

The writer displays a sufficient understanding of the assignment but fails to show any similarity between the two poems. His/her description of the differences between the two, however, is cleanly done.

Sample Response for Practice Question #1

2-Point Response

The speaker in William Shakespeare's Sonnet LXXIII and the character of the old man in the poem by Robert Frost both face the problem of growing old. But their ways of approaching this problem seem very different.

Shakespeare, or his speaker, faces things with lots of imagination. Frost's old man just clomps around a little house in a sort of quiet stupor.

From the first, Shakespeare uses great images to express the feeling of growing old. He compares himself to a tree in the winter, when the leaves are blowing off one by one. (This might also refer to the fact that Shakespeare was balding.) He says that the boughs are "where late the sweet birds sang," which brings up images of happier times, maybe a thought of spring. Shakespeare also presents beautiful images of a fading sunset and a dying fire to represent his old age and fading life. The language he uses is formal and dignified, with the ancient sound of words such as **thou** and **doth** setting the tone. He sounds like a man who has lived a full life and is now resigned to its end.

By contrast, Frost's old man is described in very plain words that seem to fit the man's plain life. The old man hears creaks and cracks of "familiar" sounds and "common things." Frost presents his sad situation of being so old and almost senile and alone in unemotional language that is quite a contrast with Shakespeare's more colorful verse. By the end, the reader realizes that the old man is either very near death or already dead. Only a log shifting in the stove spurs one last movement from the old man. Thus, Frost seems to say, does an uneventful life come to an end.

Analysis:

The writer has a basic understanding of the assignment and is able to partially fulfill its requirements. She/he fails to recognize and build upon the similarities in both poems. Static sentence structure is employed throughout.

Sample Response for Practice Question #1

1-Point Response

At first it seems like Shakespeare's sonnet and Frost's poem do not have much in common. Shakespeare's poem is dated, and uses words like **thou** and **doth**, and is full of rhyming words that sometimes seem a bit of a stretch. Frost's poem is written in more modern English and is therefore easier to understand. Also, it doesn't have rhymes, so it seems to flow like a story.

What the two works do have in common is the theme of old age, for Shakespeare seems to be describing his own old age and Frost's old man is certainly near the end. Both poems use the idea of old age being like winter, which is not a new idea by any means. Shakespeare also presents a nice picture of himself as a branch that is losing leaves and blowing in the wind. He seems to be sad that life is coming to an end, but maybe he is happy to be able to describe it in colorful words. Frost's old man doesn't speak at all in the poem, and he appears to barely understand his own situation.

Of the two, I prefer Robert Frost's poem because it is more understandable in its language and presentation. The reader feels the sad predicament of the old man clomping around in his little farmhouse. He can't comfort himself with words like Shakespeare, so he can only sit by the stove and sleep.

Analysis:

Having little understanding of the task, the writer focuses only on the superficial themes of both poems and fails to describe any deeper meaning.

Sample Response for Practice Question #2

4-Point Response

This article, "A Word of Advice for the Fracking Industry," was apparently written for the op-ed page of a newspaper, so its intended audience would be fairly well educated and well informed about current issues such as energy policies. The author argues that the new technology for obtaining natural gas, calling fracking, has some drawbacks but could also represent a boom in cheap energy for the foreseeable future. He advises the drilling companies to accept government regulations on their industry now to avoid much bigger problems in the future.

The author presents the facts clearly, but he also writes in a breezy style that can be irritating — particularly on such an important subject. For example, he describes the people in the fracking industry as having "dollar signs floating in their eyes," and later refers to them as "fretful frackers." This is amusing in small doses, but I think the author employs this irreverent tone too often.

The author does a good job of presenting the situation that the fracking industry faces, referring several times to reports from the International Energy Agency to provide solid figures and authoritative opinions. He explains that "should governments and drillers reach agreement on a set of rules," the result would be a boom in natural gas production and, presumably, large profits for the fracking companies. Thus he advises the owners of these companies to accept regulations now so they can get on with the business of drilling for the natural gas.

While this sounds plausible at first, the author seems to omit several points. Are the concerns about contamination of drinking water and potential earthquakes (which are quite alarming to begin with) the only problems that environmentalists have with fracking? And shouldn't environmental experts play more of a role in creating the proper regulations for this vast new technology? Through all his jokes and breeziness, the author never seems to consider these ideas.

Analysis:

The writer immediately identifies the intended audience and moves briskly through the required points of the essay, utilizing excellent writing skills and sound reasoning.

Sample Response for Practice Question #2

3-Point Response

The author of "A Word of Advice for the Fracking Industry" argues that the fracking industry — companies that drill for natural gas in shale-rock formations around the world — should accept new government regulations and the resulting loss of profits in order to avoid larger protests about the process and get on with their drilling. He lays out his case by explaining what fracking is, the potential problems and hazards with its implementation, and the possible boon it represents for the world's energy future.

The author writes in a casual, witty style that might cause some to doubt the seriousness of his purpose. For example, he asserts that fracking "emissions-wise [is] lower in carbon than that bete noire of the Greens, nasty old coal." And further on, he refers to "all those fretful frackers" worrying that government regulation will kill their industry.

However, he does a good job laying out the arguments for both sides of the issue. Environmentalists, he says, worry that "leaking methane from fracking sites could be more dangerous for global warming than coal." And he explains potential problems such as contamination of drinking water wells and even earthquakes in certain areas. Nevertheless, he acknowledges that should the industry reach an agreement on regulations and go ahead with drilling projects, natural gas could be the world's second largest energy source by 2035.

In advising the fracking industry to accept regulations that would shave as much as 15 percent off their bottom line, the author seems to urge a practical approach. He also says that reaching an agreement now is better than to "be blind-sided somewhere down the road." Yet the reader never seems to know exactly where the author stands on the fracking process itself. Does he see the potential problems as serious, or just a few more roadblocks to an industry that should be able to do what it wants? At times, the author seems to view environmentalists as busy bodies, and protesters as fanatics "waving their snide signs, and generally making life miserable for the poor honest fracker." While this last sentence does sound like an attempt at humor, the tone throughout this article leaves the reader wondering if there isn't a more serious examination of this issue available.

Analysis:

Displaying an overall knowledge of hydraulic fracking, the writer gives a well-thought-out summary of the article. The essayist gives clear evidence that questions the author's purpose and mindset. Both the use of rhetorical devices as well as the intended audience for the essay is never discussed.

Sample Response for Practice Question #2

2-Point Response

The article "A Word of Advice for the Fracking Industry" examines the controversy over the new drilling technology called hydraulic fracturing, or fracking. The author explains that there are environmental concerns about the process. Drillers use chemicals that could seep into drinking wells. Some environmental experts also worry about methane leaks adding to global warming problems.

The author tries to take an even-handed approach. He explains how the fracking industry fears that too much regulation could doom this potentially huge source of natural gas — or "stifle this fledgling technology in the nest," as he puts it. He then goes on to advise the industry to accept new regulations now before the political opposition really heats up.

His argument is persuasive as far as it goes. But that is not very far. Even though he explains why fracking is controversial, I think he still plays down just how determined the opposing faction is. As the writer puts it, "the Sierra Club isn't going out of business anytime soon." Nor should it, or any other environmental group, simply roll over and let the fracking industry have its way. The "golden rules" that the IEA has suggested for the fracking industry is probably a good place to start. It's **not** a good idea to end up with something like "Fracking Gone Wild."

Analysis:

The writer slides through an explanation of the author's reasoning to point out that opposing fractions aren't "going out of business soon." The persuasive impact of the essay on an audience is not discussed, and the intended audience is never identified.

Sample Response for Practice Question #2

1-Point Response

This article called "A Word of Advice for the Fracking Industry" was written for regular newspaper readers, I think. Its main point is that fracking is dangerous but should go on because we need the natural gas. The author makes some jokes about both sides of the debate, but he seems to be on the side of the fracking people.

In general, the author seems more interested in being a comedian than in explaining the problem. He breezes right over the worries about drinking water as if they are not very important. I know that clean drinking water is important to me and my family. But he also explains how fracking could produce so much new natural gas, which could help solve our country's energy problems. I would drive a car powered by natural gas if I could find one.

The author acts like it's life or death that fracking gets started right away. But it sounds like cooler heads will first write some rules and regulations that will make the process safer. This was an informative article about an important issue, but I don't think it covers both sides of the argument. A reader should probably follow up with his own research after reading it.

Analysis:

Although the writer understands the issue of fracking, and explains it fairly well, she/he fails to follow a number of the requirements for the answer—particularly that of the author's use of persuasion and rhetorical devices.

PRACTICE TEST 2

CSET: English Subtest IV

Also available at the REA Study Center (*www.rea.com/studycenter*)

This practice test is also available online at the REA Study Center. The CSET: English test is only offered as a computer-based exam; therefore, we recommend that you take the online version of the practice test to receive these added benefits:

- **Timed testing conditions** – helps you gauge how much time you can spend on each question

- **On-screen detailed analysis of sample essays** – guides you to a 3-point response

SCORING THE CSET: ENGLISH SUBTEST IV

In CSET: English Subtest IV, you will have 1 hour and 30 minutes to respond to four constructed-response writing prompts.

For each constructed-response question in Subtest IV, you should write a response of about 75–125 words, although you may write longer responses if you prefer. Your responses will be assessed according to the subject-matter knowledge and skills they demonstrate, *not* writing ability. You should, however, write clearly enough to allow for a valid judgment of your knowledge and skills regarding the subject matter. You should write for an audience of educators in the field.

Your response essays will be scored by California educators using focused holistic scoring. The scorers will evaluate the overall effectiveness of your essay responses with a focus on the performance characteristics that have been judged most important for CSET: English Subtest IV. These performance characteristics, or writing standards, are established by the California Commission on Teacher Credentialing and include the following:

> **Purpose:** The extent to which the response focuses on and accomplishes the task set by the prompt in relation to relevant CSET: English subject-matter requirements.

> **Subject-matter knowledge:** The extent to which the response applies accurate subject-matter knowledge as described in the relevant CSET: English subject-matter requirements.

> **Support:** The extent to which the response employs quality, appropriate supporting evidence in relation to CSET: English subject-matter requirements.

Your essay responses will be scored based on the following Scoring Scale:

Scoring Scale

3: To earn a **3-point score**, your response must show that you have a sophisticated grasp of the relevant knowledge and skills as defined in the subject-matter requirements for CSET: English. These include:

- The ability to address the specific purpose of the assignment comprehensively and without distractions in order to accomplish the assigned task.

- The ability to select and include relevant supporting evidence and examples that demonstrate your overall understanding of the subject matter.

A 3-point essay demonstrates that you have a thorough understanding of the assignment and the relevant subject matter.

2: To earn a **2-point score**, your response must show that you have an overall or general understanding of the relevant knowledge and skills as defined in the subject-matter requirements for CSET: English. These include:

- The ability to recognize the overall purpose of the assignment in order to accomplish the assigned task adequately.

- The ability to recognize and apply some accurate information and relevant supporting evidence to the given subject matter.

A 2-point essay demonstrates that you have an adequate or sufficient understanding of the assignment.

1: To earn a **1-point score**, your response will show that you have a basic, partial, or insufficient understanding of the knowledge and skills as defined in the subject-matter requirements for CSET: English. These include:

- The ability to address the assignment's purpose only partially or not at all.

- The ability to recognize and apply only a limited amount, if any, of relevant supporting evidence, demonstrating only a partial understanding of the subject matter.

A 1-point essay demonstrates that you have a limited, partial, or unsatisfactory understanding of the assignment.

U: A grade of **"U" (Unscorable)** is given to essays that are completely unrelated to the assignment, illegible, written in a language other than English, and/or lack a sufficient amount of your own original writing. Most problems that cause an essay to earn a "U" are solvable by simply slowing down and pacing yourself as you systematically respond to each question or prompt.

B: A grade of **"B" (Blank)** is given to essay responses left blank. Never leave a test question blank if at all possible.

CSET: English Practice Test 2, Subtest IV Communications: Speech, Media, and Creative Performance

Practice Question 1

Complete the exercise that follows.

An important part of an oral presentation is the interaction between the speaker and the audience. A speaker should be alert to various audience reactions and be able to adapt the speech accordingly. Write a response in which you:

- identify one kind of audience reaction that might occur during a speech or oral presentation; and

- describe one strategy the speaker could employ in adjusting to that audience reaction during the speech or oral presentation.

In your response, be sure to address both of the tasks described above.

Practice Question 2

Complete the exercise that follows.

Professional journalists use six basic questions (the five W's and one H) to assemble the facts they will need to write an effective article or make an effective report. However, quality journalism goes beyond simply answering these questions and includes an extra responsibility that a reporter feels toward his or her audience. Write a response in which you:

- briefly describe the idea of quality journalism as it relates to a reporter's responsibility to the audience; and

- provide an example of the difference between quality (i.e., thorough, complete) reporting and superficial (i.e., shallow, minimal) reporting.

In your response, be sure to address both of the tasks described above.

Practice Question 3

Complete the exercise that follows.

You are a director staging a drama class production of Oscar Wilde's *The Importance of Being Earnest*. You are preparing to stage the opening of Act III, the text of which is shown below.

SCENE—*Morning-room at the Manor House.* GWENDOLEN and CECILY *are at the window, looking out into the garden.*

GWENDOLEN: The fact that they did not follow us at once into the house, as anyone else would have done, seems to me to show that they have some sense of shame left.

CECILY: They have been eating muffins. That looks like repentance.

GWENDOLEN: (after a pause) They don't seem to notice us at all. Couldn't you cough?

CECILY: But I haven't got a cough.

GWENDOLEN: They're looking at us. What effrontery!

CECILY: They're approaching. That's very forward of them.

GWENDOLEN: Let us preserve a dignified silence.

CECILY: Certainly. It's the only thing to do now.

[Enter JACK followed by ALGERNON. They whistle some dreadful popular air from a British Opera.]

GWENDOLEN: This dignified silence seems to produce an unpleasant effect.

CECILY: A most distasteful one.

As director, you will base your staging decisions on the text of the play. Write a response in which you

- describe one problem related to staging this scene (e.g., direction, lighting, blocking, props, sound); and
- explain how you would solve the problem.

In your response, be sure to address both of the tasks described above.

Practice Question 4

A high school student must write and deliver a reflective narrative presentation in speech class. The presentation must examine a personal experience by using sensory language, narrative strategies, and connections to a broader theme. The student's first draft for the presentation follows.

¹ A few years ago my piano teacher enlisted me to play in a recital in front of an audience of parents and family friends. ² I was supposed to play a piece by the French composer Claude Debussy. ³ It is a beautiful piece, but not tremendously difficult. ⁴ I love many of the French composers of the late nineteenth and early twentieth century. ⁵ I think their melodies are haunting and beautiful. ⁶ I was a little nervous as the recital approached, but it didn't worry me too much.

⁷ My performance at the recital was not great, but I got through it OK. ⁸ I made a few mistakes that only someone really familiar with the piece would recognize. ⁹ After the recital, I expected my dad to congratulate me on my performance. ¹⁰ He had always been supportive of me in all my activities. ¹¹ He coached my softball team for two straight seasons. ¹² Instead of offering praise, however, my dad delivered a stern lecture on having higher standards and the need to work harder to achieve personal goals. ¹³ He saw that I hadn't taken the recital seriously enough. ¹⁴ I realized that it's not enough in life merely to get through things. ¹⁵ One should work hard to excel and try to make the most of one's abilities.

Using your knowledge of oral communication, write a response in which you:

- describe one kind of revision the student could make to improve the draft shown above; and

- explain why this kind of revision would make the presentation more effective.

Written Response Answer Sheets for CSET: English Practice Test 2, Subtest IV

Although the actual CSET: English test is computer-based and you will input your responses on a computer screen, use the answer sheets that follow to write your responses. For Subtest IV, you will have 1 hour and 30 minutes to complete the four short-response questions.

_____

_____

_____

_____

_____

_____

_____

_____

_____

_____

_____

_____

_____

_____

_____

_____

Practice Question 1

Practice Question 2

_____
_____
_____
_____
_____
_____
_____
_____
_____
_____
_____
_____
_____
_____
_____
_____
_____
_____
_____
_____
_____

Practice Question 3

_____

_____

_____

_____

_____

_____

_____

_____

_____

_____

_____

_____

_____

_____

_____

_____

_____

_____

_____

Practice Question 4

_____

_____

_____

_____

_____

_____

_____

_____

_____

_____

_____

_____

_____

_____

_____

_____

_____

_____

_____

Sample Responses for Practice Test 2, Subtest IV

Sample Response for Practice Question #1

3-Point Response

One kind of audience reaction that a speaker might face is heckling or inappropriate outbursts from a member of the audience. In response, the speaker should rely on a strategy of remaining calm and sensible. The speaker might pause after an initial outburst before resuming the speech in order to highlight the fact that the outburst is inappropriate. Should the heckling continue, the speaker might calmly note that questions and comments will be addressed after the presentation. Gentle humor might also help to ease a tense situation. By remaining calm and polite, the speaker will tend to earn the respect of other audience members, who might urge the heckler to be quiet.

Analysis:

The writer displays a clear understanding of the assignment and uses strong knowledge of the relevant subject matter to respond to both of the tasks in the prompt. The response is well organized and thorough.

Sample Response for Practice Question #1

2-Point Response

One thing that can happen is heckling from one or more of the audience members. A speaker should be ready if this problem should arise. It is very irritating when someone interrupts a speaker or insists on making comments during a speech. Such outbursts can ruin the presentation for the entire audience. There is not much a speaker can do in response without dropping to the level of the heckler. In general, the speaker should stay calm and try to reason with the person or persons who are interrupting. But even this might not be enough to save the situation.

Analysis:

The writer demonstrates a general understanding of the assignment and does identify heckling as one type of possible audience reaction to which a speaker must respond. However, the writer shows limited knowledge of the subject matter in describing how the speaker should deal with the situation effectively.

Sample Response for Practice Question #1

1-Point Response

> Audiences get bored with a tedious speech and start to make noises and get restless. I hate to have to sit through a boring presentation that I have no real interest in. It's up to the speaker to keep things interesting. Sometimes you wish you had a channel changer to flip to something more interesting than a boring speaker.

Analysis:

The writer shows a limited understanding of the assignment by responding in only a vague way to the first task of the prompt and not at all to the second part. The writer displays no knowledge of the relevant subject matter and does not provide any supporting evidence or examples.

Sample Response for Practice Question #2

3-Point Response

> Quality reporting includes presenting not just the facts pertaining to a particular story or event, but also the direct significance or impact that those facts will have on the reader or viewer. So for example, rather than just reporting, "Congress passes a voting rights bill," or "The president signs a landmark student loan bill," a thorough reporter will include the impact or significance that those events will have upon the citizen as voter, business owner, or consumer. The difference is reflected in this re-writing of the two above examples: "Voters will have new protections for their right to vote because of Congress passing this voting rights bill," or "The nation's college tuition costs may rise as a result of the president signing this landmark student loan bill."
>
> Thus, a minimal journalistic approach will include a presentation of the five W's (who, what, when, where, and why) with the occasional "how" thrown in, but ultimately will leave the audience with the task of deciding

what impact the news events will have on them personally. A complete or quality job of reporting, on the other hand, will include the significance or impact that the information has had or will have on the audience.

Analysis:

The writer exhibits a comprehensive understanding of the assignment as he/she identifies the difference between quality, or successful, news reporting and superficial reporting. The writer shows knowledge of the relevant subject matter and provides strong supporting evidence.

Sample Response for Practice Question #2

2-Point Response

Superficial or careless reporting is commonplace in today's media. It suggests that only the bare minimum of information is reported. So a careless journalist will, for example, write an article where he or she barely even includes the Five W's and the H; he or she might report that a store was robbed in a certain neighborhood, and that the robber's image was captured on the store's video camera and then omit all other facts, such as when did this robbery occur, was anyone hurt, was anyone else involved, and so forth. A truly quality reporter might do further background research to see if similar robberies had occurred in that neighborhood recently or whether nearby stores were taking additional precautions because of the incident. Audiences or readers appreciate having as much information as possible so they can make their own judgments about the news.

Analysis:

The writer shows a sufficient understanding of the assignment, explaining the difference between quality journalism and minimal reporting. Examples are generally well chosen and relevant.

Sample Response for Practice Question #2

1-Point Response

Since writing a good news story isn't brain surgery, it seems that it's up to the reporter to ask what they want to ask, and write whatever they want to write about a news story, as long as they make sure to include the five or six basic questions. If they don't include all of the basic questions, then they are writing minimally, maybe because they are too lazy or something.

Analysis:

The writer shows a poor understanding of the assignment and does not adequately describe the difference between quality reporting and superficial reporting. The writer also employs a flippant tone that is inappropriate for the essay response.

Sample Response for Practice Question #3

3-Point Response

> One problem in staging this scene has to do with blocking: where to place the actors on the stage. According to the text, Gwendolen and Cecily are watching Jack and Algernon from the window of the morning-room as they talk together. It is important for the audience to see what Gwendolen and Cecily are doing and also hear what they are saying. However, the audience need not see Jack and Algernon approaching. One solution is to place a large window-frame prop downstage right on the side so that the actors' lines are audible to the audience as they peer out the window. Then Jack and Algernon can "approach" and enter through a door that is also on the right side of the stage.

Analysis:

The writer displays a thorough understanding of the assignment by identifying a possible problem in staging the scene and then offering a solution. The writer also employs relevant subject matter knowledge about stage directing to address the prompt clearly and effectively.

Sample Response for Practice Question #3

2-Point Response

> One problem that a director would have in staging this scene is where to put the young ladies while they are looking out the window. If they are looking out a window at the back of the stage, their backs will be to the audience and no one will be able to hear them. The morning-room should be furnished with props such as an old-style mahogany desk and chairs and paintings from the nineteenth century. And the young ladies should probably speak with a British accent. There are many ways

to stage this scene, but the best way would feature the young ladies speaking out toward the audience somehow.

Analysis:

The writer shows a general understanding of the assignment, but identifies a problem with staging the scene without suggesting how the problem could be solved. The writer shows some familiarity with the appropriate subject matter, but he or she also adds irrelevant material that does not address the task in the prompt.

Sample Response for Practice Question #3

1-Point Response

The biggest problem with staging this is how dull it is. There's only so much a director can do with a scene like this. If I were the director, I'd rewrite the scene so that the audience can hear what Jack and Algernon are saying as well as what the young ladies are saying. That would make the scene more interesting for the audience. I would also leave out words like "repentance" and "effrontery" to make the scene easier to understand.

Analysis:

The writer displays very limited understanding of the assignment. Instead of following the text of the play in staging the scene, the writer intends to rewrite the text. There is no evidence of familiarity with the relevant subject matter.

Sample Response for Practice Question #4

3-Point Response

An important revision that the student could make is to eliminate unnecessary details. Whereas an oral presentation may be delivered in a more relaxed manner than a formal written essay, it should still mostly stick to the main point. Details should be chosen to support the theme of the presentation. For example, the detail that the Debussy piano piece is not tremendously difficult to play is important to the story. By contrast, the student's opinions about French composers and their melodies are unnecessary and distracting to the audience. In the same way, the fact that the student's father coached his or her softball team is irrelevant to the main theme. The overall structure of the draft would be stronger without these unnecessary details.

Analysis:

The writer displays a complete understanding of the assignment and addresses the tasks in the prompt effectively. The writer obviously knows the subject matter and uses it to support the response.

Sample Response for Practice Question #4

2-Point Response

> I think one way the student could revise this draft is to take out things that don't add to the theme. The theme, after all, is working hard to excel and making the most of oneself. But the student's story includes some details that might be interesting in themselves but add nothing to the theme. For example, the audience doesn't know or care who Claude Debussy is. Things like that could be removed to make the student's draft much better and more enjoyable for the audience.

Analysis:

The writer exhibits a general understanding of the assignment and identifies a kind of revision that would indeed improve the draft. The writer partially fulfills the second part of the prompt also by describing how the removal of details that don't belong would make the draft better and more appealing to an audience. But the writer does not correctly identify an unnecessary detail—Claude Debussy was the composer of the piece the student played, which is relevant—and includes little supporting subject matter on oral communication.

Sample Response for Practice Question #4

1-Point Response

> This draft needs plenty of work. It's such a cliché to tell yourself you need to try harder. And the story the student has to tell is too boring for an audience to pay attention to. The best revision would be a complete rewrite on another topic. Maybe a theme about finding a way to hold an audience's interest. Because that's what this student needs to learn.

Analysis:

The writer scarcely addresses the assignment and instead recommends that the student's draft be scrapped. The writer shows no understanding of the relevant subject matter and does not satisfy either part of the prompt.

Index